Syntax-based Statistical Machine Translation

Synthesis Lectures on Human Language Technologies

Editor
Graeme Hirst, *University of Toronto*

Synthesis Lectures on Human Language Technologies is edited by Graeme Hirst of the University of Toronto. The series consists of 50- to 150-page monographs on topics relating to natural language processing, computational linguistics, information retrieval, and spoken language understanding. Emphasis is on important new techniques, on new applications, and on topics that combine two or more HLT subfields.

Syntax-based Statistical Machine Translation
Philip Williams, Rico Sennrich, Matt Post, and Philipp Koehn
2016

Domain-Sensitive Temporal Tagging
Jannik Strötgen and Michael Gertz
2016

Linked Lexical Knowledge Bases: Foundations and Applications
Iryna Gurevych, Judith Eckle-Kohler, and Michael Matuschek
2016

Bayesian Analysis in Natural Language Processing
Shay Cohen
2016

Metaphor: A Computational Perspective
Tony Veale, Ekaterina Shutova, and Beata Beigman Klebanov
2016

Grammatical Inference for Computational Linguistics
Jeffrey Heinz, Colin de la Higuera, and Menno van Zaanen
2015

Automatic Detection of Verbal Deception
Eileen Fitzpatrick, Joan Bachenko, and Tommaso Fornaciari
2015

Natural Language Processing for Social Media
Atefeh Farzindar and Diana Inkpen
2015

Semantic Similarity from Natural Language and Ontology Analysis
Sébastien Harispe, Sylvie Ranwez, Stefan Janaqi, and Jacky Montmain
2015

Learning to Rank for Information Retrieval and Natural Language Processing, Second Edition
Hang Li
2014

Ontology-Based Interpretation of Natural Language
Philipp Cimiano, Christina Unger, and John McCrae
2014

Automated Grammatical Error Detection for Language Learners, Second Edition
Claudia Leacock, Martin Chodorow, Michael Gamon, and Joel Tetreault
2014

Web Corpus Construction
Roland Schäfer and Felix Bildhauer
2013

Recognizing Textual Entailment: Models and Applications
Ido Dagan, Dan Roth, Mark Sammons, and Fabio Massimo Zanzotto
2013

Linguistic Fundamentals for Natural Language Processing: 100 Essentials from Morphology and Syntax
Emily M. Bender
2013

Semi-Supervised Learning and Domain Adaptation in Natural Language Processing
Anders Søgaard
2013

Semantic Relations Between Nominals
Vivi Nastase, Preslav Nakov, Diarmuid Ó Séaghdha, and Stan Szpakowicz
2013

Computational Modeling of Narrative
Inderjeet Mani
2012

Syntax-based Statistical Machine Translation

Philip Williams, Rico Sennrich, Matt Post, and Philipp Koehn

ISBN: 978-3-031-01036-1   paperback
ISBN: 978-3-031-02164-0   ebook

DOI 10.1007/978-3-031-02164-0

A Publication in the Springer series
SYNTHESIS LECTURES ON HUMAN LANGUAGE TECHNOLOGIES

Lecture #33
Series Editor: Graeme Hirst, *University of Toronto*
Series ISSN
Print 1947-4040   Electronic 1947-4059

Syntax-based Statistical Machine Translation

Philip Williams
University of Edinburgh

Rico Sennrich
University of Edinburgh

Matt Post
Johns Hopkins University

Philipp Koehn
Johns Hopkins University

SYNTHESIS LECTURES ON HUMAN LANGUAGE TECHNOLOGIES #33

ABSTRACT

This unique book provides a comprehensive introduction to the most popular syntax-based statistical machine translation models, filling a gap in the current literature for researchers and developers in human language technologies. While phrase-based models have previously dominated the field, syntax-based approaches have proved a popular alternative, as they elegantly solve many of the shortcomings of phrase-based models. The heart of this book is a detailed introduction to decoding for syntax-based models.

The book begins with an overview of synchronous-context free grammar (SCFG) and synchronous tree-substitution grammar (STSG) along with their associated statistical models. It also describes how three popular instantiations (Hiero, SAMT, and GHKM) are learned from parallel corpora. It introduces and details hypergraphs and associated general algorithms, as well as algorithms for decoding with both tree and string input. Special attention is given to efficiency, including search approximations such as beam search and cube pruning, data structures, and parsing algorithms. The book consistently highlights the strengths (and limitations) of syntax-based approaches, including their ability to generalize phrase-based translation units, their modeling of specific linguistic phenomena, and their function of structuring the search space.

KEYWORDS

statistical machine translation, syntax, synchronous grammar formalisms, natural language processing, computational linguistics, machine learning, statistical modeling

Contents

Preface

Statistical machine translation takes a complex human skill and frames it as a clean, crisp mathematical equation. Expressed in words, this equation asks the following question.

> Given a text in the source language, what is the most probable translation in the target language?

For the most part, researchers and practitioners do not worry about the linguistic and philosophical question of what it means to talk about language and cognition as being probabilistic processes. Instead they view statistical models as tools with which to attack a complex and poorly understood problem. The interpretation is pragmatic: how should one construct a statistical model that assigns high probabilities to "good" translations and low probabilities to "bad" translations? Of course, no such model will be perfect. Unavoidably, it will have blind spots and shortcomings, and it will sometimes assign high probabilities to sentences that no human would conceive of uttering.

Restated in more formal terms, here is how statistical machine translation frames the translation problem:

$$t^* = \arg\max_t p(t|s).$$

The variables s and t are strings of tokens in the source and target language, respectively. Typically, the tokens represent words and the strings represent sentences. The statistical model that we want to construct is of the conditional distribution $p(t|s)$.

Since the inception of the field at the end of the 1980s, the most popular models for statistical machine translation—the models of $p(t|s)$—have been sequence-based. In these models, the basic units of translation are words or sequences of words (called phrases). Sequence-based n-gram language models are a core feature. These kinds of models are simple and effective, and they work well for many language pairs, but they exhibit weaknesses inherent to their sequence-based nature. For instance, they are blind to the global structure of the target sentence, and translation decisions are made based on a narrow window of adjacent words. They also do not take into account the cross-lingual syntactic divergences observed by linguists, such as that English is subject-verb-object (SVO) and Japanese subject-object-verb (SOV). Furthermore, heuristics used to rein in the complexity of the search problem in phrase-based translation often preclude the correct translation.

Despite the empirical success of sequence-based models, these deficiencies make them unsatisfying from a scientific perspective. This is especially true when we consider how much work has been independently undertaken in modeling the syntactic structure of language, both natural and formal. It is therefore unsurprising that the last 20 years have also seen fruitful research on translation models that are in some way based on the syntactic structure of the source and/or target sentences. Incorporating syntactic structure into the translation process allows reordering between languages to be informed by that structure. It also permits long-distance dependencies to be used in selecting translations of ambiguous source-language words, and can help promote fluent translations beyond the local window of phrases and n-grams. Since models that produce target-side syntactic structure are naturally extended with syntactic language models, this provides a means of improving global fluency and addressing problems that are morphosyntactic in nature, such as agreement.

Research into syntax-based translation has not just scratched a scientific itch. The effectiveness of syntax-based approaches has been demonstrated in shared translation tasks such as OpenMT12[1] and the yearly WMT evaluations [Bojar et al., 2014, 2015]. These successes have been borne out in automatic and human evaluations. Output from syntax-based systems has long been observed to have a different feel from that of sequence-based models, and, as might be hoped, to improve grammaticality. And while not always empirically the best choice, syntax has been shown to be superior across a range of situations, in high-resource settings and low, between languages disparate and similar.

Sequence-based models, however, remain the default. And while statistical machine translation is a large and important enough area of research to have garnered lengthy surveys and a textbook, syntax-based approaches have to date received little in the way of introductory presentation. We hope this book fills that gap.

OVERVIEW OF THIS BOOK

This book introduces the reader to core models and algorithms that have emanated from research on syntax-based statistical machine translation, and have found their use in different varieties of syntax-based translation models. While we cannot cover every aspect of this subject in a book of this size, we aim to provide coverage that is sufficiently broad and sufficiently in-depth to open up the research literature for further study and to provide a solid foundation for beginning experimental work.

The main focus of this book is models based on *synchronous context-free grammars* (SCFG) and *synchronous tree-substitution grammars* (STSG). Historically, most research in statistical machine translation has focused on translation into English and most syntax-based approaches have been based on constituency. This book reflects that bias. Nonetheless, we hope that readers interested in dependency-based approaches will not feel discouraged: despite their roots in constituency grammar, the methods described here have been successfully adapted and applied to dependency-based translation.

We have tried to keep this book as self-contained as possible; however, we do assume some background knowledge in mathematics and computer science. In particular, we assume that the

---

[1]http://www.nist.gov/itl/iad/mig/openmt12results.cfm

reader has at least a passing familiarity with basic concepts from probability theory, set theory, graph theory, and algorithms. Any previous exposure to natural language processing, and specifically statistical machine translation, is likely to be helpful but is not essential. For readers looking for a succinct crash course to the field of machine translation, we recommend the survey of Lopez [2008]. For a more in-depth introduction focusing on phrase-based translation, the reader would do well to consult the textbook, *Statistical Machine Translation* [Koehn, 2010].

Here is a sketch of what is to come.

Chapter 1 introduces the syntactic and statistical building blocks that make up a syntax-based model. We introduce SCFG and STSG formally and then discuss the role they play in statistical models. With these formal foundations in place, we begin to introduce the family of model types that exist in the wild. We begin with a high-level classification of approaches, before giving a brief history of syntax-based statistical machine translation.

Chapter 2 describes how the synchronous grammars that serve as translation models can be learned from parallel text. We discuss extraction algorithms for three popular grammars: hierarchical phrase-based grammars, syntax-augmented grammars, and GHKM grammars.

Chapter 3 is the first of three chapters devoted to decoding—the task of finding the most probable translation of a source sentence for a given model. For syntax-based models, decoding is based on a generalization of the graph called a hypergraph. This chapter introduces basic definitions and algorithms on hypergraphs.

Chapter 4 discusses tree decoding, i.e., decoding when the input sentence has already been parsed. It introduces the basic decoding algorithm, and discusses the inclusion of non-local features such as n-gram language models. Non-local features break the independence assumptions that allow for efficient exact decoding with rule-locally weighted grammars. We discuss common approximations made for the sake of efficiency, in particular beam search and cube pruning.

Chapter 5 describes string decoding, i.e., decoding with a string input. While the basic algorithms from the previous two chapters carry over to string decoding, the chapter discusses how to tackle the higher computational complexity of string decoding. The chapter covers topics such as stronger search approximations, grammar binarization and pruning, and efficient parsing algorithms and data structures for non-binary grammars.

Chapter 6 delves into a selection of further topics. We begin by discussing some important extensions of the core models and algorithms. For the most part, these extensions are aimed at relaxing the constraints imposed by constituency. We then move onto alternative grammar formalisms, including the use of dependency structure. Several prominent translation systems are based on dependency syntax, and we discuss dependency-based machine translation, comparing it to the algorithms introduced previously. Finally, we highlight some linguistic phenomena that have proven challenging for statistical machine translation, especially sequence-based models, but have seen progress through the use of syntax-based approaches.

Chapter 7 wraps up the book with closing remarks, discussing some limitations of syntax-based machine translation, and speculating on its future.

Acknowledgments

Work on the material for this book began with the preparation of a tutorial on syntax-based SMT delivered by two of the authors (Williams and Koehn) at EMNLP 2014. We would like to thank the tutorial attendees for their feedback and questions, and our editor, Graeme Hirst, for proposing that we develop the tutorial into a Synthesis lecture.

The initial draft of this book was improved greatly by the numerous corrections and many thoughtful suggestions of the two anonymous reviewers. We are indebted to them for the time and care they took in thoroughly reviewing the book. We would also like to thank Gillian Foy and Keisuke Sakaguchi, who carefully read through preliminary drafts and provided many helpful suggestions and corrections.

Finally, our thanks to the staff at Morgan and Claypool for their assistance (and patience) throughout the preparation of this book.

Philip Williams, Rico Sennrich, Matt Post, and Philipp Koehn
May 2016

CHAPTER 1

Models

During the last 20 years, researchers have proposed a wide range of syntax-based approaches to statistical machine translation. While a core set of methods has now crystallized and become dominant, much of the diversity of those approaches is still reflected in the models that are in current use. In this chapter, we describe the common components that make up a modern syntax-based model. We will focus initially on the formal syntactic and mathematical building blocks before introducing the family of model types. We will not say too much about specific models—that will come in the next chapter.

In a syntax-based model, the basic units of translation are synchronous grammar rules. We begin by introducing these rules informally in Section 1.1, showing how they compare to phrase pairs, which are the basic translation unit in the dominant phrase-based approach. We proceed in Section 1.2 by formalizing the description, introducing the basic concepts of two synchronous grammar formalisms: synchronous context-free grammar (SCFG) and synchronous tree-substitution grammar (STSG).

In formal grammar, a primary concept is that of derivation. In the current context this roughly means a sequence of translation steps. Once equipped with a formal conception of derivation, we have something over which to define a statistical model. In Section 1.3, we will describe the two main types of statistical modeling framework: the generative noisy-channel framework and the discriminative log-linear framework.

Having covered these foundational topics, we give a classification of syntax-based models in Section 1.4. As with classification in general, the criteria for classifying syntax-based models are somewhat subjective. The specific approach we take is not particularly important. Rather, the main purpose of this section is to introduce and contrast the range of features that can be found in current models.

Finally, in Section 1.5, we give a brief history of syntax-based statistical machine translation, with pointers to many of the seminal papers in the field.

1.1 SYNTACTIC TRANSLATION UNITS

In phrase-based models, the basic unit of translation is the *phrase pair*. A phrase pair is simply a pairing of a sequence of tokens in the source language with a sequence of tokens in the target language. We will write phrase pairs in the form ⟨ *source* | *target* ⟩. For instance, the pair ⟨ ein groß | a big ⟩ represents a translation unit in which the German fragment ein groß is mapped to the English fragment a big.

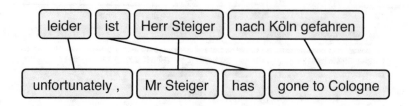

Figure 1.1: A derivation using phrases.

In syntax-based models, the translation unit can be thought of as an extended version of the phrase pair. There is not one type of syntactic translation unit. Rather, there is a family of related types, with different syntax-based models using different types. Within this family, one property can be considered fundamental: the phrases can contain *gaps*. The introduction of gaps allows for the nesting of phrases within phrases and corresponds directly to the notion of recursion in natural language. There are two other main types of extension: the first is *labeling*—the association of phrases with labels; the second is *internal tree structure*—the association of phrases with syntactic tree fragments.

Before we see how these notions are defined formally, let us take a look at some examples of different types of translation units and see how each of them functions as part of a translation. In the examples that follow, we will show a decomposition into translation units of the following German-English translation:[1]

(1) leider ist Herr Steiger nach Köln gefahren
    unfortunately has Mr Steiger to Cologne gone
(2) unfortunately, Mr Steiger has gone to Cologne

Our example sentence pair exhibits one of the features of German-English translation that has proven problematic for statistical machine translation: the movement of the main verb from a position just after the subject in English to the end of the clause in German. In the example, the verb does not have far to move, but in longer sentences the distance can be considerable—much further than is allowed by the hard reordering limit imposed by typical phrase-based models.

1.1.1   PHRASES

Figure 1.1 shows a possible derivation of our example sentence pair using phrase pairs. By choosing different segmentations, many alternative derivations are of course possible. When given a choice, longer phrases are usually preferable because they include more context, but in practice a

---

[1]We have decapitalized the first word of each sentence. Normalizing letter case helps to improve the generality of translation units and is common practice in statistical machine translation (see, for example, Koehn et al. [2008]).

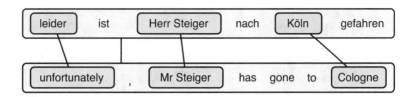

Figure 1.2: A derivation using phrases with gaps.

model must draw from the limited pool of phrase pairs that were observed in training. This means that the context encoded in an individual phrase pair rarely extends beyond three or four words.

For the issue of verb movement in English-German translation, moving the main verb within a phrase pair may be possible for very short distances, as in the example sentence, which uses the phrase pair ⟨ `nach Köln gefahren | gone to Cologne` ⟩. However, for movement over longer distances, it becomes increasingly unlikely that a suitable phrase pair will exist, meaning that the model must instead reorder phrases.

1.1.2   PHRASES WITH GAPS

Our second derivation, shown in Figure 1.2, uses phrases with gaps. On the German side, the phrases `leider`, `Herr Steiger`, and `Köln` are nested inside the larger sentence-level phrase ◇ `ist` ◇ `nach` ◇ `gefahren` (where the ◇ symbol represents a gap). Unlike the previous example, all reordering is now internal to the translation units. The decision about how to move the verbs is encoded within the outermost translation unit. Importantly, the verbal translation is now captured within a single operation:

⟨ ◇ `ist` ◇ `nach` ◇ `gefahren` | ◇ `,` ◇ `has gone to` ◇ ⟩

Notice also that the insertion of a comma is now contextualized within a unit that covers the entire sentence.

While gaps allow the generalization of long phrase pairs, they also carry a danger of over-generalization since there is no restriction on the form of the phrase pair that fills a gap. For instance, suppose that we wish to translate the sentence:

(3) leider ist Herr Steiger **nicht** nach Köln gefahren
    *unfortunately has Mr Steiger **not** to Cologne gone*

The outermost translation unit can be overlaid onto this sentence just as well as for the original sentence. Now suppose that during training the model had learned the phrase pair:

⟨ `Herr Steiger nicht | Mr Steiger does not` ⟩

Figure 1.3: An alternative derivation using phrases with gaps. In this instance the English sentence is ungrammatical.

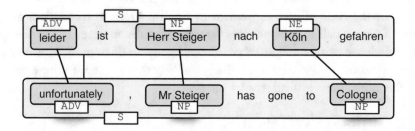

Figure 1.4: A derivation using phrases with labels.

This is a perfectly reasonable translation unit. However, the translation units do not produce a good translation in combination: the resulting sentence, shown in Figure 1.3, is ungrammatical and difficult to make sense of.

1.1.3   PHRASES WITH LABELS

Our third derivation, shown in Figure 1.4, adds labels to the phrases. The labels in this example happen to be treebank constituent labels, but in principle, they could be anything: CCG supertags, dependency relations, semantic roles, and so on. Adding labels can go some way to addressing the overgeneralization problem. For instance, the outermost translation unit requires the second gap to be filled by a phrase pair that is labeled NP (for "noun phrase") on both the source and target side. This rules out the problematic phrase pair from the previous example, since neither phrase is a noun phrase.

    Notice that there can be differing labels for the source and target phrases (in the example, Köln is labeled NE and Cologne is labeled NP). As we will see later, this is a modeling decision: some models require matching source and target labels.

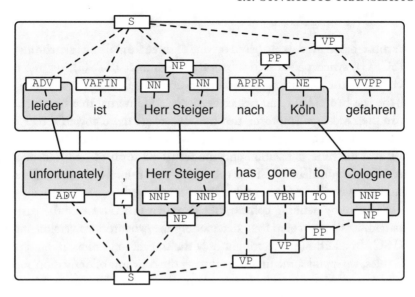

Figure 1.5: A derivation using phrases with internal tree structure.

Now that we are introducing syntactic annotation into the rules, it is natural to take this a step further and fill in the missing tree structure.

1.1.4   PHRASES WITH INTERNAL TREE STRUCTURE

Our final derivation adds internal tree structure (Figure 1.5). We have already showed how gaps in phrase pairs allow us to capture a generalization about verb phrase translation in a single operation. By adding labeled gaps and tree structure, we are in theory able to extend this ability to capture phenomena like paired predicate-argument structure. In the example, it is possible to capture paired tree fragments that explain how the past participle construction of verbs changes from German to English. It can also help disambiguate between syntactic relations. For instance, consider the following sequence of labeled gaps: V NP PP. Does the PP attach to the NP or to the V? Correctly translating a sentence may depend on knowing the correct attachment—a detail that can be encoded in the internal tree structure.

Syntax in rules has other practical advantages. On the source side, syntax-directed rule selection can be used to reduce the search space to enable faster decoding (Section 1.4). On the target side, the syntax can be used to inform scoring features. For instance, a syntactic language model can be used to encourage the generation of syntactically well-formed sentences.

1.2   GRAMMAR FORMALISMS

Most syntax-based models are based on one of three formalisms: synchronous context-free grammar (SCFG), synchronous tree-substitution grammar (STSG), or tree transducers. The first, SCFG, allows the definition of translation units containing gaps, which can optionally be labeled; the last two, STSG and tree transducers, add internal tree structure.

In their most general form, tree transducers are more powerful than STSG, adding operations such as node copying or deletion. However, these facilities have so far not been employed in statistical machine translation and the restricted form of tree transducer rules that are used in practice are equivalent to STSG rules with only minor technical differences. To simplify the presentation, we will use STSG throughout this book.[2]

We begin by defining context-free grammar (CFG). Once the basics of CFG have been understood, it is a short step to understanding the synchronous version and then to understanding STSG. In addition to describing how the translation units can be represented as SCFG or STSG rules, we spend some time introducing the concepts of derivation and weighted grammars, and introducing related terminology and notation. These are prerequisites for the description of statistical models in the following section and decoding algorithms in Chapters 3–5. Rather than scattering the material through the book, we have tried to provide a self-contained introduction here. If these concepts are new to you and some details pass you by on first reading, then you can always return to this section later.

1.2.1   CONTEXT-FREE GRAMMAR

We suspect that most readers will have at least some familiarity with context-free grammar. For those readers, let us bring CFG back into sharp focus with a formal definition. Even if you have not seen CFG before, the basic concepts should quickly become clear.

Definition 1.1   (Context-Free Grammar).   A *context-free grammar (CFG)* is a 4-tuple $G = \langle T, N, S^\dagger, R \rangle$, where T is a finite set of terminal symbols; N is a finite set of non-terminal symbols that is disjoint from T; $S^\dagger \in N$ is a start symbol; and R is a set of production rules defined over $N \cup T$. Each rule has the form $A \to \alpha$, where A is a non-terminal and α is a string of terminals and non-terminals.

In the context of natural language processing, the terminals of a CFG typically represent the words of a language and the non-terminals represent grammatical categories. The categories might be those delineated by a linguistic theory or might be derived by other means (for example, using unsupervised machine learning methods). The production rules collectively specify the ways in which the words of the language can be combined. For instance, a CFG for English might contain a production rule S → NP VP specifying that a noun phrase (NP) can be combined with a verb

---

[2]For readers wishing to learn more about tree transducer formalisms, see Knight and Graehl [2005] for an excellent overview.

phrase (VP) to produce a sentence (S). In turn, further production rules specify precisely how NPs and VPs can be constructed and exactly what combinations of words they can contain.

The flip side to describing how words combine is that CFGs also describe how strings of words can be broken apart. We will focus in this section on the combinatorial aspect: how a CFG combines words into strings through the process of *derivation*. We will return later to the process of *parsing*, which is concerned with breaking down a string into its constituent parts.

Derivation is a sequential process that operates on a symbol string (i.e., a string of terminals and non-terminals). At each step, the symbol string is transformed by rewriting a single non-terminal, A, as a string of symbols, α. Rewriting is constrained by the grammar's set of production rules: a rewrite of non-terminal A with symbol string α is only allowed if the grammar includes the production rule $A \rightarrow \alpha$. For many grammars, the derivation process can continue indefinitely (for instance by continually rewriting a non-terminal X as Y then as X again), but for the most part we are only concerned with finite derivations. We are particularly interested in derivations that begin with a single non-terminal and end with a string of terminals. When a derivation yields a string of terminals, the process *must* end since there is no way of further rewriting the string. When a derivation begins with the grammar's start symbol and ends with a string of terminals, the resulting string is called a *sentence* ("sentence" is a formal term here: a sentence in this sense need not be a sentence in the natural language sense).

Example 1.2   If a CFG G has terminal symbols $T = \{$a, beastie, bold, timorous$\}$ and non-terminal symbols $N = \{$ADJ, DET, NOUN, NP$\}$, of which $S^\dagger = $ NP is designated the start symbol, and if G contains the production rules:

$$\begin{aligned} \text{NP} &\rightarrow \text{DET ADJ NOUN} \\ \text{DET} &\rightarrow \text{a} \\ \text{ADJ} &\rightarrow \text{bold} \\ \text{ADJ} &\rightarrow \text{timorous} \\ \text{NOUN} &\rightarrow \text{beastie} \end{aligned}$$

then the two sentences "a timorous beastie" and "a bold beastie" (and only those two sentences) are derivable from G. Here is one way of deriving the first sentence.

1. Starting from the string "NP," rewrite it as "DET ADJ NOUN" by applying the first production rule.

2. Next, rewrite the intermediate string to "DET timorous NOUN" (using the fourth rule).

3. Then rewrite that to "DET timorous beastie" (using the fifth rule).

4. Finally, rewrite the string to "a timorous beastie" (using the second rule).

By applying the production rules in different orders, there are six (trivially) distinct ways to derive the sentence.

In Example 1.2, the start symbol NP, the intermediate strings, and the sentence are all examples of *sentential forms*. For any grammar G, a sentential form is either G's start symbol $S^\dagger$ or a sequence of terminals and non-terminals that can be derived from $S^\dagger$ via a sequence of one or more rule applications.

If a symbol string, α, can be rewritten as a second, β, using a single production rule then we say that β is *immediately derivable* from α and denote this relation $\alpha \Rightarrow \beta$. We use the symbol $\overset{*}{\Rightarrow}$ to indicate that a symbol string can be rewritten as another via a sequence of zero or more rule applications (naturally, an application of zero rules leaves the string unchanged).

The derivation process has a hierarchical nature: when a non-terminal symbol is rewritten, we can think of that non-terminal being the parent of the symbols that replace it; and in turn, any child non-terminal symbols being the parents of the symbols that replace them. The resulting hierarchical object is referred to as a *derivation tree*.

Example 1.3   The six derivations from Example 1.2 all share the following derivation tree:

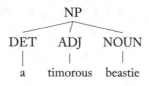

If two derivations result in the same derivation tree then the differences in the order of rewrites are usually of little interest. By adopting a convention of, for instance, always rewriting the leftmost non-terminal in a symbol string, we can uniquely associate a single *canonical derivation* with each distinct derivation tree. In Example 1.2, the two sentences ("the timorous beastie" and "the bold beastie") have a single canonical derivation each.

As well as referring to a process, the word "derivation" is also used to refer to an entity, which can be thought of as the trace of the process:

Definition 1.4 (CFG Derivation).   A (finite) *CFG derivation* is a sequence of sentential forms $\sigma = \gamma_1, \gamma_2, \ldots, \gamma_k$ defined over some CFG such that $\gamma_i \Rightarrow \gamma_{i+1}$ for all $1 \leq i < k$. If a canonical derivation form is assumed then σ can equivalently be expressed as a sequence of production rules $r_1, r_2, \ldots, r_{k-1}$, where r_i is the (unique) rule that rewrites γ_i to γ_{i+1}.

The use of a canonical form of derivation is so common that it frequently goes unstated. Often the word "derivation" is used without qualification to mean a canonical derivation or to refer to a derivation tree. Throughout the remainder of this book, unless specified otherwise, we will use the term in this second, order-independent sense.

Having defined a CFG derivation, we can define the *language* of a grammar.

Definition 1.5 (Language of a CFG).   Let G be a context-free grammar with start symbol $S^\dagger$. The *language* of G, denoted $\mathcal{L}(G)$, is the set of sentences that can be derived from $S^\dagger$.

At this point, our examples have exhibited an implicit constraint on their form. For a rule $A \to \alpha$, the right-hand side α has been either (a) a single terminal symbol or (b) a sequence of one or more non-terminals. Definition 1.1 does not constrain α in this way, but instead states that α is a sequence of one or more symbols drawn from $N \cup T$. We can produce a variation of the grammar from Example 1.2 that combines some of the rules:

$$
\begin{array}{rcl}
\text{NP} & \to & \text{a ADJ beastie} \\
\text{ADJ} & \to & \text{bold} \\
\text{ADJ} & \to & \text{timorous}
\end{array}
$$

The first rule here is reminiscent of the labeled gaps discussed above. The language of this grammar is exactly the same as that of Example 1.2: the sentences *a bold beastie* and *a timorous beastie*. This is true despite the fact that the derivations that produce these sentences will differ between the grammars; the first grammar takes four productions per string, while the second takes only two. Because these grammars have identical languages, they are considered to be *weakly equivalent*; if they were isomorphic (up to a relabeling), they would also be *strongly equivalent*.

Definition 1.6 (Equivalence).   Two grammars G_1 and G_2 are *weakly equivalent* if $\mathcal{L}(G_1) = \mathcal{L}(G_2)$. They are *strongly equivalent* if every derivation in G_1 is isomorphic to a derivation in G_2, and vice versa.

As we will see later in this book, the form of a grammar's rules can have implications for computational complexity. One important property is the number of non-terminals on the rule's right-hand side. This is referred to as the rule's *rank*.

Definition 1.7 (CFG Rank or Arity).   The *rank* (equivalently, *arity*) of a CFG rule is the number of non-terminals on its right-hand side. The rank of a grammar is the maximum rank of any rule in the grammar.

1.2.2 SYNCHRONOUS CONTEXT-FREE GRAMMAR

Having defined CFG, we can now define the synchronous version.

Definition 1.8 (Synchronous Context-Free Grammar). A *synchronous context-free grammar* (SCFG) is a 4-tuple $G = \langle T, N, S^\dagger, R \rangle$ where T, N, and $S^\dagger$ are defined as for CFG (Definition 1.1) and R is a set of synchronous rules. Each rule $r \in R$ is a pair of CFG production rules $A \to \alpha$ and $B \to \beta$, A and B being non-terminals, α and β strings of terminals and non-terminals, with the property that α and β contain the same number of non-terminals, and each non-terminal in α is paired exclusively with one non-terminal in β.

In the context of statistical machine translation, the first production rule, $A \to \alpha$ is a CFG rule in the source language and the second, $B \to \beta$, is a CFG rule in the target language. The terminal set T comprises the combined vocabularies of the source and target languages (as observed in the data from which the rules are learned). The contents of the non-terminal set N depends on the type of model: in models that use unlabeled gaps, N will typically contain a single generic non-terminal (commonly X) and a separate start symbol (commonly S). In models that use labeled translation units, N will contain symbols derived from linguistic categories for either the source or target language, or (less commonly) both.

We will write a general SCFG rule in the following format:

$$A \;\to\; \alpha \;\;,\;\; B \;\to\; \beta$$

using subscripted indices to indicate the non-terminal links.

Example 1.9 The translation units from Example 1.4 can be written as the following SCFG rules:

ADV	$\to$	leider	,	ADV $\to$	unfortunately
NP	$\to$	Herr Steiger	,	NP $\to$	Mr Steiger
NE	$\to$	Köln	,	NP $\to$	Cologne
S	$\to$	ADV_1 ist NP_2 nach NE_3 gefahren	,	S $\to$	ADV_1 , NP_2 has gone to NP_3

It is often necessary to refer individually to the source or target components of a SCFG rule or grammar. These components are referred to as the source and target projections and are denoted using a function called proj.

Definition 1.10 (Source and Target Projections). If $G = \langle T, N, S^\dagger, R \rangle$ is a SCFG and $r = \langle A \to \alpha, B \to \beta \rangle \in R$ then the *source projection* and *target projection* of r, $\text{proj}_s(r)$ and $\text{proj}_t(r)$, are

$A \rightarrow \alpha$ and $B \rightarrow \beta$, respectively. The source and target projections of G, $\text{proj}_s(G)$ and $\text{proj}_t(G)$, are the CFGs with the rule sets $\{\text{proj}_s(r) \mid r \in R\}$ and $\{\text{proj}_t(r) \mid r \in R\}$.

Given a CFG rule q, the *inverse* source (or target) projection returns the set of SCFG rules for which q is the source (or target) side component. Of course, the inverse projection must be applied with respect to a particular SCFG.

Definition 1.11   (Inverse Source and Target Projections).   If $G = \langle T, N, S^\dagger, R \rangle$ is a SCFG and $q = \langle C \rightarrow \gamma \rangle$ is a CFG rule then the *inverse source projection* and *inverse target projection* of q with respect to G, $\text{proj}'_s(q)$ and $\text{proj}'_t(q)$, are the rule sets $\{r \mid q = \text{proj}_s(r), r \in R\}$ and $\{r \mid q = \text{proj}_t(r), r \in R\}$, respectively.

Derivation with a SCFG G involves the rewriting of a pair of symbol strings $\langle \gamma_s, \gamma_t \rangle$, where γ_s contains only symbols that occur on the source-side of G's production rules and γ_t contains only symbols that occur on the target-side. As with the production rules, γ_s and γ_t are required to contain the same number of non-terminals, and each non-terminal in γ_s is paired exclusively with one non-terminal in γ_t. A rewrite using a rule $\langle A \rightarrow \alpha, B \rightarrow \beta \rangle$ is allowed if γ_s contains the non-terminal A, γ_t contains the non-terminal B, and A and B are paired with each other.

Example 1.12   Using the SCFG rules from Example 1.9, and assuming S to be the start symbol, we can derive a pair of source and target sentences as follows:

S_1, S_1

$\Rightarrow$ ADV$_2$ ist NP$_3$ nach NE$_4$ gefahren ,
        ADV$_2$, NP$_3$ has gone to NP$_4$

$\Rightarrow$ leider ist NP$_3$ nach NE$_4$ gefahren ,
        unfortunately , NP$_3$ has gone to NP$_4$

$\Rightarrow$ leider ist Herr Steiger nach NE$_4$ gefahren ,
        unfortunately , Mr Steiger has gone to NP$_4$

$\Rightarrow$ leider ist Herr Steiger nach Köln gefahren ,
        unfortunately , Mr Steiger has gone to Cologne

Just as a CFG derivation has an associated tree, a SCFG derivation has an associated pair of trees, one for the source-side and one for the target-side. Each non-terminal node of the source tree is linked with a single non-terminal node of the target tree. Equivalently, a SCFG derivation can be expressed as a single tree where the nodes are labeled with rule identifiers and each node has one child for each non-terminal pair in the corresponding rule. The ordering of a node's children can follow the source or target non-terminal order, as long as the ordering scheme is consistent across the tree. As with CFG derivations, if a canonical derivation form is assumed then a SCFG derivation can be expressed as a sequence of SCFG rules.

Example 1.13   The derivation from Example 1.12 corresponds to the following pair of trees. Non-terminal links are indicated using co-index boxes:

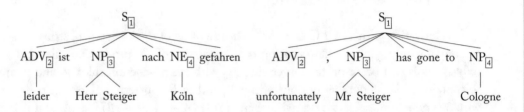

Equivalently, if we use the identifiers $r_1 - r_4$ to refer to the SCFG rules from Example 1.9 (in the order they are listed) then the derivation can be written:

The concepts of language, equivalence, and rank generalize naturally from CFG to SCFG.

Definition 1.14   (Language of a SCFG).   Let G be a SCFG with start symbol $S^\dagger$. The *language* of G, denoted $\mathcal{L}(G)$, is the set of sentence pairs that can be derived from $S^\dagger$.

Definition 1.15   (SCFG Rank).   The *rank* of a SCFG rule is the number of non-terminal pairs on its right-hand side. The rank of a SCFG is the maximum rank of any rule in the grammar.

The definition of equivalence is exactly as for CFG and so we do not repeat it here (see Definition 1.6).

There is a widely used variant of SCFG that we will refer to as *shared-category* SCFG. Shared-category SCFG is defined identically to the *distinct-category* version of Definition 1.8, except that the paired CFG rules have the same left-hand side and every non-terminal in α is paired with an identical non-terminal in β. When writing shared-category SCFG rules, we will drop the target left-hand side:

$$A \rightarrow \alpha \, , \beta$$

Distinct-category SCFGs are a natural choice for models in which the translation units are labeled on both the source and target sides, since the two languages are likely to use differing grammatical categories. When only one side is labeled—which is by far the more common case in practice—shared-category SCFGs are usually used.

While the expressivity of distinct-category SCFG is attractive for certain kinds of model, it is sometimes more convenient to work with a shared-category SCFG. We can convert any distinct-category SCFG to shared-category form by conjoining each pair of non-terminals to create a hybrid "source and target" non-terminal.[3]

Example 1.16   The SCFG from Example 1.9 can be expressed in shared-category form as follows:

$$(ADV, ADV) \rightarrow \text{leider} \qquad\qquad , \text{ unfortunately}$$
$$(NP, NP) \rightarrow \text{Herr Steiger} \qquad , \text{ Mr Steiger}$$
$$(NE, NP) \rightarrow \text{Köln} \qquad\qquad , \text{ Cologne}$$
$$(S, S) \rightarrow (ADV, ADV)_1 \text{ ist } (NP,NP)_2 \quad , \quad (ADV, ADV)_1 , (NP,NP)_2 \text{ has}$$
$$\text{nach } (NE,NP)_3 \text{ gefahren} \qquad \text{gone to } (NE,NP)_3$$

Note that the notation (A, B) is for our convenience only. Formally, the name is arbitrary: we could equally have chosen a symbol like X_{482}.

1.2.3 SYNCHRONOUS TREE-SUBSTITUTION GRAMMAR

Using SCFG, we can define translation units with labeled gaps. Synchronous tree-substitution grammar (STSG) allows us to add internal tree structure. This is possible since STSG rules are pairs of tree fragments.

Definition 1.17   (Synchronous Tree-Substitution Grammar).   A *synchronous tree-substitution grammar* (STSG) is a 4-tuple $G = \langle T, N, S^\dagger, R \rangle$ where T, N, and $S^\dagger$ are defined as for CFG (Definition 1.1) and R is a set of synchronous rules. Each rule $r \in R$ is a pair of trees α and β in which the root and interior nodes are non-terminals drawn from N and each leaf node is either a terminal drawn from T or a non-terminal drawn from N. Each non-terminal leaf in α is paired exclusively with one non-terminal leaf in β.

In the context of machine translation, α is a tree in which the terminals represent tokens in the source language and non-terminals represent grammatical categories. Similarly, the termi-

---

[3]As this conversion makes clear, the distinct-category version does not provide any additional formal expressiveness over its shared-category counterpart.

nals and non-terminals of β represent tokens and grammatical categories in the target language. Typically, the trees are fragments of parse trees over source and target sentences in the training data.

　　We will write a general STSG rule as a pair of comma-separated trees, using index boxes to indicate the non-terminal links.

Example 1.18　　An example of an STSG. The translation units from Figure 1.5 correspond to the rules r_1, r_2, r_3, and r_5.

$$r_1 = \begin{array}{c} \text{ADV} \\ | \\ \text{leider} \end{array}\ ,\ \begin{array}{c} \text{ADV} \\ | \\ \text{unfortunately} \end{array}$$

$$r_2 = \begin{array}{c} \text{NP} \\ \diagup\diagdown \\ \text{NN}\quad\text{NN} \\ |\qquad| \\ \text{Herr}\ \ \text{Steiger} \end{array}\ ,\ \begin{array}{c} \text{NP} \\ \diagup\diagdown \\ \text{NNP}\quad\text{NNP} \\ |\qquad| \\ \text{Mr}\ \ \text{Steiger} \end{array}$$

$$r_3 = \begin{array}{c} \text{NE} \\ | \\ \text{Köln} \end{array}\ ,\ \begin{array}{c} \text{NP} \\ | \\ \text{NNP} \\ | \\ \text{Cologne} \end{array}$$

$$r_4 = \begin{array}{c} \text{VVPP} \\ | \\ \text{gefahren} \end{array}\ ,\ \begin{array}{c} \text{VBN} \\ | \\ \text{gone} \end{array}$$

$r_5 =$

Left tree:
```
              S
   ┌──────┬──────┬───────────┐
 ADV□1  VAFIN  NP□2          VP
          |              ┌────┴────┐
         ist            PP       VVPP
                      ┌──┴──┐      |
                    APPR  NE□3   gefahren
                      |
                    nach
```
,
Right tree:
```
         S
   ┌───┬────┬──────┐
 ADV□1 ,  NP□2     VP
              ┌─────┴─────┐
            VBZ          VP
             |        ┌───┴───┐
            has     VBN      PP
                     |     ┌──┴──┐
                   gone   TO   NE□3
                           |
                           to
```

$r_6 =$

Left tree:
```
              S
   ┌──────┬──────┬───────────┐
 ADV   VAFIN  NP□1           VP
  |      |              ┌─────┴─────┐
leider  ist           PP         VVPP□3
                    ┌──┴──┐
                  APPR  NE□2
                    |
                  nach
```
,
Right tree:
```
         S
   ┌───┬────┬──────┐
 ADV   ,  NP□1     VP
  |             ┌─────┴─────┐
unfortunately  VBZ         VP
                |      ┌────┴────┐
               has   VBN□3      PP
                            ┌────┴────┐
                           TO       NE□2
                            |
                           to
```

As for SCFG, it is convenient to have a notation for referring individually to the source and target components of a STSG rule. We will define the analogous projection functions here. Just as the source and target components of a SCFG rule are CFG rules, the components of a STSG rule are tree-substitution grammar (TSG) rules. The relationship between the TSG and STSG formalisms is essentially the same as the relationship between CFG and SCFG. We will therefore leave the definition of TSG implicit, except to note that the projection of a STSG rule is more usually referred to as an *initial tree* or an *elementary tree*, rather than a rule. For uniformity, we will use the term *rule* since many of the methods that we will present later in this book are (more or less) interchangeable between CFG and TSG formalisms (or SCFG and STSG).

Definition 1.19 (Source and Target Projections (STSG)). If $G = \langle T, N, S^\dagger, R \rangle$ is a STSG and $r = \langle \alpha, \beta \rangle \in R$ then the *source projection* and *target projection* of r, $\text{proj}_s(r)$ and $\text{proj}_t(r)$, are α and β, respectively. The source and target projections of G, $\text{proj}_s(G)$ and $\text{proj}_t(G)$, are the TSGs with the rule sets $\{\text{proj}_s(r) \mid r \in R\}$ and $\{\text{proj}_t(r) \mid r \in R\}$.

Given a TSG rule q, the inverse source (or target) projection returns the set of STSG rules for which q is the source (or target) side component. The inverse projection must be applied with respect to a particular STSG.

Definition 1.20 (Inverse Source and Target Projections (STSG)). If $G = \langle T, N, S^\dagger, R \rangle$ is a STSG and $q = \gamma$ is a TSG rule then the *inverse source projection* and *inverse target projection* of q with respect to G, $\text{proj}'_s(q)$ and $\text{proj}'_t(q)$, are the rule sets $\{r \mid q = \text{proj}_s(r), r \in R\}$ and $\{r \mid q = \text{proj}_t(r), r \in R\}$, respectively.

Derivation with a STSG G involves the rewriting of a pair of trees $\langle \gamma_s, \gamma_t \rangle$. Whereas an SCFG rewrite replaces a pair of non-terminals with a pair of symbol strings, an STSG rewrite replaces a pair of non-terminals with a pair of trees. A rewrite using a rule $\langle \alpha, \beta \rangle$ is allowed if γ_s contains the non-terminal A, where $A = \text{root}(\alpha)$, γ_t contains the non-terminal B, where $B = \text{root}(\beta)$, and the sentential form's A and B are paired with each other. The rewrite operation is called synchronous tree substitution. As with SCFG, γ_s and γ_t are required to contain the same number of non-terminals and each non-terminal in γ_s is paired exclusively with one non-terminal in γ_t.

Like CFG and SCFG, a STSG derivation has an associated derivation tree. The derivation tree is distinct from the derived trees and care must be taken to avoid confusing the two types of object.

Example 1.21 Two sentential derivations are possible using the grammar rules from Example 1.18. Their derivation trees are

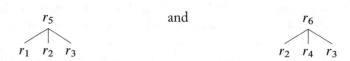

Notice that the two derivations have the same source and target derived trees. The left derivation corresponds to the derivation shown in Figure 1.5.

Language, equivalence, and rank are defined for STSG exactly as for SCFG (see Definitions 1.14, 1.6, and 1.15, respectively).

Like with SCFG, we will distinguish between shared-category and distinct-category forms of STSG. The examples we have given so far have used the distinct-category form. In the shared-category form, it is typical that the tree structure on either the source or target side of a rule is derived from a parse tree; the other side of the rule has a flat structure with non-terminal labels that double those of their counterparts.

Example 1.22 A shared-category version of rule r_6 from Example 1.18 that uses source-side structure only would be:

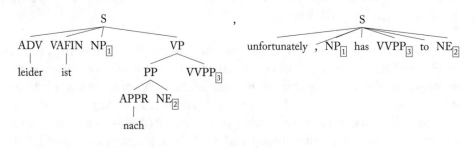

1.2.4 PROBABILISTIC AND WEIGHTED GRAMMARS

Probabilistic and weighted variants have been developed for CFG, SCFG, and STSG. Among these, the most frequently encountered are probabilistic CFGs (PCFGs), which are widely used in natural language processing, most notably for phrase-structure parsing.

In this book, we will follow recent work in parsing by defining rule weights abstractly as elements of a weight set $\mathbb{K}$. For a particular application, the weight set might contain probabilities, real numbers, Booleans, vectors, or some more exotic type. At this level of abstraction, the definitions of rule weights and weighted grammars are essentially the same, regardless of the underlying formalism. In the following definition we will use the word "grammar" to mean any of CFG, SCFG, or STSG and the word "rule" to mean a rule of one of those grammars.

Definition 1.23   (Rule Weight Function and Weighted Grammar).   Given a rule set R, a *rule weight function* for R is a function $W_R : R \to \mathbb{K}$. A *weighted* grammar is a pair $\langle G, W_R \rangle$, where G is a grammar with rule set R and W_R is a rule weight function for R.

A probabilistic grammar is a weighted grammar $\langle G, P \rangle$ with a probabilistic rule weight function P. Specifically, P is a probability mass function that gives the probability of a rule conditioned on its left-hand-side. To put that another way, suppose that midway through a CFG derivation, we have arrived at a symbol string α, and we want to rewrite the leftmost non-terminal. If G's production rules allow us to derive β in the next step ($\alpha \Rightarrow \beta$) then P gives us the probability of this event (as opposed to any alternative the grammar might allow). The same interpretation applies for synchronous grammars except that then we are dealing with pairs of sentential forms and pairs of non-terminals.

Definition 1.24   (Probabilistic Context-Free Grammar (PCFG)).   A *probabilistic context-free grammar (PCFG)* is a pair $\langle G, P \rangle$, where $G = \langle T, N, S^\dagger, R \rangle$ is a CFG (Definition 1.1) and $P : R \to [0, 1]$ is a rule weight function such that for any $A \in N$,

$$\sum_\alpha P(A \to \alpha) = 1.$$

Probabilistic SCFGs and STSGs are defined in a similar way to PCFGs. Instead of conditioning on a single left-hand side non-terminal, the SCFG rule probability function conditions on a pair of left-hand side non-terminals. The STSG rule probability function conditions on a pair of root non-terminals.

If we assume that rule applications are independent events, then the probability of a derivation is simply the product of the probabilities of its component rules. While this independence assumption is clearly unrealistic in practice—for example, rewriting a NOUN as "tiger" is going to be more probable if a previous derivation step rewrote the preceeding word as "fierce" rather than "cloudy"—, assuming independence between rule applications greatly simplifies language modeling and this assumption is widely used. The problem of overgeneralization can be ameliorated by using more specific categories. For instance, the category-refinement approach of the Berkeley parser [Petrov et al., 2006] dramatically improves over a basic probabilistic PCFG, bringing the model close to state of the art performance.

While it is often useful to assume independence, there are situations where this assumption is too strong and needs to be relaxed. In this case we can use an alternative derivation weighting function (and possibly an alternative rule weight function). In general, the weight of a derivation is not necessarily the product of the component rule's weights.

Definition 1.25 (Derivation Weight Function). Given a derivation set D, a *derivation weight function* on D is a function $W_D : D \to \mathbb{K}$ that assigns a weight to every derivation $d \in D$.

1.3 STATISTICAL MODELS

We now return to the fundamental problem of modeling the distribution $p(t|s)$. Using the concepts from the previous section, we are now in a position to formulate a model that expresses the probability of a translation in terms of rules, derivations, and weights.

As in statistical machine translation generally, the first statistical syntax-based models proposed in the literature were generative models—that is, they modeled the joint probability distribution $p(s, t)$. A generative model of translation describes a process that generates a pair (s, t) via a sequence of steps—it provides a *generative story*. We have already seen one example: probabilistic synchronous grammar.

In contrast, discriminative models directly model the distribution of interest: $p(t|s)$. They dispense with the notion of a generative story and instead calculate a conditional probability for a translation in terms of weighted features. It is up to the model's designer to designate a set of features that they deem relevant to the problem. During training, the model learns to weight the features in order that it can discriminate good translations from bad ones.

Following the pattern in phrase-based modeling, generative models have now been supplanted by discriminative ones, with the conditional log-linear approach of Och and Ney [2002] being the dominant approach. Since generative models are no longer widely used, we will not describe them in detail. Nonetheless, we feel it is instructive to examine an example in order to see some of the decisions made in the modeling process. Here we give a representative example, which is due to Galley et al. [2006]. We then move on to discriminative models, focusing on the log-linear framework.

1.3.1 GENERATIVE MODELS

Applied to statistical machine translation, a generative model is a model of the joint probability distribution $p(s, t)$. The distribution of primary interest to us is $p(t|s)$, and the two distributions are related by the chain rule:

$$p(t|s) = \frac{p(s, t)}{p(s)}. \tag{1.1}$$

Since the denominator, $p(s)$, is fixed for a given input sentence, s, we can substitute a generative model directly into our objective function:

$$t^* = \arg\max_t p(t|s) \tag{1.2}$$

$$= \arg\max_t p(s, t). \tag{1.3}$$

We have already seen a simple means of modeling $p(s,t)$: probabilistic synchronous grammar (recall that these grammars define a probability distribution over derivations; this implicitly defines a distribution over string pairs since for any string pair we can obtain its probability by summing up the probabilities of derivations yielding that pair).

Given a probabilistic SCFG or STSG (or data from which to estimate one) we could stop at this point. However, probabilistic synchronous grammars have been found to make poor translation models on their own. Instead, generative statistical machine translation models generally follow the noisy channel approach[4] from information theory. Returning to the chain rule (Equation 1.1), if we switch the s and t variables and rearrange terms, then we get

$$p(s,t) = p(s|t)p(t). \tag{1.4}$$

Substituting into Equation 1.1, we arrive at

$$p(t|s) = \frac{p(s|t)p(t)}{p(s)} \tag{1.5}$$

and our objective function becomes

$$t^* = \arg\max_t p(s|t)p(t). \tag{1.6}$$

Equation 1.5 is known as Bayes' rule and lies at the heart of the seminal IBM word-based models [Brown et al., 1993] and early phrase-based models [Koehn et al., 2003, Marcu and Wong, 2002]. It may not be immediately obvious how applying Bayes' rule can help. After all, for sentences s and t in two arbitrarily chosen natural languages, there is no reason to think that modeling $p(s|t)$ is likely to be any more straightforward than modeling $p(t|s)$, and now there is an additional term, $p(t)$. The motivation for this approach lay in its successful use in the field of automatic speech recognition, where a distribution analogous to $p(t)$ had been modeled using a n-gram language model. Intuitively, it might seem that modeling two distributions, $p(s|t)$ and $p(t)$, instead of one, $p(t|s)$, will lead to a weaker model due to the increasing scope for the introduction of errors. Instead, automatic speech recognition had shown that modeling two components independently led to a more robust model. In the absence of a reliable model of the translation distribution (either $p(t|s)$ or $p(s|t)$), the addition of a language model component proves essential for finding well-formed translations. The language model can be seen as a filter that weeds out ill-formed candidate strings.

It is at this point that the formulation of word-based, phrase-based, and syntax-based models diverges. Let us continue with the syntax-based model by Galley et al. [2006], which as-

---

[4]Taken literally, the noisy channel approach interprets translation as the task of recovering a corrupted message: the string s is taken to be a version of t that has been garbled during its transmission across a noisy channel (i.e., its expression in the source language). Given a source string, s, the task is to recover the most probable target string, t, given what we know probabilistically about the action of the noisy communication channel and what we know about the probability distribution of strings in the target language.

sumes that we are using a STSG-based translation grammar[5] (for presentations of word-based and phrase-based models, see Brown et al. [1993] and Koehn et al. [2003]).

Applying Bayes' rule splits our model into two components, a translation model, $p(s|t)$, and a language model, $p(t)$. Galley et al. introduced a third component, $p(\pi|t)$, which we will call the tree model. They do this by splitting the translation model through the application of the sum rule:

$$p(s|t) = \sum_{\pi} p(s|\pi)p(\pi|t), \tag{1.7}$$

where π is any target-side derived tree occurring in the set of all derivations in G. (Recall that in STSG a derived tree is distinct from a derivation tree.) Notice that the term $p(\pi|t)$ is exactly the distribution that is modeled by a probabilistic parsing model, such as a PCFG. The motivation for adding this term is the same as for the introduction of the language model: to increase the robustness of the overall model by injecting a source of external modeling knowledge. Loosely speaking, the role of the tree model is to ensure that, all else being equal, translations for which there are plausible parse trees get higher probabilities than translations for which the parse trees are ill-formed.

Now, what about the term $p(s|\pi)$? In general, a single target-side derived tree π can result from multiple STSG derivations, even if the source sentence s is fixed. If we write $D(s, \pi)$ to denote the set of all derivations in G for which the source yield is s and the target derived tree is π then

$$p(s|\pi) = \sum_{d} p(d|\pi), \tag{1.8}$$

where $d \in D(s, \pi)$. To model the term $p(d|\pi)$, Galley et al. [2006] make the assumption that a derivation's rules are independent of one another. This is the standard independence assumption that we encountered in Section 1.2.4.

$$p(s|\pi) = \frac{1}{Z} \sum_{d} \prod_{r} p(\alpha|\beta), \tag{1.9}$$

where $r \in d$ and α and β are the source and target components of rule r. Notice the introduction of the term $1/Z$. This is a normalization factor, which is required to ensure that $\sum_{s'} p(s'|\pi) = 1$ (where s' is any source sentence in G).

Galley et al.'s presentation goes on to propose two methods for estimating $p(\alpha|\beta)$ from data, one based on relative frequency estimation and the other based on expectation maximization. In a typical training scenario, estimation is non-trivial since only sentence pairs are provided, not their derivations. For the remaining details of the model, we refer the reader to the original paper.

The example here demonstrates the distinguishing features of generative syntax-based models.

---

[5]Technically, Galley et al. [2006] assume a tree transducer, but the distinction is unimportant here.

1. The probability distribution over translations, $p(s, t)$, is broken down into a function of distributions over smaller units. This is primarily to facilitate the reliable estimation of statistics from data. In the example model, the language model distribution, tree distribution, and rule probability distribution are much more amenable to machine learning approaches than the original distribution.

2. The model combines independent distributions that each serve a distinct role in discriminating between translations: the language model discriminates for fluency, the tree model for syntactic well-formedness, and the translation model for translational equivalence.

1.3.2 DISCRIMINATIVE MODELS

In contrast to generative approaches, which model $p(t|s)$ indirectly in terms of $p(s, t)$, discriminative approaches to statistical machine translation directly model the conditional distribution. We will focus on the log-linear formulation, which was proposed for use in machine translation by Och and Ney [2002], and is now the most widely used approach in both phrase-based and syntax-based approaches.

Let us begin by defining the conditional log-linear model in general.

Definition 1.26 A conditional log-linear model is a conditional probability distribution of the form

$$p_\Lambda(x|y) = \frac{\exp\left(\sum_{m=1}^M \lambda_m h_m(x, y)\right)}{\sum_{x'} \exp\left(\sum_{m=1}^M \lambda_m h_m(x', y)\right)}, \tag{1.10}$$

where $h_1, \ldots, h_M$ are real-valued functions, often referred to as feature functions, and $\Lambda = \lambda_1, \ldots, \lambda_M$ are real-valued constants, often referred to as weights or scaling factors.[6] The denominator is a sum over every event x' that is possible given y.

Typically, a conditional log-linear model $p_\Lambda(x|y)$ is used to approximate a conditional distribution $p(x|y)$ that cannot be estimated directly. In principle, the feature functions, $h_1, \ldots, h_M$, can be any real-valued functions: the task of defining them is the responsibility of the model designer. Once the feature functions have been defined, the scaling factors $\lambda_1, \ldots, \lambda_M$ are determined by a learning algorithm that attempts to fit the model to data (according to some metric of model fit).

In statistical machine translation, a log-linear model is used to define the conditional probability of a translation, $p(t|s)$, in terms of the probabilities of individual derivations. Plugging s

---

[6]We will use the term "scaling factor" to avoid any confusion with rule weights.

and t into Equation 1.10 we get[7]

$$p(t|s) = \frac{\exp\left(\sum_{m=1}^{M} \lambda_m h_m(s, t)\right)}{\sum_{s'} \exp\left(\sum_{m=1}^{M} \lambda_m h_m(s', t)\right)}. \tag{1.11}$$

In a syntax-based system, every possible source and target string is the yield of some derivation in a synchronous grammar. By marginalizing over derivations, we get

$$p(t|s) = \frac{\sum_{d} \exp\left(\sum_{m=1}^{M} \lambda_m h_m(d)\right)}{\sum_{d'} \exp\left(\sum_{m=1}^{M} \lambda_m h_m(d')\right)}, \tag{1.12}$$

where $d \in D(s, t)$ and $d' \in D$ is any derivation with source yield s. In the context of search, the denominator is fixed and can be dropped (just as we dropped the $p(s)$ term in the generative approach).

$$t^* = \arg\max_t \left(\sum_d \exp\left(\sum_{m=1}^{M} \lambda_m h_m(d)\right)\right), \tag{1.13}$$

where $d \in D(s, t)$. For models based on SCFG or STSG, the number of derivations in $D(s, t)$ is exponential with respect to the source sentence length. Calculating the outer sum by enumeration is therefore intractable, but depending on the choice of features, it may be possible to perform the calculation in polynomial time using dynamic programming. Unfortunately, this turns out to be too computationally expensive for models that include a n-gram language model (we will discuss the computational cost of including a n-gram language model in Chapter 4). In practice, therefore, the search objective is usually approximated using a single derivation:

$$d^* = \arg\max_d \left(\exp\sum_{m=1}^{M} \lambda_m h_m(d)\right), \tag{1.14}$$

where d is any derivation with source yield s. This is sometimes referred to as the *max-derivation* objective, in contast to the *max-translation* objective of Equation 1.13. Mathematically, the max-derivation objective is an extremely crude approximation to the max-translation objective, taking the largest element of the sum as an approximation of the whole sum. However, the use of better (and more computationally expensive) approximations has so far only led to minor improvements in translation quality in practice.[8]

We can make a further simplification: since the exponential function is monotonic, $\arg\max_x e^{f(x)}$ is equivalent to $\arg\max_x f(x)$ for any function $f(x)$. Applying this to Equa-

---

[7]We will drop the $p_\Lambda(t|s)$ notation and write $p(t|s)$ from here on.
[8]See, for example, Blunsom and Osborne [2008] and Arun et al. [2009].

tion 1.14 gives our final version of the objective search function:

$$d^* \;=\; \arg\max_d \left(\sum_{m=1}^{M} \lambda_m h_m(d) \right). \tag{1.15}$$

Having defined the general form of the model, we can turn to the definition of feature functions. One possibility is to define three functions that are analogous to the translation model, tree model, and language model components of Galley et al. [2006]'s generative model. The first (the translation model) is the log probability of the derivation given the target-side tree:

$$h_1(d) = \log p(d|\pi) = \sum_{r \in d} \log p(\alpha|\beta), \tag{1.16}$$

where π is d's target-side derived tree and $r \in d$ is a rule $\langle \alpha, \beta \rangle$. The log of the probability is used for two reasons: first, since the calculations typically involve extremely small numbers, summing log probabilities is less likely to lead to arithmetic underflow than multiplying probabilities; second, applying a nonlinear transformation to the probability (of which the logarithm is just one possibility) makes the function more amenable to learning from data.[9]

The second feature function (the tree model) is the log probability of the target-side tree given the target-side sentence:

$$h_2(d) = \log p(\pi|t), \tag{1.17}$$

where t is the target-side yield of d. The third (the language model) is the log probability of the target-side sentence:

$$h_3(d) = \log p(t). \tag{1.18}$$

Slotting these in to Equation 1.15 gives

$$d^* = \arg\max_d \left(\lambda_1 \cdot \sum_{r \in d} \log p(\alpha|\beta) + \lambda_2 \cdot \log p(\pi|t) + \lambda_3 \cdot \log p(t) \right). \tag{1.19}$$

An important advantage of this model over a generative model is that the scaling factors can be tuned to increase or decrease the influence of each component. Scaling of this kind is crucial in a model where the component distributions are poor approximations of the true distributions making it likely that some are more reliable than others. A further advantage of the log-linear model is that there is (at least mathematically) no limit to the number of feature functions. Since the functions are not required to be statistically independent of each other, the scaling factors can serve to counter redundancy if there is a strong correlation between feature functions.

---

[9]See Clark et al. [2014] for a detailed discussion of feature non-linearity in log-linear SMT models.

Dense Features

Most syntax-based models include a small number of core features that are analogous to features used in phrase-based models. These are sometimes called *dense* features (for reasons that will become clear once we describe *sparse* features). They include:

- $\log p(d|d_s)$ and $\log p(d|d_t)$, the log-probabilities of the derivation conditioned on the source or target derivation tree. These are usually the sums of rule-level log-probabilities. Our earlier example used the target-conditioned form only, but empirically it has been found that including both improves translation quality;

- $\log p(t|s)$ and $\log p(s|t)$, word-level translation probabilities, in both directions. These features are sometimes called lexical smoothing features since they are estimated from richer statistics than the rule-level translation probabilities and can compensate for sparsity-related issues that arise in the estimation of rule probabilities;

- $\log p(t)$, the language model log-probability of the target string;

- $|t|$, the length of the target string. This allows the model to correct any bias toward producing overly long or short sentences. For instance, the language model will favor short sentences over long sentences on average, and a strongly-weighted language model might result in words being dropped; and

- $|d|$, the number of rules in the derivation. This allows the model to learn a preference for using large or small rules. Large rules have the advantage that they include more contextual information, but usually at the cost of using less reliable statistics.

Other possible dense features include a penalty for rule rarity and the probability of the derived tree. The dense feature set may also include model-specific features. We will say more about dense features when we discuss how rules are learned from data in the next chapter.

Sparse Features

Dense features tend to resemble scores: they provide real-valued answers to questions like: how probable is the target sentence? How many rules does the derivation use? In contrast, sparse features answer binary questions about the individual rules of a derivation. These questions may be highly specific: does the target-side of the rule include the word "archival"? Does the source-side tree fragment include the production NP → NP PP? In any given derivation, the answer to most questions of this type is no, so that these features are most efficiently represented via sparse data structures.

Individual sparse features are usually instantiations of a general template feature. For instance, one such template may be:

$$h(r) = \begin{cases} 1, & \text{if the target-side of } r \text{ contains the terminal } w \\ 0, & \text{otherwise.} \end{cases}$$

From this template, there could be a sparse feature for every possible target-side word w (or perhaps the most frequent 100 or 1000). As such, a model may include hundreds, thousands, or even tens of thousands of sparse features.

Unlike dense features, there is not a common core of sparse features (or feature templates). For a good example of the types of feature used in a real model, we refer the reader to Chiang et al. [2009]. While the use of sparse features has been shown to significantly improve translation quality for some models, their adoption has been patchy. Frequently cited problems include the overfitting of scaling factors during tuning and a lack of generalization across language pairs. For a discussion of these issues (in the context of phrase-based statistical machine translation), see Green et al. [2014].

1.4   A CLASSIFICATION OF SYNTAX-BASED MODELS

Syntax-based models can be classified along multiple dimensions. Unfortunately, different researchers choose to distinguish among models using subtly different criteria, sometimes using the same names in different ways. As a result, the terminology in the literature can be inconsistent and confusing. Here we will present our own take on classification. Three of the names we use—string-to-tree, tree-to-string, and tree-to-tree—are widely used (albeit not entirely consistently). The other—string-to-string—is somewhat rarer.[10] Our usage is consistent with much of the literature, but unavoidably there are cases where our usage disagrees with that of other authors.

Our classification rests on whether the source derived tree, the target derived tree, or both, are intended to resemble a parse tree as observed in the training data. This single (sometimes fuzzy) criterion is applied regardless of whether source or target syntactic annotation is used in the rules.[11]

Of course, there is little to be gained from obsessing over terminology. The main purpose of this section is to introduce, at a high-level, the diverse family of syntax-based approaches and to highlight and contrast the distinguishing features of different approaches.

1.4.1   STRING-TO-STRING

String-to-string models produce derivations in which there is no requirement or expectation that the derived trees should resemble linguistic parse trees. Naturally, this category includes models that use unlabeled hierarchical phrases where there is no representation of linguistic categories. This category can also include models that do make limited use of syntactic annotation and that use linguistic parse trees in training. In this case, the crucial distinction is in how the rules are learned and applied: unlike in the other categories, there is no requirement that a string-to-string model can reproduce the parse trees observed in the training data.

---

[10]We can recall at least two occasions where this term has arisen in discussion and the researchers involved have failed to agree on what it means. This, we think, reflects the subtle differences in usage of these names.

[11]To instead differentiate models based on the presence of syntactic annotation in the rules, we suggest using the convention proposed in the Moses Syntax Tutorial [Moses Contributors] and avoiding the X-to-Y names.

String-to-string models are almost universally based on SCFG, usually in a highly restricted form with limits on the size of a rule and the number of non-terminals it can use. Decoding is based on parsing the input string.

1.4.2   STRING-TO-TREE

String-to-tree models produce derivations in which the target-side derived trees resemble the linguistic parse trees observed in the data. Galley et al. [2006]'s model, which we used as our example in Section 1.3, is an archetypal string-to-tree model: the rules contain tree fragments on the target side, which are fitted together during decoding and scored according to a model that takes into account the probability of the resulting derived tree.

String-to-tree models are either based on STSG with tree fragments on the target-side or alternatively they use a flattened SCFG form (produced by discarding the internal tree structure of the tree fragments). When SCFG is used, the grammar rules are usually less constrained than in string-to-string models. Like string-to-string models, decoding is based on parsing the input string. To make parsing tractable, the grammar rules are often binarized prior to decoding.

1.4.3   TREE-TO-STRING

Tree-to-string models produce derivations in which the source-side derived trees resemble the linguistic parse trees observed in the data. This configuration makes the model amenable to an alternative two-phase decoding algorithm: the input string is first parsed by the same statistical parser that was used to parse the training data and the resulting parse tree then becomes the input to the second phase, which is sometimes called *tree parsing*. In tree parsing, the source-sides of rules are matched against the input tree and synchronous derivations are constructed by combining the rules' target-sides. Search in the second phase is therefore restricted to derivations in which the source-side derived tree matches the input tree. This substantially reduces the search space and in practice tree-to-string decoding is usually much faster than string-to-string or string-to-tree decoding.

Most tree-to-string models are based on STSG, with tree fragments on the source-side. Decoding is usually the two-phrase tree decoding approach we have just described, although sometimes the string parsing and tree parsing phases are performed jointly.

1.4.4   TREE-TO-TREE

Tree-to-tree is the least used of the four classes. The requirement that rules can produce linguistically well-formed derived trees on both sides turns out to be extremely limiting due to the non-isomorphism of source and target parse trees in practice (which can result from arbitrary differences in the annotation applied to the two languages, or may be due to deeper linguistic differences). Non-isomorphism can in theory be handled by STSG rules provided it is localized to the rules' fragments. Nonetheless, learning rules from data has proven to be problematic in practice due to the increased data sparsity arising from this constraint.

As a result of the sparsity issue, the pure tree-to-tree approach is usually eschewed in favor of one of the previous three approaches, but with "soft" or "fuzzy" use of syntax on the string side (or both sides in the string-to-string case). In soft syntactic approaches, the matching of linguistic categories at non-terminal substitution sites is no longer a binary decision, but is always permitted, with the similarity (or dissimilarity) of the non-terminals rewarded (or penalized) by the statistical model. In line with our previously stated classification criterion, if a model, for example, uses soft syntactic constraints on the source side and hard syntactic constraints on the target side, then we will classify it as string-to-tree model and not a tree-to-tree model.

Decoding in tree-to-tree models can use the efficient tree-decoding approach of tree-to-string. The difference is that the target sides of rules must have matching non-terminals at the root and substitution site if they are to combine to form a derivation.

1.5 A BRIEF HISTORY OF SYNTAX-BASED SMT

This section provides a brief history of syntax in statistical machine translation, with pointers to many of the papers that underlie the work presented in this chapter.

The use of syntax in machine translation extends back to its earliest days. Weaver [1955] speculated about the utility of language structure for translation in his letter proposing the idea of automatic translation, and a 1957 paper laid out a general approach [Yngve, 2003]. This is unsurprising because the use of syntax is obvious: languages have structural differences that are often used in their characterizations (e.g., SVO vs. SOV), and the syntactically motivated reorderings between language pairs are clear to the student of a foreign language (e.g., pre- vs. post-positions for noun adjective modifiers). Subsequent years, however, saw a story unfold that is familiar to historians of machine translation: the facility that humans have with languages both in isolation and in translation, and the readiness of ideas for how the mechanize the process of translation, proved to belie the actual difficulties in formulating rules for doing so. Many attempts were made at describing syntax-based systems (e.g., Kaplan et al. [2003], Kay [1984], Landsbergen [2003]), but these were encumbered by the same problems hampering direct-transfer systems, namely, the lack of any means of easily extending them from simple motivating examples to broad-coverage scenarios.

Everything changed when the statistical approach to machine translation was invented in the early 1990s. A fundamental idea contributed by this revolution—which provides an answer to the problem that concluded the previous paragraph—might be stated as *simplify your models and learn them from data*. To be clear, this is not to say that complicated methods should be eschewed entirely, or that there are no insights or linguistically informed constraints that might be useful. It is better thought of as a rough guide or core lesson that should be considered before moving further on. Successful approaches to syntax in MT have taken this lesson to heart. And over the years, as the research community's understanding has grown, these simple models have in turn grown in complexity, with the difference being that they are anchored to data and corpus-based training methods.

The first use of syntax in statistical machine translation was in the **Inversion Transduction Grammar (ITG)** formalism [Wu, 1995, 1997]. An ITG is a restricted form of SCFG that has productions of two types: terminal productions, which pair a single source symbol with a single target symbol (either of which may be a special "empty" symbol to allow for insertion and deletion); and non-terminal productions, which contain sequences of paired non-terminals. These latter productions can be of any length, but the reordering between the source and target side is required to be monotonic: either *straight* or *inverted*. Despite this constraint, the reordering patterns permitted by ITG have been found to match well with actual reorderings occurring in parallel texts, at least for some language pairs [Cherry and Lin, 2006, Wellington et al., 2006]. Importantly, this restriction permits ITG grammars to be binarized and thus parsed efficiently. It was in ITG that techniques for intersecting a CFG with a finite-state machine were first applied to machine translation, enabling integration of a target-side bigram language model with the parsing-based search procedure [Wu, 1996].

A restricted form of ITG, called **Bracketing Transduction Grammar (BTG)**, permits only a single non-terminal label (typically X). Although motivated with linguistically informed examples, ITG was typically used in the BTG form; under our classification, it can therefore be considered to be a string-to-string model, with the hierarchical structure induced by the rules serving mostly to structure the search space.

The first successors of ITG sought to incorporate syntax in a more systematic way. Yamada and Knight [2001] proposed a generative, string-to-tree noisy-channel model that transformed parse trees in the target language to strings in the source language, using simple insertion, deletion, translation, and reordering operations that worked on the children of a single node at a time. Their model was first proposed for alignment, and then quickly extended to decoding in a noisy-channel framework that sought to restore the hidden parse tree that was imagined to have produced (under the model operations) an observed source string [Yamada and Knight, 2002]. This was later extended to explicitly include probabilities from a bilexicalized CFG parsing model [Charniak, 2001] employed as a syntax-based language model [Charniak et al., 2003].

Formally, these models were SCFGs. By then, the limitations of the formalism were starting to show. The incorporation of syntax had revealed clashes between the target-side structure and alignments that blocked the capture of many potentially useful rules. A push to work with larger portions of trees therefore ensued. Poutsma [2000] introduced **Data-Oriented Translation**, a STSG-based tree-to-tree model, rooted in data-oriented parsing (DOP) and relying on manually-aligned tree data. Later, Eisner [2003] presented a sketch of an EM-based algorithm for learning STSG rules from unaligned data. The tree-to-tree trend has not caught on, for a number of reasons: the need for parsers in two languages is often problematic, and the brittleness and complexity of tree-pair extraction techniques are further impediments. However, the approach remains scientifically interesting. More recent work has found some success in loosening the tree constraints by allowing rules to apply despite mismatched labels, incurring (after learning) penalties for particular mismatches [Chiang, 2010].

Motivated by a thorough study of phrasal coherence between French and English [Fox, 2002], one of the first successful STSG approaches limited itself to trees on the target side only. **GHKM** [Galley et al., 2004, 2006] described a process taking an aligned parse tree and sentence pair and learning STSG fragments, which permitted orderings across all levels of a parse tree. GHKM has remained one of the most interesting formalisms to work with; the principled formation of target-language structure, for example, provides a solid foundation for syntax-based language modeling. In the meantime, the original word-based approaches to translation had given way to the intuitions and empirical success of phrase-based approaches [Koehn et al., 2003]. Chiang [2005]'s **Hierarchical Phrase-Based Model (Hiero)** brought phrase-based approaches into the sphere of syntax-based translation by extending the standard phrase-pair extraction method to instead learn hierarchical phrase-based rules—phrase pairs with gaps. Chiang [2007] presented a major update to the parsing-based decoding approach with the introduction of **cube pruning**, which allowed fast, approximate integration of an n-gram language model.

Like BTG, Hiero does not use syntactic annotation. A variant called **Syntax-Augmented Machine Translation (SAMT)** soon followed [Zollmann and Venugopal, 2006]. It used categories from a target-side parse tree to refine the single non-terminal used in Hiero.

An alternative to parsing the input string into a target-side tree representation is the **Syntax-Directed Translation** approach, which transforms a source-language tree into a string. This input tree can take the form of a dependency tree (the **Dependency Treelet** approach [Quirk et al., 2005]) or a constituent tree [Huang et al., 2006]. Once learned, rules can be matched against the source-language tree in a bottom-up parsing-based approach (used by the treelet approach and also by Liu et al. [2006]), or using a tree parsing framework [Huang et al., 2006].

Tree-to-string translation suffers from the fact that the source-language tree is produced automatically, and is therefore likely to have mistakes. This is the case in many natural language pipelines. One approach to dealing with this is the **Forest-to-String** model, which exposes the parse forest (or a pruned sub-forest) to the decoder [Huang and Chiang, 2007]. This is the same idea underlying lattice-based approaches to translating the output of automatically-segmented text, or the output of a speech recognition system.

Finally, another appealing use of syntax is in explicitly modeling the structure of the target-language sentence. Such efforts had been successfully used in speech recognition [Chelba and Jelinek, 1998] (although at great computational cost) and it stands to reason that their utility would increase in light of MT's reordering problem. The string-to-tree approaches do this implicitly, but the system's rules are learned from aligned parallel text, and thus the primary role of the syntax is to learn reorderings between words and phrases in the two languages. The first approach to explicitly incorporate **syntax-based language modeling** was that of Charniak et al. [2003], described above, which rescored a simple string-to-tree model with scores from a monolingual bilexicalized parser. A manual analysis suggested the decoder was producing translations with a decidedly different feel, but that were not reflected in the BLEU scores. A subsequent effort examined the use of scores from probabilistic parsers (PCFGs) to rerank the 1,000-best output of a machine translation system, and found (rather infamously) that such scores could not even be used to discriminate between MT output and the reference translation Och et al. [2004]. It is possible, however, to train the weights of a monolingual CFG to do much better at this task [Cherry and Quirk, 2008].

A common complaint about reranking approaches is that n-bests list produced by an n-gram based decoder represent only a small corner of the search space, and one unlikely to be chosen by a syntax-based language model. However, attempts to incorporate parsing models into the decoder search have not been successful. Post and Gildea [2008] added a vanilla PCFG model in an ITG framework, to no avail, and Schwartz et al. [2011a], who used a syntactic language model in a phrase-based translation system, similarly found no improvement [Schwartz et al., 2011b]. In addition, incorporating these models explodes the search space and running time (the latter reported a 6,000-fold increase), a common issue that is sometimes swept under the rug. In contrast, syntax-based language models that simply score the syntactic structures produced by a string-to-tree decoder are more efficient. Collectively, these efforts demonstrated the large gap between the optimization goals of monolingual syntactic structure when used for parsing (where the goal is to discover the best structure over a fixed, grammatical string) and language modeling (where the latent structure is used to try to discriminate among competing strings).

Attempts at syntax-based language modeling have not been wholly without success. Shen et al. [2010] incorporated a trigram dependency model on top of a Hiero model, improving performance in a large-data Chinese—English translation task. More recently, explicit linguistic models of difficult problems in German have improved performance in English—German translation, particularly when evaluated against human judgment [Williams and Koehn, 2014].

CHAPTER 2

Learning from Parallel Text

The previous chapter provided formal foundations for syntax-based translation models, along with a taxonomy of formalism types. But where do grammars come from? In this chapter, we describe the concrete methods that are used to automatically extract grammar rules from aligned parallel text. We focus our attention on three predominant instantiations of these formalisms: hierarchical phrase-based grammars (Section 2.2), syntax-augmented grammars (Section 2.3), and GHKM, which can be used for both string-to-tree and tree-to-string decoding (Section 2.4). As with the learning of phrase-based models, the extraction of these grammars is laden with a host of heuristics that have been shown to work in practice. As such, we present these three extraction methods in light of specific proposals in the literature that have been shown to be successful over the years.

2.1 PRELIMINARIES

Extracting grammars from parallel text works on large collections of word-aligned sentence pairs. These are pairs of sentence translations that have been automatically aligned with an alignment tool such as GIZA++ [Och and Ney, 2003] or the Berkeley aligner [Liang et al., 2006]. Some of the grammars additionally make use of a parse tree over the source or target side.

We begin with an example and some definitions, which will be used for describing the extraction procedures in the rest of this chapter. Figure 2.1 contains a visualization of a source language sentence s (here, German), a target language sentence t (here, and by convention, En-

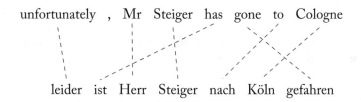

Figure 2.1: A sentence pair with word alignment.

glish), and an alignment $\mathcal{A}$ between the words in s and t. Both s and t are sequences of words under a single vocabulary, $\mathcal{V}$. From these, we can define the concepts of phrases and phrase pairs.

Definition 2.1 (Phrase). A *phrase* is a sequence of contiguous words in one language. When working with a specific sentence, a phrase is denoted as s_i^j for the source language sentence, s, and $t_{i'}^{j'}$ for the target language, t, for a phrase starting at word i (i') and ending with word j (j'). For a generic phrase not rooted in a particular sentence, we use $\bar{s}$ and $\bar{t}$.

Definition 2.2 (Phrase pair). A *phrase pair* is a pair of phrases, $(\bar{s}, \bar{t})$.

For any sentence pair, there are $\mathcal{O}(|s|^2|t|^2)$ possible phrase pairs. However, not all of these will be good phrase pairs. The subset of all phrase pairs that will serve as the basis for building syntactic rules are those that are consistent with the alignment. The word alignment, $\mathcal{A}$, is a set of *alignment points*, which are pairs of indices (k, k'), $1 \leq k \leq |s|$ and $1 \leq k' \leq |t|$, each connecting a single word in s with a single word in t. There are no restrictions on the alignment; each word on either side can be aligned to zero or more on the other side. The word alignment is used to filter the full set of phrase pairs down to a subset that are consistent with the alignment.

Definition 2.3 (Consistent alignment point). An alignment point (k, k') is *consistent* with respect to a phrase pair $(s_i^j, t_{i'}^{j'})$ if and only if

$$i \leq k \leq j \wedge i' \leq k' \leq j'$$

or

$$(k < i \vee k > j) \wedge (k' < i' \vee k' > j').$$

In other words, both ends of the alignment point must be either entirely inside or entirely outside of the phrase pair. A consistent alignment point that meets the first condition is a *positive* alignment point, and one that meets the second condition is a *negative* alignment point.

Definition 2.4 (Consistent phrase pair). A phrase pair $(\bar{s}, \bar{t})$ is *consistent* with respect to an alignment $\mathcal{A}$ if all the alignment points within $\mathcal{A}$ are consistent (under Definition 2.3).

Figure 2.2 contains a two-dimensional visualization of the sentence alignment in Figure 2.1. It highlights both a consistent and an inconsistent phrase pair. For any aligned sentence pair, there will be many consistent phrase pairs, and these will overlap.

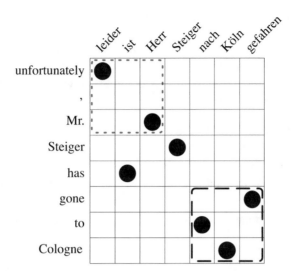

Figure 2.2: A two-dimensional representation of the aligned sentence pair in Figure 2.1. The dashed box (lower right) marks a consistent phrase pair. The dotted box (upper left) marks an inconsistent phrase pair. Inconsistent phrase pairs can be easily identified by looking for alignment points above, below, left, and right of the alignment box.

2.2   HIERARCHICAL PHRASE-BASED GRAMMAR

Chiang's hierarchical phrase-based model (often referred to simply as "Hiero") was not the first syntax-based statistical machine translation model; that credit goes to Wu [1997]'s Stochastic Inversion Transduction Grammar (ITG) model. Nonetheless, Hiero can be considered the forerunner of most current models. It was the first to bring together many necessary components for state-of-the-art translation performance for SCFG, including a linear model and the combination of beam search and cube pruning for n-gram language model integration. Crucially, Hiero also introduced a method for learning hierarchical grammars from parallel text that was based on *phrases* as the fundamental unit of translation, instead of words. Hiero's phrases are phrases that have been generalized to include gaps, which allow for their recursive nesting.

2.2.1   RULE EXTRACTION

The phrase extraction process begins by identifying *initial phrase pairs*, which are a subset of all possible phrase pairs meeting the following conditions:

1. the phrase pair is consistent;

2. the phrase pair contains at least one positive alignment point; and

3. there are no unaligned words at the boundary of the phrase in either language.

The sentence pair in Figures 2.2 permits the extraction of fourteen initial phrase pairs (seven phrase pairs with one word on each side, and seven with more than one word). Each of these becomes a terminal production in an SCFG grammar, with a left-hand side symbol of X. Here are those rules, excluding rules representing singleton pairs and the entire sentence pair:

X	→	leider ist Herr Steiger	, unfortunately , Mr Steiger has
X	→	ist Herr Steiger	, Mr Steiger has
X	→	nach Köln	, to Cologne
X	→	nach Köln gefahren	, gone to Cologne
X	→	ist Herr Steiger nach Köln gefahren	, Mr Steiger has gone to Cologne
X	→	Herr Steiger	, Mr Steiger

Once the set of initial phrase pairs has been identified, hierarchical phrases can be created through a process that can be thought of as *phrase subtraction*, whereby shorter initial phrase pairs embedded in longer ones are removed and replaced with non-terminals. These removed phrases become substitution points that are labeled with the same label, X. For example, we can build the rule below from the following sequence:

X	→	ist Herr Steiger nach Köln gefahren	, Mr Steiger has gone to Cologne
− X	→	Herr Steiger	, Mr Steiger
= X	→	ist X_1 nach Köln gefahren	, X_1 has gone to Cologne

For initial phrase pairs that are long enough, multiple non-terminals can be created by repeatedly subtracting initial phrases. For instance, we can subtract out another initial phrase pair from the rule we just produced:

X	→	ist X_1 nach Köln gefahren	, X_1 has gone to Cologne
− X	→	Köln	, Cologne
= X	→	ist X_1 nach X_2 gefahren	, X_1 has gone to X_2

These two rule subtractions are depicted visually in Figure 2.3.

Allowing all possible initial phrases and all possible substitutions would lead to an unusably large grammar and many undesirable rules. Chiang [2007] provides the following heuristic constraints:

1. the maximum length of the initial phrase pairs is set to ten;

2. there can be no more than five symbols (terminal or non-terminal) on the source side;

3. unaligned words are not permitted on initial phrase pair boundaries;

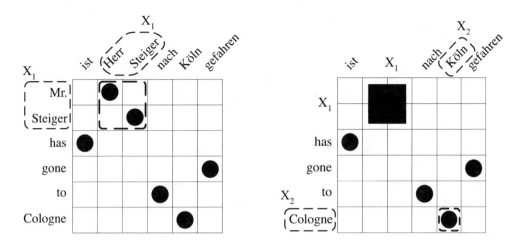

Figure 2.3: The Hiero rule extraction process. On the left, an initial phrase pair is extracted from a larger one to form a rule with a single gap. On the right, that rule in turn has a second initial phrase pair removed from it to form a rule with two gaps.

4. the number of substitution points per rule is limited to two; and

5. source-side non-terminals are not permitted to be adjacent.

The last two restrictions on non-terminals limit the complexity of parsing with the source-side projection of these grammars. Altogether, 50 grammar rules can be extracted from our working example sentence pair under these extraction heuristics (compared to 16 phrases without gaps that are extracted under Moses' default extraction heuristics).

The automatically extracted rules can then be used to translate new sentences at test time with a decoding algorithm. However, it is often the case that new sentences cannot be parsed with a single-rooted hierarchical analysis. This is due in part to the restriction on the maximum length of initial phrase pairs,[1] but also due to efficiency considerations at decoding time. Hiero imposes a *maximum span* constraint, which limits the span over which hierarchical rules can apply (many decoders use a default value of 20). Sentences longer than this cannot be parsed entirely hierarchically, but must instead join together adjacent derivations of the input sentence. To make this possible, Hiero also manually defines a simple set of *glue rules*:

$$S \rightarrow \langle s \rangle \quad , \quad \langle s \rangle$$
$$S \rightarrow S_1 X_2 \quad , \quad S_1 X_2$$
$$S \rightarrow S_1 \langle /s \rangle \quad , \quad S_1 \langle /s \rangle.$$

---

[1]It is not only new sentences that cannot be parsed in this way; the constraint also prevents many sentence pairs in the training data from being covered with a structure.

These rules begin by parsing the start-of-sentence symbol, $\langle s \rangle$. They then allow the combination (without reordering) of any number of subderivations, by allowing hierarchical substructures from adjacent source-side spans to be "glued" together. The glue grammar makes use of the additional non-terminal symbol S, which is the SCFG's start symbol. Glue rules thus help control the computational complexity of decoding, which is cubic in N, the size of the maximum span. They also provide a backoff mechanism for situations where no derivation can be found using automatically extracted rules alone.

Finally, during decoding, another set of rules is assumed to exist for handling unknown words. Unknown words on the input are treated as if there was a singleton rule in the grammar which has the unknown word on the source and target side; they are thus "pushed through" by the decoder. Together, the automatically learned rules and the glue rules constitute a synchronous context-free grammar of the form presented in the previous chapter.

2.2.2   FEATURES

The product of the extraction procedures in this chapter are not just rules, but also a set of dense feature values associated with each rule. These feature values are multipled against weights in the decoder's linear model in order to help steer the decoder's search procedure toward good derivations. It is possible to compute many different kinds of features over these rules. Feature sets are typically split into two groups: *dense features*, which have values for every rule, and *sparse features*, which typically only apply to small subsets of the total set of rules. The exact set of features extracted depends on the tool used. The following are common ones:

- $P(s \mid t)$ and $P(t \mid s)$, the conditional phrase probabilities [Och and Ney, 2002];

- $P_{lex}(s \mid t)$ and $P_{lex}(t \mid s)$, the lexical phrase probabilities [Koehn et al., 2003], which estimate how well the words of each rule translate, in each direction; and

- $\exp(1)$, which serves as a count of how many rules are used in a derivation, and which can be used by the model to prefer longer or shorter derivations.

2.3   SYNTAX-AUGMENTED GRAMMAR

Syntax-augmented machine translation (SAMT) was proposed soon after Hiero [Zollmann and Venugopal, 2006], and occupies an interesting place between Hiero and other tree-based models. It is linguistically informed because it makes use of a parse tree over the target side of the training data. The motivation for this was a step in the direction of syntax-based language modeling, where the target-side tree structure ostensibly guides decoding. However, SAMT extends directly from Hiero; its fundamental notion of phrase, therefore, does not derive from a linguistic notion of constituents, but instead from the consistent phrase pair concept defined in the previous section. Many of the phrase pairs extracted are therefore not syntactic (in the linguistic sense); SAMT retains such phrase pairs by using a set of extended categories formed by combining non-terminal labels. For that reason, its use of parse tree labels is better viewed as a kind of symbol refinement.

SAMT grammar differs from Hiero in three important ways:

1. the use of constituent labels to assign category labels;

2. a change in the extraction heuristics; and

3. the use of many more features.

2.3.1   RULE EXTRACTION

Rule extraction proceeds in much the same way as it did for Hiero. We begin with the set of initial phrase pairs, and repeatedly subtract an initial phrase pair from another. However, instead of using the default non-terminal X, the gaps are assigned labels from the constituent parse tree according to the following rules:

1. if the removed initial phrase pair is a constituent, assign the constituent label;

2. if the phrase pair exactly extends across multiple constituents $A_1 \ldots A_N$ that are not themselves a constituent, assign a *concatenated label* of the form "$A_1 + \cdots + A_N$;"

3. if the phrase pair is a complete constituent A except for a single missing constituent B to the right or left, assign a *partial label* "A/B" or "$B \backslash A$," respectively;

4. finally, if none of the above situations applies, assign the default label, X.

Figure 2.4 contains a version of our working example augmented with a parse tree. Word-word aligned pairs are trivially assigned the label of the preterminal above the target-language word. SAMT also produces the following set of initial rules:

$$
\begin{aligned}
\text{S/VP} &\rightarrow \text{leider ist Herr Steiger} & , & \text{ unfortunately , Mr Steiger has} \\
\text{NP+VBZ} &\rightarrow \text{ist Herr Steiger} & , & \text{ Mr Steiger has} \\
\text{ADV+COMMA} &\rightarrow \text{leider} & , & \text{ unfortunately ,} \\
\text{COMMA+NP} &\rightarrow \text{Herr Steiger} & , & \text{ , Mr Steiger} \\
\text{COMMA+NP+VBZ} &\rightarrow \text{ist Herr Steiger} & , & \text{ , Mr Steiger has} \\
\text{PP} &\rightarrow \text{nach Köln} & , & \text{ to Cologne} \\
\text{VP}\backslash\text{VBN} &\rightarrow \text{nach Köln} & , & \text{ to Cologne} \\
\text{VP} &\rightarrow \text{nach Köln gefahren} & , & \text{ gone to Cologne} \\
\text{ADV}\backslash\text{S} &\rightarrow \text{ist Herr Steiger nach Köln} & , & \text{ , Mr Steiger has gone to} \\
& \text{gefahren} & & \text{Cologne} \\
\text{NP+VP} &\rightarrow \text{ist Herr Steiger nach Köln} & , & \text{ Mr Steiger has gone to} \\
& \text{gefahren} & & \text{Cologne} \\
\text{NP} &\rightarrow \text{Herr Steiger} & , & \text{ Mr Steiger}
\end{aligned}
$$

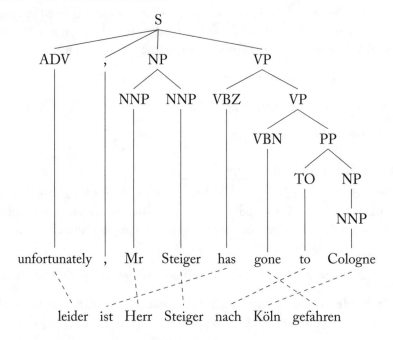

Figure 2.4: An aligned sentence pair with a target-side parse tree.

The above list is larger than the Hiero list. This is because, in addition to labeling, SAMT changes the heuristics used to derive initial phrases. First, unaligned words are permitted at rule boundaries, and since attachment is ambiguous, this leads to multiple extracted phrases (as with the COMMA symbol above). SAMT also imposes some of its own constraints. For example, in an effort to reduce the already-large number of symbols, it is common to permit only one label concatenation per rule. In that case, the "COMMA+NP+VBZ" rule above would become X instead. Rules assigned the default label in this way are ineligible for further subtraction.

Deriving hierarchical rules then proceeds in the same way as before: all initial phrase pairs are added to the grammar. Further rules are then created by subtracting initial phrases, and adding the results to the grammar until there are no more ways to do so.

SAMT also makes use of glue rules to ensure that a derivation can be produced. The glue grammar is much larger than for Hiero because it must include a rule for every non-terminal symbol N in the grammar:

$$
\begin{aligned}
S^\dagger &\rightarrow \langle s \rangle &, \ \langle s \rangle \\
\forall X \in N \ \ S^\dagger &\rightarrow S^\dagger {}_1 X_2 &, \ S^\dagger {}_1 X_2 \\
S^\dagger &\rightarrow S^\dagger {}_1 \langle /s \rangle &, \ S^\dagger {}_1 \langle /s \rangle .
\end{aligned}
$$

If the symbol S occurs in the training data as a constituent label, then typically a different, otherwise unused, symbol (such as TOP, ROOT, or GOAL) is chosen as the start symbol $S^{\dagger}$.

2.3.2 EXTRACTION HEURISTICS

As we showed in the example above, SAMT significantly alters Hiero's extraction heuristics. The differences outlined in the original article include the following. SAMT

- permits adjacent non-terminals on the source language side;

- increases the maximum length of initial phrase pairs from 10 to 12;

- allows unaligned words at phrase boundaries; and

- allows the extraction of abstract rules (ones with no terminals symbols on the source language side).

These changes result in a much larger number of extracted rules. Whereas Hiero extraction produces 50 rules from this sentence, SAMT extraction produces 147. Furthermore, the extraction of rules with adjacent non-terminals means that the decoding algorithm has to search over the split point when applying such rules. The larger number of rules and symbols, together with the admission of adjacent non-terminals, have a deleterious effect on parsing complexity. On the other hand, they have often been found to produce improved BLEU scores over Hiero [Baker et al., 2009, Weese et al., 2011], although it is difficult to evaluate whether this is due to the label projection or the revised extraction and decoding constraints.

2.3.3 FEATURES

Finally, SAMT in practice uses a much larger number of features for each rule than the standard implementation of Hiero. These include a number of binary-valued features. The following list is included in the original formulation of SAMT and in Thrax [Weese et al., 2011], a grammar extraction tool:

- Binary-valued features indicating

  - whether the rule is purely lexical (contains only terminal symbols),

  - whether there are terminals on the source but not the target (and vice versa),

  - whether the rule is abstract (contains no terminal symbols),

  - for binary rules, the permutation between the terminals (straight or inverted),

  - whether the rule contains adjacent non-terminals, and

  - whether the rule was assigned the default non-terminal;

- counters for

  – the number of unaligned words,

  – the number of target-side words, and

- a constant phrase penalty.

2.4   GHKM

The Hiero model is syntactic in a generic sense of having structure: its rules apply hierarchically, and translation under the model (Chapter 5) involves parsing the source-language string. However, it is not syntactic in the traditional sense of providing a linguistic explanation of the constituent structure of either the source or target sentence. In fact, since Hiero is based on the phrase-based model—which explicitly rejects such syntactic restraints [Koehn et al., 2003]—there is no notion of linguistics at all. And we have already noted how SAMT is better viewed as symbol refinement of Hiero's rules than as a linguistically-motivated alternative.

String-to-tree models are different. They provide a view of translation based on linguistically-motivated transformations between strings and parse trees. The most well-known instance of string-to-tree models is GHKM [Galley et al., 2004, 2006].[2] Formally, GHKM is based on the STSG formalism, and defines a mapping between strings and tree *fragments* of arbitrary size. GHKM grammar comprises pairs of tree fragments and strings. Consider the following rule:

$$\text{NP}_1 \text{ ont ADVP}_2 \text{ signé }._3 \rightarrow$$

$$\begin{array}{c} \text{S} \\ \diagup \quad | \quad \diagdown \\ \text{NP}_1 \quad \text{VP} \quad ._3 \\ \diagup \quad | \quad \diagdown \\ \text{VBD} \quad , \quad \text{ADVP}_2 \\ | \qquad | \\ \text{signed} \quad , \end{array}$$

This can also be written in a version of our SCFG format that has been extended to include tree fragments:

  S → NP$_1$ ont ADVP$_2$ signé PUNC$_3$, NP$_1$ (VP (VBD signed) (, ,) ADVP$_2$) PUNC$_3$.

But we will prefer an equivalent and more compact format, which emphasizes the transformation from a source-language string to a target-language structure:

  NP$_1$ ont ADVP$_2$ signé PUNC$_3$ → (S NP$_1$ (VP (VBD signed) (, ,) ADVP$_2$) PUNC$_3$).

This rule takes a sequence of unparsed French words and already-parsed constituents to produce a new constituent labeled with the S symbol. Both the string side of the rule and the leaves of the tree fragment on the target side of the rule contain a mixture of terminals and non-terminals. The

---

[2]Named for its authors, Galley, Hopkins, Knight, and Marcu.

leaf non-terminals are co-indexed and bijective, which permits them to be reordered (although there is no reordering in this rule). Each side can have zero or more terminal symbols, which may or may not be aligned. The use of fragments allows the leaf non-terminals to be reordered across multiple levels of the tree, which is an important flexibility over earlier models [Yamada and Knight, 2001] that were limited to deletions, insertions, and reorderings of the children of a single syntactic node.

We emphasize that at decoding time, the rules of GHKM grammar can be used in either direction: as described here, transforming an input string into a target-language tree in a parsing-based framework (Chapter 5), or in the other direction, transforming an input source-language tree into a target-language string as a tree transduction task (Chapter 4).

Example rules of this sort are learned from the same kind of aligned tree pair presented in the previous section. However, the manner in which rules are extracted is quite different from Hiero. GHKM outlines a multi-step procedure for learning translation grammars.

1. Determine the set of *frontier nodes*, which are the constituents in the parse tree whose leaves are consistent phrase pairs.

2. From these, extract the *minimal set* of rules that explain the complete derivation.

3. Build a set of *composed rules* that provide for more general coverage and which reduce the independence of rule application.

Figure 2.5 contains a new aligned tree pair. We will now step through a GHKM extraction procedure using it as an example.

2.4.1   IDENTIFYING FRONTIER NODES

Informally, *frontier nodes* are internal nodes of the parse tree whose (target-side) yield form a consistent phrase pair (according to Definition 2.4) with their aligned source words. They are important because each frontier node will serve as the root of a minimal rule, and also as substitution points among the leaves of other rules. Figure 2.5 identifies frontier nodes by placing boxes around them.

Formally, GHKM extracts rules from tuples $(\pi, s, \mathcal{A})$. s and $\mathcal{A}$ are the source language sentence and alignment, as defined before (Section 2.1), and π is a parse tree whose leaves are the words of t. Together, we can consider the tuple as a directed, acyclic graph, $\mathcal{G}$. Edges in the parse tree point from parent to child, and edges in $\mathcal{A}$ point from words in t to words in s. Note that the graph is not necessarily connected, since there may be words in s that are unaligned. For each non-leaf node of the parse tree $N \in \{\pi - t\}$, GHKM defines two properties:

- the *span*, span(N), a range from the minimum to the maximum indices of words in s that are reachable from N;[3] and

---

[3]Galley et al. [2004] defines this as closure(span(N)).

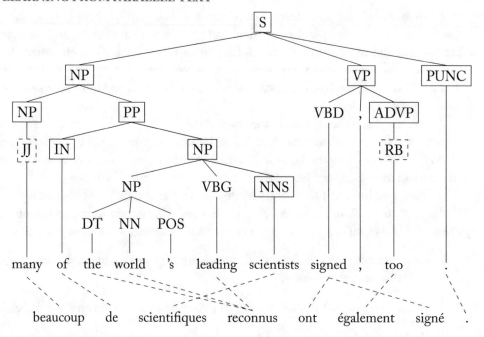

Figure 2.5: An aligned sentence pair with a parse tree over the target side. Boxed nodes denote frontier nodes; the dashed nodes mark frontier nodes that were removed to avoid unary cycles.

- the *complement set,*[4] $\overline{\mathrm{span}}(N)$, which is the set of spans produced by taking the union of the spans of all nodes N' in π that are neither descendants nor ancestors of N.

The set of frontier nodes is then the set of nodes N such that

$$\mathrm{span}(N) \cap \overline{\mathrm{span}}(N) = \emptyset.$$

Put another way, this definition of frontier node enforces that the range of words a node covers in the target language is not interrupted by any node that is not its ancestor or descendant. Frontier nodes thus project downward onto consistent phrase pairs. The set of phrase pairs covered by frontier nodes, however, is a subset of all possible consistent phrase pairs, and therefore fewer rules will be extracted than would be from Hiero.

Chung et al. [2011] recommends one further modification to the definition of frontier nodes: if the span of a frontier node is the exact same as its parent span, then the child node is no longer considered to be a frontier node. This removes unary rules, which complicate decoding. The dashed RB node in Figure 2.5 is one such node.

---

[4]Galley et al. [2006] calls this the *complement span*, but it is actually a set of one or more spans.

2.4.2   EXTRACTING MINIMAL RULES

Each frontier node becomes the root of a rule that extends its reach along the graph, terminating in (a) other frontier nodes, (b) unaligned words in t, or (c) words in s. Together, the set of rules extracted from frontier nodes define a minimal, complete derivation of the alignment pair. These rules are STSG rules comprising a left-hand side, additional internal structure, and source and target transformations. The complete set of minimal GHKM rules from Figure 2.5 are listed here:

$$
\begin{aligned}
NP_1\ VP_2\ PUNC_3 &\rightarrow (S\ NP_1\ VP_2\ PUNC_3) \\
NP_1\ PP_2 &\rightarrow (NP\ NP_1\ PP_2) \\
beaucoup &\rightarrow (NP\ (JJ\ many)) \\
IN_1\ NP_2 &\rightarrow (PP\ IN_1\ NP_2) \\
de &\rightarrow (IN\ of) \\
NNS_1\ reconnus &\rightarrow (NP\ (NP\ (DT\ the)\ (NN\ world)\ (POS\ 's))\ (VBG\ leading)\ NNS_1) \\
scientifiques &\rightarrow (NNS\ scientists) \\
ont\ ADVP_1\ signé &\rightarrow (VP\ (VBD\ signed)\ (,\ ,)\ ADVP_1) \\
également &\rightarrow (ADVP\ (RB\ too)) \\
. &\rightarrow (PUNC\ .)
\end{aligned}
$$

These rules are different from the Hiero rules above in a number of ways. The main difference is that the target-side is no longer flat but contains tree structure, depicted here in Penn Treebank [Marcus et al., 1993] format. Other differences are due to heuristic extraction decisions: for example, Hiero as originally formulated did not permit adjacent non-terminals, for parsing efficiency. GHKM rules do not have restrictions on non-terminal adjacency, or indeed on the number of non-terminals in the right-hand side.[5]

2.4.3   UNALIGNED SOURCE WORDS

Unaligned target-side words are easily incorporated into the minimal rule rooted in the nearest frontier node (and from there, merged into combined rules). Unaligned source-side words, however, often present an ambiguity. There are often many minimal rules they could be attached to without violating the notion of consistent phrase pair. Consider the example fragment shown in Figure 2.6. Where should the unaligned comma be attached? We could create any of the following rules:

$$
\begin{aligned}
NP_1\ ,\ VP_2 &\rightarrow (S\ NP_1\ VP_2) \\
DT_1\ poste\ , &\rightarrow (NP\ DT_1\ post\ office) \\
,\ c'\ est &\rightarrow (VBZ\ is)
\end{aligned}
$$

A principled approach is to maintain counts for each possible attachment and let statistics over the whole corpus make the determination. Galley et al. [2006] described a solution using a derivation forest to represent the possibilities while ensuring that each complete derivation permits only a

---

[5]However, in practice, string-to-tree decoding filters out rules whose parsing complexity is too high (Section 5.3).

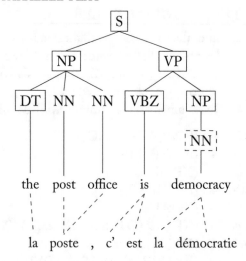

Figure 2.6: An example training fragment containing an unaligned source word.

single attachment point of the unaligned word. A much simpler approach is to heuristically attach unaligned words. For example, the Moses GHKM extractor [Williams and Koehn, 2012] uses the following heuristic: if there are aligned source words to both the left and the right of an unaligned source word, then attach it to the lowest common ancestor of its nearest such left and right neighbors; otherwise, attach it to the root of the parse tree.

2.4.4   COMPOSED RULES

The procedure above extracts the minimal set of rules that explain the derivation. In many cases, these rules are fairly small, and fail to capitalize on the ability to capture larger tree-based patterns. For this reason, it is effective to combine minimal rules into *composed rules*. In theory, there is nothing preventing the extraction of entire parse trees as rules. In practice, the formation of the set of composed rules is constrained by a number of factors. The generalizability of composed rules degrades as their size increases. Furthermore, the computational complexity of parsing with large rules is exponential in the length of sequences of non-terminals uninterrupted by terminals. For these reasons, composed rules are capped by a number of heuristically-determined thresholds. The Moses GHKM extractor imposes the following constraints: the maximum distance from fragment root to any of its leaves is limited to 4; the maximum number of nodes is 15; and the number of nodes (excluding pre-terminal and leaf nodes) is limited to 3. Those constraints lead to the extraction of the following composed rules:

$$NP_1\ VP_2\ . \quad \rightarrow \quad (S\ NP_1\ VP_2\ (PUNC\ .))$$
$$NP_1\ PP_2\ VP_3\ . \quad \rightarrow \quad (S\ (NP_1\ PP_2)\ VP_3\ (PUNC\ .))$$

$$NP_1 \text{ ont } ADVP_2 \text{ signé } PUNC_3 \rightarrow (S\ NP_1\ (VP\ (VBD\ signed)\ (,\ ,)\ ADVP_2)\ PUNC_3)$$
$$NP_1 \text{ ont } ADVP_2 \text{ signé }. \rightarrow (S\ NP_1\ (VP\ (VBD\ signed)\ (,\ ,)\ ADVP_2)\ (PUNC\ .))$$
$$NP_1 \text{ de } NP_2 \rightarrow (NP\ NP_1\ (PP\ (IN\ of)\ NP_2))$$
$$\text{beaucoup } PP_1 \rightarrow (NP\ (JJ\ many)\ PP_1)$$
$$\text{beaucoup } IN_1\ NP_2 \rightarrow (NP\ (NP\ (JJ\ many))\ (PP\ IN_1\ NP_2))$$
$$\text{beaucoup de } NP_1 \rightarrow (NP\ (JJ\ many)\ (PP\ (IN\ of)\ NP_1))$$
$$\text{scientifiques reconnus} \rightarrow (NP\ (NP\ (DT\ the)\ (NN\ world)\ (POS\ 's))$$
$$(VBG\ leading)\ (NNS\ scientists))$$
$$\text{de } NP_1 \rightarrow (PP\ (IN\ of)\ NP_1)$$
$$IN_1\ NNS_2 \text{ reconnus} \rightarrow (PP\ IN_1\ (NP\ (NP\ (DT\ the)\ (NN\ world)\ (POS\ 's))$$
$$(VBG\ leading)\ NNS_2))$$
$$IN_1 \text{ scientifiques reconnus} \rightarrow (PP\ IN_1\ (NP\ (NP\ (DT\ the)\ (NN\ world)\ (POS\ 's))$$
$$(VBG\ leading)\ (NNS\ scientists)))$$
$$\text{de } NNS_1 \text{ reconnus} \rightarrow (PP\ (PP\ (IN\ of)\ (NP\ (NP\ (DT\ the)\ (NN\ world)$$
$$(POS\ 's))\ (VBG\ leading)\ NNS_1)))$$
$$\text{de scientifiques reconnus} \rightarrow (PP\ (PP\ (IN\ of)\ (NP\ (NP\ (DT\ the)\ (NN\ world)$$
$$(POS\ 's))\ (VBG\ leading)\ (NNS\ scientists))))$$
$$\text{ont également signé} \rightarrow (VP\ (VBD\ signed)\ (,\ ,)\ (ADVP\ (RB\ too))))$$

2.4.5 FEATURES

As with the other grammars, any number of features can be computed over the extracted fragments. The existence of parse tree fragments with internal structure practically begs for the use of tree-conditioned weights. One common feature is $P_{CFG}(f)$, defined as the sum of the log probabilities of the depth-one CFG rules constituting each fragment f. These probabilities can be estimated from the parsed training data using the maximum likelihood estimator. It is also common to add the left-hand side label to the conditionining information for the phrase probabilities; that is, instead of computing Hiero's $P(s \mid t)$ and $P(t \mid s)$, we compute $P(s \mid t, \text{label}(f))$ and $P(t \mid s, \text{label}(f))$.

2.5   A COMPARISON

We extracted Hiero, SAMT, and GHKM grammars from a number of different corpora in order to provide a comparison on grammar size. For reference, we also extract a Moses phrase table. The Hiero and SAMT grammars were extracted with Thrax, and the GHKM grammar with Moses' `extract-ghkm` tool. We used default extraction settings in all scenarios.[6] The Berkeley parser [Petrov et al., 2006] was used to parse the English corpora, and BitPar[7] [Fraser et al., 2013] to parse the German corpus. Statistics on the number of rules extracted are listed in Table 2.3.

---

[6]For phrase extraction, the maximum phrase length = 7. Defaults for the others are given in their respective sections.
[7]http://www.ims.uni-stuttgart.de/tcl/SOFTWARE/BitPar.html

Language pair	description	# rules (millions)				sentence stats	
		phrase	Hiero	SAMT	GHKM	#	mean len.
Spanish–English	speech	2	22	32	3	137k	12.7
Turkish–English	newswire	7	15	80	9	200k	20.9
Chinese–English	newswire	12	62	82	44	1,861k	18.4
English–German	gov't, web	186	786	1,756	494	4,434k	25.1

Table 2.3: Sizes of extracted grammars using the Hiero, SAMT, and GHKM algorithms.

For all languages, the hierarchical and syntactic models are much bigger than their phrase-based counterparts. SAMT, in turn, always produces larger grammars compared to Hiero, because of its loosened extraction heuristics. In contrast, the requirement that consistent phrase pairs be constituents reduces the size of GHKM grammars compare to Hiero, even allowing for the fact that larger rules can be formed from composed rules. However, this GHKM story is complicated a bit by two extremes. For Spanish–English, relatively few GHKM rules are extracted, due to a combination of very short sentences and possibly to repetitive speech data. For English–German, a different parser, together with longer sentence lengths combine with the combinatorics of both span projection (SAMT) and composed rule formation (GHKM), yielding massive grammars. Of course, grammar size is affected by many factors and is hard to characterize precisely, and these numbers can therefore vary widely when extraction parameters are altered. We present these numbers here to give the reader a rough idea of model sizes under common heuristic defaults.

2.6   SUMMARY

We have reviewed the methods for extracting three different grammars that have been proposed in the literature. Of these three grammars, Hiero has been the most popular. The label projection techniques stemming from SAMT have provided some gains over Hiero, but in general, the approach is not widely used, and it is difficult to know precisely how much of the score differences are due to label projection and how much are due to the relaxed extraction constraints and much deeper search. GHKM grammars are much smaller than Hiero and SAMT grammars; they are still based on the notion of consistent phrase pairs, but enforce a constituency constraint from a source- or target-language parse tree. In the past few years, rich syntactic approaches based on GHKM have done very well in shared tasks; for example, English–German string-to-tree systems were tied for best in the human evaluation of the WMT14 and WMT15 translation tasks.[8] On the downside, GHKM grammars exhibit higher computational complexity for parsing due to the presence of multiple adjacent nonterminals, but this can be limited with rule filtering and efficient decoding.

---

[8]http://statmt.org/wmt14/results.html and http://statmt.org/wmt15/results.html.

CHAPTER 3

Decoding I: Preliminaries

Decoding in statistical machine translation is the computational process of searching for the most probable translation (or k most probable translations) of a source sentence according to a model. For the models described in the previous two chapters, the search space is so large that search is only made possible through heavy use of dynamic programming techniques. Unfortunately, as we will see, the use of non-local features means that these models are not ideally suited to dynamic programming and require the use of approximate search algorithms.

Broadly speaking, decoding for syntax-based models falls into two categories: *string decoding* and *tree decoding*. String decoding, which is used for hierarchical phrase-based and string-to-tree models, takes a string as input and applies a heuristic search algorithm based on monolingual parsing and beam search. Tree decoding, which is used for tree-to-string and tree-to-tree models, takes a parse tree as input and applies a heuristic search algorithm based on rule matching (sometimes called tree parsing) and beam search.

The two approaches have a lot in common. Both are based on hypergraph algorithms, which follows from the fact that the models define a hypergraph-shaped search space. While we assume that most readers are familiar with graphs, we do not assume familiarity with hypergraphs and so this chapter, the first of three chapters on decoding, is dedicated to basic definitions and algorithms. In the next chapter, we move onto tree decoding. We start with a simple algorithm for decoding with local features and gradually build up to state-of-the-art decoding methods. Most of the methods introduced in that chapter are common to both decoding approaches. The final decoding chapter covers string decoding. It builds on the material from the tree decoding chapter, adding techniques for dealing with the efficiency issues that arise from the larger search space of string decoding.

3.1 HYPERGRAPHS, FORESTS, AND DERIVATIONS

3.1.1 BASIC DEFINITIONS

Hypergraphs generalize the concept of the graph: whereas a graph has edges that connect pairs of vertices, a hypergraph has hyperedges that connect sets of vertices. Just like graphs, hypergraphs can be directed or undirected. While undirected hypergraphs have important applications in other fields, all of the hypergraphs that we will encounter in this book will be directed. We therefore provide only a brief definition of undirected hypergraphs and move straight on to directed hypergraphs.

Definition 3.1   (Undirected Hypergraph).   An *undirected hypergraph H* is a pair $\langle V, E \rangle$ where V is a finite set of *vertices* and E is a finite set of *undirected hyperedges*. Each hyperedge $e \in E$ is a subset of V.

Because their definition is so broadly encompassing, undirected hypergraphs are commonplace even if we do not recognize them as such. For example, consider the frontier graph fragments generated by the GHKM algorithm (Section 2.4): each of these fragments is a subset of the alignment graph's vertex set, and so the alignment graph's vertex set, together with its set of frontier graph fragments, can be characterized as an undirected hypergraph.

Definition 3.2   (Directed Hypergraph).   A *directed hypergraph H* is a pair $\langle V, E \rangle$, where V is a finite set of *vertices* and E is a finite set of *directed hyperedges*. Each directed hyperedge $e \in E$ is a pair $\langle \text{head}(e), \text{tail}(e) \rangle$, where $\text{head}(e)$ and $\text{tail}(e)$ are subsets of V.

From here on, we will drop the qualifier "directed" and just write hypergraph and hyperedge. In figures we will depict hyperedges using multi-headed and multi-tailed arrows.

Example 3.3   Let H be a hypergraph with five vertices, $V = v_1, v_2, v_3, v_4, v_5$, and five hyperedges, $E = e_1, e_2, e_3, e_4, e_5$, such that:

$$\begin{aligned}
\text{head}(e_1) &= \{v_2, v_3\} &,&\quad \text{tail}(e_1) = \{v_1\} \\
\text{head}(e_2) &= \{v_1\} &,&\quad \text{tail}(e_2) = \{v_2\} \\
\text{head}(e_3) &= \{v_2\} &,&\quad \text{tail}(e_3) = \{v_3\} \\
\text{head}(e_4) &= \{v_4, v_5\} &,&\quad \text{tail}(e_4) = \{v_4, v_5\} \\
\text{head}(e_5) &= \varnothing &,&\quad \text{tail}(e_5) = \{v_1, v_3\}.
\end{aligned}$$

We can depict H as follows:

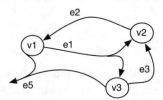 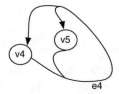

In Example 3.3, we used arbitrary names $(v_1, v_2, \ldots)$ to refer individually to each vertex and hyperedge. For some applications, it will be necessary to attach a *label* to every vertex or to every hyperedge (or to both). In these cases, the label will be considered an integral part of the hypergraph. When labeled hyperedges are used, we will allow multiple hyperedges to have the same head and tail. (Technically, this makes the structure a hyperedge-labeled multi-hypergraph, but we will not worry about making the distinction when the type is clear from the context.)

As well as potentially having a label, a hyperedge will often be assigned a weight. Like with the weighted grammars of Section 1.2.4, we define weights abstractly as elements of a weight set $\mathbb{K}$. Hyperedge weights are given by a weight function.

Definition 3.4 (Hyperedge Weight Function).   Given a set of hyperedges E and a weight set $\mathbb{K}$, a *hyperedge weight function* for E is a function $W_E : E \to \mathbb{K}$ that assigns a weight to every hyperedge $e \in E$.

A hypergraph with weighted hyperedges is called a *weighted hypergraph*.

Definition 3.5 (Weighted Hypergraph).   A *weighted hypergraph* is a pair $\langle H, W_E \rangle$, where $H = \langle V, E \rangle$ is a hypergraph and $W_E : E \to \mathbb{K}$ is a weight function for H's hyperedge set.

3.1.2   PARSE FORESTS

One application of hypergraphs that we will encounter numerous times in this book is the representation of *parse forests*. A parse forest is a set of parse trees for a single sentence, produced from a single grammar. A parse forest can be represented by a hypergraph in which the sink vertices (those with no incoming hyperedges) represent the words of the sentence and the non-sink vertices represent parsing states (a non-terminal and span). The hyperedges represent parsing steps, where one or more words or parsing states are connected to a successor state. If the trees of the parse forest are weighted, then the weighting can be preserved in the hypergraph (by assigning each hyperedge the weight of the corresponding parsing step).

Example 3.6   A parse forest for the sentence "the giant drinks" might consist of the following two CFG parse trees:

The hypergraph representation of this parse forest is:

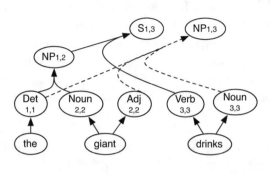

A key property of parse trees is that they are ordered (i.e., the children of a node have a fixed ordering). In general, hypergraphs are unordered, but notice that for a parse forest hypergraph an implicit ordering is defined by the spans encoded in the vertex labels. For a general hypergraph, we can impose an explicit ordering by defining an ordering relation for every hyperedge tail. A hyperedge with an ordered tail is called an *ordered hyperedge*.

Definition 3.7   (Ordered Hyperedge).   An *ordered hyperedge* is a pair $\langle e, \preceq_e \rangle$, where e is a directed hyperedge and $\preceq_e$ is a total order on tail(e).

If $\langle e, \preceq_e \rangle$ is an ordered hyperedge, then we will use the notation $\mathrm{pred}(e, \preceq_e, i)$ to refer to the ith tail vertex of e. For example, in Example 3.6, if e is the incoming hyperedge of the vertex with label $(\mathtt{S}, 1, 3)$, then $\mathrm{pred}(e, \preceq_e, 2)$ refers to the predecessor vertex with label $(\mathtt{Verb}, 3, 3)$. Notice that we just used $\preceq_e$ without explicitly defining it: if a hyperedge, e, belongs to a parse forest, then we will use $\preceq_e$ to refer to the implicit ordering relation.

A hypergraph with ordered hyperedges is called an *ordered hypergraph*.

Definition 3.8   (Ordered Hypergraph).   An *ordered hypergraph* is a pair $\langle H, \preceq_E \rangle$, where $H = \langle V, E \rangle$ is a directed hypergraph and $\preceq_E$ is a function that assigns a tail ordering relation $\preceq_e$ to every $e \in E$.

By the nature of their construction, the hypergraphs used to represent parse forests have a quite specific form: they are directed, acyclic, vertex-labeled, and (implicitly) ordered; their hyperedge tails are non-empty; and their hyperedge heads contain exactly one vertex each. A directed hyperedge with this last property is given a special name: it is called *backward* hyperedge (or *B-hyperedge*).

Definition 3.9   (Backward Hyperedge).   A *backward* hyperedge, or *B-hyperedge*, is a directed hyperedge e for which head(e) is a singleton. A *backward* directed hypergraph, or *B-hypergraph*, is a directed hypergraph for which all hyperedges are backward hyperedges.

Looking back to Example 3.3, hyperedges e_2 and e_3 are backward hyperedges, but e_1, e_4, and e_5 are not. The hypergraph is not a backward hypergraph due to the presence of non-backward hyperedges.

3.1.3   TRANSLATION FORESTS

A *translation forest* is a set of linked tree pairs for a single source sentence, produced from a single synchronous grammar. A translation forest can be represented as a hypergraph using a similar construction to that of a parse forest. It differs in two ways: first, the vertex labels encode a pair of source and target non-terminals (at least in the case of a distinct-category SCFG; for a shared-category SCFG there is only one); second, the hyperedges are labeled with rule identifiers.

Example 3.10   Consider the following two pairs of linked trees. Each tree pair represents a different German translation of our ambiguous English example, "the giant drinks" (incidentally, the resulting German translations do not share the ambiguity of the source sentence).

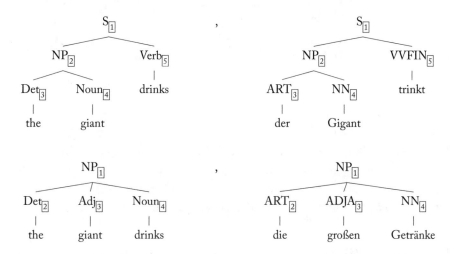

The two tree pairs could be produced by a SCFG or STSG. In the SCFG case, a minimal grammar that derives the two tree pairs contains the following rules:

r_1:	Det	$\rightarrow$	the	,	ART	$\rightarrow$	der
r_2:	Det	$\rightarrow$	the	,	ART	$\rightarrow$	die
r_3:	Noun	$\rightarrow$	giant	,	NN	$\rightarrow$	Gigant
r_4:	Adj	$\rightarrow$	giant	,	ADJA	$\rightarrow$	große
r_5:	Verb	$\rightarrow$	drinks	,	VVFIN	$\rightarrow$	trinkt
r_6:	Noun	$\rightarrow$	drinks	,	NN	$\rightarrow$	Getränke
r_7:	NP	$\rightarrow$	$\text{Det}_1\ \text{Noun}_2$	,	NP	$\rightarrow$	$\text{ART}_1\ \text{NN}_2$
r_8:	NP	$\rightarrow$	$\text{Det}_1\ \text{Adj}_2\ \text{Noun}_3$	,	NP	$\rightarrow$	$\text{ART}_1\ \text{JJ}_2\ \text{NN}_3$
r_9:	S	$\rightarrow$	$\text{NP}_1\ \text{Verb}_2$	,	S	$\rightarrow$	$\text{NP}_1\ \text{VVFIN}_2$

The hypergraph representation is then:

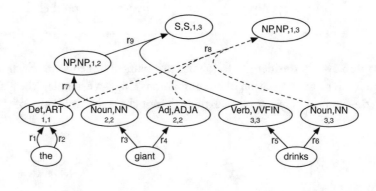

3.1.4 DERIVATIONS

If we were defining graphs then at this point it would be natural to define the concept of a path. For directed hypergraphs, there are several possible ways of defining a path-like object, but there is not a direct analog of the familiar digraph path. One path-like object that is particularly useful for parse forest hypergraphs and related structures is the *derivation*.

Definition 3.11 (Derivation).   A *derivation* takes the form of a pair $\langle e, S \rangle$ where e is a (directed) hyperedge and S is itself a set of derivations (referred to as the *subderivations*). For a given vertex v in a directed hypergraph H, the set of derivations of v, denoted $D(v)$, is defined recursively as follows:

$\langle e, S \rangle$ is a derivation of v iff e is an incoming hyperedge of v and S is a set comprising exactly one derivation $d \in D(u)$ for each non-sink predecessor $u \in tail(e)$.

If $tail(e)$ is empty or if every $u \in tail(e)$ is a sink node then $\langle e, \varnothing \rangle$ is a derivation of v.

Example 3.12   The following hypergraph has four derivations.

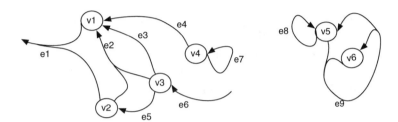

- The vertices, v_4, v_5, and v_6, do not have any derivations. In all three cases, this is because the vertex is part of a cycle.

- The vertices v_2 and v_3 have one derivation each. The derivation of v_3 is $\langle e_6, \varnothing \rangle$ and this is a subderivation of v_2's derivation, which is $\langle e_5, \{\langle e_6, \varnothing \rangle\} \rangle$.

- The vertex v_1 has two derivations: $\langle e_3, \{\langle e_6, \varnothing \rangle\} \rangle$ (which contains the derivation of v_3 as a subderivation) and $\langle e_2, \{\langle e_5, \{\langle e_6, \varnothing \rangle\} \rangle, \langle e_6, \varnothing \rangle\} \rangle$ (which contains the derivations of both v_2 and v_3 as subderivations). e_4 is not part of a third derivation because its tail node, v_4, is not a sink node and has no derivations.

Of course, it is no coincidence that the hypergraph derivation object shares its name with the grammar formalism object. For a parse forest, the hypergraph definition of a derivation coincides with the CFG definition of a derivation (assuming a canonical form for the CFG derivations). In other words, every hypergraph derivation corresponds to a parse tree or subtree; conversely, every CFG parse tree and subtree is represented by a derivation in the hypergraph. For a SCFG or STSG translation forest, a hypergraph derivation corresponds to a SCFG or STSG derivation.

3.1.5   WEIGHTED DERIVATIONS

In many applications, derivations have an associated weight and we are interested in finding the derivation (or derivations) with the highest weight. Often this weight is a probability. For instance, a statistical parsing model assigns a probability to each derivation tree and the job of a statistical parser is to find the tree with the highest probability.

A derivation weight function can be any function that takes a derivation as input and produces a weight as output.

Definition 3.13   (Derivation Weight Function).   Given a derivation set D and a weight set $\mathbb{K}$, a *derivation weight function* on D is a function $W_D : D \rightarrow \mathbb{K}$ that assigns a weight to every derivation $d \in D$.

In practice, a derivation weight function may be subject to strict constraints in order that it can be used in a particular algorithm or in order that its value can be computed efficiently. Two such constraints are *decomposability* and *monotonicity*. Informally, a derivation weight function is decomposable if the weight of a derivation can be calculated given only the weight of the incoming hyperedge and the subderivation weights.

Definition 3.14   (Decomposability).   Let W_D be a weight function for the derivation set D and let W_E be a weight function for E, the set of hyperedges occurring in D. Let $w(d)$ be the function that for any $d = \langle e, S \rangle \in D$ yields the set containing the weight of the hyperedge e and the weights of the subderivations in S:

$$w(d) = \{W_E(e)\} \cup \left[\bigcup_{d' \in S} W_D(d') \right].$$

The function W_D is *decomposable* iff it can be expressed as a composed function $f \circ w : D \rightarrow \mathbb{K}$

Informally, a decomposable weight function is *monotonic* if it has the additional property that, all else being equal, increasing the weight of a derivation's incoming hyperedge or of a subderivation results in an increase in the overall weight of the derivation.

Definition 3.15   (Monotonicity).   Let $W_D : D \rightarrow \mathbb{K}$ be a decomposable derivation weight function for the derivation set D, let $W_E : E \rightarrow \mathbb{K}$ be a hyperedge weight function for E, the set of hyperedges occurring in D, and let $\preceq$ be a total order on $\mathbb{K}$. Now let $d_1 = \langle e_1, S \rangle$ and $d_2 = \langle e_2, S \rangle$ be any pair of derivations in D that differ only in the hyperedge and let $d_3 = \langle e, S_1 \rangle$ and $d_4 = \langle e, S_2 \rangle$ be any pair of derivations in D that differ only in the set of subderivations by a single element (there is a single subderivation s_1 that occurs in S_1 but not S_2 and a single subderivation s_2 that occurs in S_2 but not S_1). W_D is *monotonic* iff it satisfies both of the following conditions:

1. $W_E(e_1) \preceq W_E(e_2) \Rightarrow W_D(d_1) \preceq W_D(d_2)$

2. $W_D(s_1) \preceq W_D(s_2) \Rightarrow W_D(d_3) \preceq W_D(d_4)$

In probabilistic parsing models, the—often implicit—derivation weight function simply multiples the incoming hyperedge weight with the weights of the subderivations. Clearly this function is both decomposable and monotonic. This property also makes the parsing problem amenable to the application of a variety of efficient algorithms.

3.2   ALGORITHMS ON HYPERGRAPHS

In this section, we describe a small selection of hypergraph algorithms. The first is the topological sort algorithm for graphs adapted for use with hypergraphs. Many hypergraph algorithms perform operations on vertices in topological order and so a topological sort of a hypergraph's vertices frequently appears as a substep in other algorithms.

We then give two algorithms for finding a hypergraph's maximally weighted derivation. We will refer to this type of algorithm as a *max-derivation* algorithm. The first, a variant of the Viterbi algorithm, is the more general of the two: it assumes a directed acyclic hypergraph as input, along with an associated derivation weight function. While the Viterbi max-derivation algorithm is a natural fit for parsing problems, it makes no assumptions about the structure of the hypergraph, other than that it is directed and acyclic. The second—the weighted CYK algorithm—deals with the specific case of parse forest hypergraphs that are produced by parsing a string with a weighted CFG.

Finally, we describe a pair of algorithms for generating the k-best derivations of a hypergraph (according to some monotonic derivation weight function).

3.2.1   THE TOPOLOGICAL SORT ALGORITHM

Topological sorting for hypergraphs is essentially the same as for graphs. The algorithm visits the hypergraph's vertices in any order it likes, but at each vertex v it checks if it has visited v's predecessors. If not, then the algorithm takes a detour to visit the unvisited predecessors (recursively checking their predecessors) before proceeding. A Boolean flag (initially false) is used to indicate whether or not a vertex has been visited.

Pseudocode is shown in Algorithm 1. Our version of the algorithm does not produce a stored representation of the sorted vertex sequence; instead, it takes a procedure, *op*, as an input parameter and applies *op* once at every vertex (in topological order). Of course, an implementation could choose to define *op* such that it adds its vertex argument to a list, resulting in a topologically sorted list of vertices.

3.2.2   THE VITERBI MAX-DERIVATION ALGORITHM

The Viterbi max-derivation algorithm—shown in Algorithm 2—is the first of the two max-derivation algorithms. As input, it takes a directed acyclic hypergraph H together with a monotonic derivation weight function W_D, where D is the set of all derivations over H.

Algorithm 1 Topological Ordering

Input : Directed acyclic hypergraph H; procedure *op* taking a single vertex parameter
Output : None (but calls *op* once for each vertex of H (in topological order))

TOPOLOGICAL-PROCESS(H, op)

1 **for** v **in** H's vertex set
2      $visited[v] = $ FALSE
3 **for** v **in** H's vertex set
4   **if** $visited[v] = $ FALSE
5   VISIT(v, op)

VISIT(v, op)

1 $visited[v] = $ TRUE
2 **for** u **in** v's predecessor set
3   VISIT(u)
4 **call** op, v

Algorithm 2 Viterbi Max-derivation Algorithm

Input : Directed acyclic hypergraph H, monotonic derivation weight function W_D
Output : None (but $best[v]$ contains max-derivation for every vertex v)

VITERBI-DERIVATION(H, W_D)

1 **for** v **in** H's vertex set
2      $best[v] = $ NULL
3 TOPOLOGICAL-PROCESS(H, FIND-BEST)

FIND-BEST(v)

1 **for** each incoming hyperedge e of v
2      $S = \varnothing$
3   **for** each vertex u **in** $tail(e)$
4   **if** u is not a sink vertex
5              $S = S \cup \{best[u]\}$
6      $candidate = \langle e, S \rangle$
7   **if** $best[v] = $ NULL **or** $W_D(best[v]) \preceq W_D(candidate)$
8          $best[v] = candidate$

The algorithm makes use of the Algorithm 1's generic Topological-Sort, defining *op* to be a function that records for each vertex the current best-known derivation. Initially this is set to NULL (lines 1 and 2 of Viterbi-Derivation) to indicate that no derivations have yet been considered. Each vertex is then visited in topological order (line 3 of Viterbi-Derivation) and the max-derivation is determined from the set of candidate derivations, one per incoming hyperedge (lines 1 to 8 of Find-Best). At line 7, the relation $\preceq$ is a total order on $\mathbb{K}$, the codomain of the weight function W_D.

The correctness of Find-Best relies on the weight function being monotonic: by visiting the vertices in topological order, the algorithm already knows the optimal subderivations to use for each candidate derivation and monotonicity guarantees that the optimal derivation will include the optimal subderivations (in dynamic programming terms, this is referred to as the property of optimal substructure).

3.2.3   THE CYK MAX-DERIVATION ALGORITHM

Whereas the Viterbi max-derivation assumes that the input hypergraph has already been constructed, the CYK max-derivation algorithm interweaves two processes: the construction of the hypergraph and the max-derivation search itself. Furthermore, the algorithm (as presented here) only constructs part of the hypergraph, disregarding portions that can be determined not to belong to the optimal derivation.

Before presenting the full version of the algorithm, we will describe the simpler CYK recognition algorithm. This algorithm takes as input a string, s, and a CFG, G, which must be in a restricted form known as Chomsky normal form. The algorithm returns a Boolean value indicating whether or not the string belongs to the language defined by G. The core of the two CYK algorithms is identical, but the recognition version is shorter and more readable. Once the main ideas of the recognition algorithm are understood, the max-derivation version can be seen as a simple variant.

First let us examine the requirement that the input grammar is in Chomsky normal form (CNF). A CNF grammar is a CFG grammar (Definition 1.1) in which all rules are of the form $A \rightarrow BC$ or $A \rightarrow w$, where A, B, and C are non-terminals and w is a terminal. To all intents and purposes, any CFG grammar can be transformed into a weakly-equivalent CNF grammar.[1] Furthermore, there are standard[2] conversion algorithms that are reversible: if a CFG grammar G is converted to a CNF grammar G', then G can be recovered from G', and a parse tree for G' can be converted to an equivalent parse tree for G. Thus, the CYK algorithm can be used with any CFG provided the grammar is first normalized and (for the max-derivation version) the resulting hypergraph is de-normalized (or "flattened").

---

[1]The only exceptions are CFGs that can generate the empty string. In that case, a grammar, G, has an *almost* weakly-equivalent CNF grammar, G', such that $\mathcal{L}(G') = \mathcal{L}(G) - \{\epsilon\}$.

[2]Details of the conversion process are covered in most introductory textbooks on formal language theory.

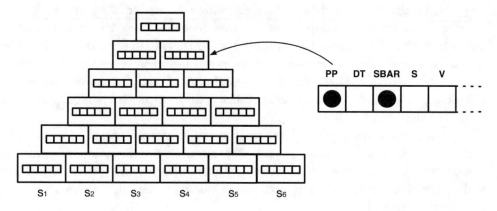

Figure 3.1: A chart for the CYK recognition algorithm.

The CYK algorithm belongs to a family of parsing algorithms that use a *chart* data structure. The chart contains a cell for each substring of the input string. So, for an input string s, it contains $|s|$ cells for the words of the string, $|s| - 1$ cells for the two-word substrings, $|s| - 2$ cells for the three-word substrings, and so on. The contents of the cells depends on the exact variant of the algorithm. For the recognition algorithm, each cell contains a vector of Boolean values, with one element for each non-terminal in the input grammar. For a particular element, the value is true if and only if $A \overset{*}{\Rightarrow} s'$, where A is the non-terminal and s' is the substring of the input corresponding to the chart cell.

Figure 3.1 depicts a chart for an input string of six words. The example cell entry indicates that among all the possible derivations of the substring $s_2 \ldots s_6$, there is at least one beginning with the symbol PP, there are none beginning DT, there is at least one beginning SBAR, and so on.

The CYK algorithm visits the cells of the chart in order of increasing subspan width. For each cell in the bottom layer, the algorithm must determine if the corresponding input word s_i is derivable from A, for each non-terminal $A \in N$ (where N is the grammar's non-terminal set). Since the input grammar is in Chomsky Normal Form, all this requires is a simple check for the existence of a rule $A \rightarrow s_i$.

The other CNF rule form, $A \rightarrow BC$, is used for cells in the higher chart layers. For a cell covering substring $s_i \ldots s_j$ $(j > i)$, the algorithm must determine for each non-terminal $A \in N$ whether there is (i) a rule $A \rightarrow BC$ in the grammar and (ii) a pair of adjacent subderivations that derive B and C, where the first derives the substring $s_i \ldots s_{x-1}$ and the second derives the substring $s_x \ldots s_j$, for some value $i < x \leq j$. The first condition simply involves a check of the grammar's rule set. The second additionally involves consulting the lower, previously-computed, cells of the chart for each possible value of x.

Algorithm 3 The CYK Recognition Algorithm

═══

Input : String s; CFG, G, in Chomsky normal form
Output : Boolean indicating whether s belongs to language defined by G

CYK-RECOGNIZE(G, s)

1   Initialize all entries in *chart* to FALSE
2   **for** $i = 1$ **to** $|s|$
3   **for** each rule $A \rightarrow s_i$ in G
4           $chart[i, i, A] =$ TRUE
5   **for** $width = 2$ **to** $|s|$
6   **for** $i = 1$ **to** $|s| - width + 1$ // i = span start
7           $j = i + width - 1$ // j = span end
8   **for** $x = i + 1$ **to** j // x = split-point
9   **for** each rule $A \rightarrow BC$ in G
10   **if** $chart[i, x - 1, B]$ **and** $chart[x, j, C]$
11                      $chart[i, j, A] =$ TRUE
12 **return** $chart[1, |s|, S^\dagger]$

═══

Pseudocode is shown in Algorithm 3. The chart is represented by a three-dimensional array which is indexed by three values i, j, and A, where i and j are the first and last index of the substring and A is the non-terminal. For example, the SBAR flag from the example in Figure 3.1 would be indexed as $chart[2, 6, \text{SBAR}]$.

The two forms of CNF grammar rule are handled separately by the two top-level for loops: the loop from lines 2–4 fills the cells for single-word substrings, using rules of the form $A \rightarrow w$; the loop from lines 5–11 handles the remaining cells, using the rules of the form $A \rightarrow BC$.

At the end of the algorithm, the cell $chart[1, |s|, S^\dagger]$ contains the value TRUE if s is derivable from $S^\dagger$, or FALSE otherwise.

The worst-case time complexity of the algorithm is $\mathcal{O}(|N|^3 \cdot |s|^3)$, where N is the number of distinct non-terminal symbols in G and $|s|$ is the length of the input string. To see this, consider that for each of the chart's $\mathcal{O}(|s|^2)$ cells, the algorithm must try $\mathcal{O}(|s|)$ split points, and for each split point it must try $\mathcal{O}(|N|^3)$ rules (since there are $\mathcal{O}(|N|)$ possible non-terminal symbols for each of A, B, and C). It is assumed that checking the existence of a rule in the grammar has constant cost (which is easily achieved by storing the rules in a hash table[3]).

The max-derivation version of the algorithm is essentially the same as the recognition algorithm except that instead of containing vectors of Boolean flags, the cells of the chart contain

---

[3]Since the grammar is fixed during parsing, perfect hashing can be used to guarantee constant-time lookup in the worst case.

Algorithm 4 The CYK Max-derivation Algorithm

Input :	s	a string
	G	a CFG in Chomsky normal form
	W_D	a monotonic derivation weight function
Output :	d^*	the max-derivation of s (or NULL if s is not in $\mathcal{L}(G)$)

CYK-MAX-DERIVATION(G, s)

1 Initialize all entries in *chart* to NULL
2 **for** $i = 1$ **to** $|s|$
3   **for** each rule $A \rightarrow s_i$ in G
4      $head = \{vertex[i, i, A]\}$
5      $tail = \{vertex[i, i, s_i]\}$
6      $e = \langle head, tail \rangle$
7      $S = \varnothing$
8      $chart[i, i, A] = \langle e, S \rangle$
9 **for** $width = 2$ **to** $|s|$
10   **for** $i = 1$ **to** $|s| - width + 1$ // i = span start
11      $j = i + width - 1$ // j = span end
12   **for** $x = i + 1$ **to** j // x = split-point
13   **for** each rule $A \rightarrow BC$ in G
14   **if** $chart[i, x - 1, B] =$ NULL **or** $chart[x, j, C] =$ NULL
15   **continue**
16          $head = \{vertex[i, j, A]\}$
17          $tail = \{vertex[i, x - 1, B], vertex[x, j, C]\}$
18          $e = \langle head, tail \rangle$
19          $S = \{chart[i, x - 1, B], chart[x, j, C]\}$
20          $candidate = \langle e, S \rangle$
21          $chart[i, j, A] = \max_{W_D}(chart[i, j, A], candidate)$
22 **return** $chart[1, |s|, S^\dagger]$

---

vectors of derivations (one for each non-terminal $A \in N$). The vector elements perform an equivalent role to the *best*[v] variables in Viterbi algorithm, recording the current best derivation for a single non-terminal and span.

Pseudocode is presented in Algorithm 4. The algorithm constructs a portion of the parse forest hypergraph that contains (at least) the best derivation. The forest's vertices are assumed to exist at the start of the algorithm (alternatively, they could be created on-demand). Vertices are addressed using the three-dimensional array, *vertex*, which is indexed in the same way as *chart*.

Hyperedges and derivations are created as the algorithm proceeds, but only the (locally) best derivations are retained. At the end of the algorithm, the cell $chart[1, |s|, S^\dagger]$ contains the best sentential derivation of the input string s, or NULL if s is not derivable from $S^\dagger$.

3.2.4   THE EAGER AND LAZY k-BEST ALGORITHMS

The objective of a k-best algorithm is to find the k-best derivations of some target vertex t in a directed hypergraph H. By "best derivation" we mean the derivation that has the maximum weight according to a derivation weight function W_D. Finding the k-best derivations is a common requirement in NLP, for instance when re-ranking the output of a statistical parser or in feature weight optimization in SMT.

We will describe two closely related algorithms, both of which are due to Huang and Chiang [2005]. In the original article, these are Algorithms 2 and 3. Both algorithms generate the same output, but Algorithm 3 does so more efficiently. Algorithm 3 is described by the authors as taking lazy computation "to an extreme" and so we will refer to this as the "lazy" k-best derivation algorithm. Algorithm 2, although still admirably economical, is over-eager in comparison and so we will refer to this as the "eager" k-best derivation algorithm. (See Huang and Chiang [2005] for detailed comparisons of the algorithms' theoretical time complexity and empirical performance.)

While the lazy algorithm would seem to make the eager version redundant, we choose to describe both algorithms in detail since they turn out to be of interest beyond k-best extraction: the eager algorithm is the basis of the cube pruning algorithm [Chiang, 2007], which is widely used for language model integration and that we will describe later in this chapter; the lazy algorithm is the basis of the cube growing algorithm, which aims to give a better trade-off in search accuracy against time [Huang and Chiang, 2007].

The Eager k-best Derivation Algorithm

Before presenting the algorithm, let us spend a little time exploring the problem. Consider the hypergraph fragment shown in Figure 3.2, which we will imagine to be part of a much larger hypergraph (for instance, if the hypergraph were a CFG parse forest, then there could be hundreds of thousands of hyperedges). Suppose that we wish to find the k-best derivations of vertex v, considering only a single incoming hyperedge e. Huang and Chiang's algorithms require the derivation weight function to be monotonic, so let us assume that to be the case.

There are three vertices in e's tail, each of which may have many derivations of their own. Suppose that we have already found the k-best derivations of v_1, v_2, and v_3 (in dynamic programming terms, we have solved the subproblems). We can immediately generate the 1-best derivation of v: it is $\langle e, S \rangle$ where S is the set of 1-best derivations from v_1, v_2, and v_3 (this is exactly what we did in the Viterbi max-derivation algorithm). Now suppose that we want to generate the 2-best derivation. This requires a little more work: there are three candidate derivations and the only way to find the best of the three is to generate them all and compute their weights. The three candidates are $\langle e, S_1 \rangle$, $\langle e, S_2 \rangle$, and $\langle e, S_3 \rangle$, where

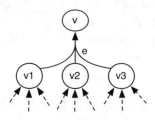

Figure 3.2: A hypergraph fragment.

- S_1 contains the 2-best derivation of v_1 and the 1-best derivations of v_2 and v_3;

- S_2 contains the 2-best derivation of v_2 and the 1-best derivations of v_1 and v_3; and

- S_3 contains the 2-best derivation of v_3 and the 1-best derivations of v_1 and v_2.

(The fact that one of these derivations is the 2-best follows directly from the monotonicity of the weight function.) Suppose that the 2-best derivation turns out to be S_2. What is the 3-best derivation? It could be one of the two existing candidates, $\langle e, S_1 \rangle$ or $\langle e, S_3 \rangle$, or it could be one of three new candidates, $\langle e, S_4 \rangle$, $\langle e, S_5 \rangle$, or $\langle e, S_6 \rangle$, where:

- S_4 contains the 2-best derivation of v_2, the 1-best derivations of v_1, and the 2-best derivation v_3;

- S_5 contains the 2-best derivation of v_2, the 2-best derivations of v_1, and the 1-best derivation v_3; and

- S_6 contains the 3-best derivation of v_2, the 1-best derivations of v_1, and the 1-best derivation v_3.

The only way to determine which of the five candidates is the 3-best derivation is by generating $\langle e, S_4 \rangle$, $\langle e, S_5 \rangle$, and $\langle e, S_6 \rangle$ then computing their weights.

This process can be repeated until we have found the k-best derivation (or run out of candidates). At each step, three new candidate derivations are revealed (these are always the "neighbors" of the last candidate that was chosen). The weights of the newly uncovered candidates are computed and then one of the candidates is chosen (and removed from the pool of candidates). To keep the candidates in order, we can store them in a max-priority queue, where the priority is the weight of the derivation.

With only minor changes, this search procedure can be extended to accommodate vertices with multiple incoming hyperedges. Suppose that vertex v has n incoming hyperedges, as depicted in Figure 3.3. We can begin by priming our priority queue with the single-best derivation for each of the n hyperedges, since we know that one of those must be the overall 1-best. The first pop

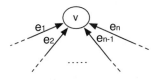

Figure 3.3: A vertex with multiple incoming hyperedges.

Algorithm 5 Partial sketch of the k-best search procedure.

Input :	v, a vertex
	k, an integer ≥ 1
Output :	*kbest*, a list of the k-best derivations of v

EAGER-K-BEST-VERTEX(v, k)

1   *kbest* = *cand* = $\varnothing$
2   **for** each incoming hyperedge e of v
3   d = the best derivation of v along e
4   PUSH(*cand*, d)
5   **while** $|kbest| < k$ **and** $|cand| > 0$
6   d = POP-MAX(*cand*)
7   append d to *kbest*
8   PUSH-NEIGHBORS(*cand*, d)
9   **return** *kbest*

---

from the queue therefore yields the 1-best derivation of v. Now the 2-best derivation must either be one of the candidates remaining in the queue *or* a neighbor of the 1-best derivation. The next step is therefore to generate the neighbors of the freshly popped derivation and push them to the queue. Popping from the queue will now yield the 2-best derivation. This process of popping derivations and then pushing their neighbors can be repeated until we either have k derivations or run out of candidates. The monotonicity of the derivation weight function guarantees that this method will yield the derivations in the correct order.

Algorithm 5 is a pseudocode version of the search procedure as described so far. EAGER-K-BEST-VERTEX assumes that the k-best subderivations have already been found for all predecessor vertices. Lines 2–4 prime the priority queue,[4] *cand*, which is keyed on the derivation

---

[4]Huang and Chiang [2005] use a more efficient queue priming method, which is based on the observation that when v has more than k incoming hyperedges, we need only push the best k derivations to *cand*. For n hyperedges, we can select the best k derivations in $\mathcal{O}(n)$ time and the cost of priming the queue becomes $\mathcal{O}(n) + \mathcal{O}(k \cdot \log k)$. This is an improvement

weight (in pseudocode, the calculation of the derivation weight will be implicit). Lines 5–8 repeatedly carry out the pop derivation/push neighbors method until either the list *kbest* has been filled or there are no more candidate derivations.

To define the PUSH-NEIGHBORS function, we require an algorithmic means of generating a derivation's neighbors. We first need to introduce an alternative representation for derivations.

Definition 3.16   (Derivation with Back-Pointers).   A *derivation with back pointers* is a triple $\langle e, \preceq_e, \mathbf{x} \rangle$, where $\langle e, \preceq_e \rangle$ is an ordered hyperedge and $\mathbf{x}$ is a coordinate vector in which each element x_i indicates the position of the ith subderivation in its respective k-best list. Note that the ordering relation $\preceq_e$ is only required to link subderivations with elements of $\mathbf{x}$. If a hyperedge is not already ordered then the relation can be defined arbitrarily. As a notational convenience, we will drop the ordering relation and write $\langle e, \mathbf{x} \rangle$ when the relation can be unambiguously inferred from context.

In our example, $\langle e, S_1 \rangle$ would be represented as $\langle e, \preceq_e, (1, 1, 1) \rangle$ and $\langle e, S_5 \rangle$ would be represented as $\langle e, \preceq_e, (2, 2, 1) \rangle$, assuming that $\preceq_e$ puts *tail*(e) in the order v_1, v_2, v_3.

Algorithm 6 gives pseudocode for the full eager k-best derivation algorithm. The input hypergraph is required to be acyclic. It is also required to be ordered, but only for the purposes of pairing up subderivations with elements of the coordinate vectors. For an unordered hypergraph, an arbitrary ordering can be imposed.

The top-level function, EAGER-K-BEST, uses the VISIT procedure from Algorithm 1. This calls EAGER-K-BEST-VERTEX on vertex t, the target vertex, but only after first calling EAGER-K-BEST-VERTEX on every predecessor of t (in topological order).

The EAGER-K-BEST-VERTEX procedure is identical to the version we have just described except for the use of the back pointer representation of derivations and the use of a global, vertex-specific k-best list. At line 3, the symbol $\mathbf{1}$ indicates a vector of length $|\text{tail}(e)|$ in which every element has the value 1. The derivation $\langle e, \mathbf{1} \rangle$ is therefore the best derivation of v along that particular hyperedge.

Finally, the EAGER-PUSH-NEIGHBORS procedure loops over the predecessors of e, generating one new derivation for each. At each iteration, the current subderivation for the ith predecessor is replaced with its next best subderivation. This requires that we increment element x_i in the coordinate vector. In the pseudocode, this is achieved by summing $\mathbf{x}$ and $\mathbf{b_i}$, where the latter is defined to be a vector of length $|\mathbf{x}|$, which contains the value 1 at position i and 0 everywhere else. The resulting neighbors are added to the priority queue subject to two conditions, both given in line 3. The first condition is that there are sufficient subderivations for the new coordinates to be valid—if a predecessor vertex only has 17 derivations then we cannot generate a neighbor with coordinate 18. The second condition is that the neighbor has not already been added (since a derivation can neighbor more than one other derivation).

---

over the $\mathcal{O}(n \cdot \log n)$ cost of pushing all n derivations to the heap. For readability, we will use the simpler (but less efficient) method in pseudocode.

Algorithm 6 Eager k-best Extraction

Input :	$\langle\langle V, E\rangle, \preceq_E\rangle$, an ordered directed acyclic hypergraph
	W_D, a monotonic derivation weight function
	t, a target vertex
	k, an integer ≥ 1
Output :	k-best derivations of t

Eager-K-Best($\langle\langle V, E\rangle, \preceq_E\rangle, W_D, t, k$)

1 **for** $v \in V$
2      $visited[v] = $ FALSE
3   VISIT(t, EAGER-K-BEST-VERTEX)   // See Algorithm 1
4   **return** $kbest[t]$

EAGER-K-BEST-VERTEX(v)

1   $kbest[v] = cand = \varnothing$
2   **for** each incoming hyperedge e of v
3   PUSH($cand, \langle e, \mathbf{1}\rangle$)
4   **while** $|kbest[v]| < k$ **and** $|cand| > 0$
5       $\langle e, \mathbf{x}\rangle = $ POP-MAX($cand$)
6   append $\langle e, \mathbf{x}\rangle$ to $kbest[v]$
7   EAGER-PUSH-NEIGHBORS($cand, \langle e, \mathbf{x}\rangle$)

EAGER-PUSH-NEIGHBORS($cand, \langle e, \mathbf{x}\rangle$)

1   **for** $i = 1 \ldots |e|$
2       $v_i = \text{pred}(e, \preceq_e, i)$
3   **if** $x_i < |kbest[v_i]|$ **and** $\langle e, \mathbf{x} + \mathbf{b_i}\rangle \notin cand$
4   PUSH($cand, \langle e, \mathbf{x} + \mathbf{b_i}\rangle$)

The Lazy k-best Derivation Algorithm

The lazy k-best derivation algorithm is based on the observation that the vast majority of derivations generated and added to $kbest[v]$ lists at the "bottom" of the forest will never become subderivations of derivations at the "top" of the forest. The eager generation of those lower derivations is therefore wasted effort. In fact, even for our tiny example the effect is striking. Consider again the hypergraph fragment in Figure 3.2. If k is 100 then, in the average case, v's 100 best derivations will only use 4 or 5 derivations each from v_1, v_2, and v_3 (since $3^4 < 100 < 3^5$).

The lazy k-best derivation algorithm eliminates this wasted effort by operating top-down from the target vertex and only generating subderivations on demand. For instance, the 8-best

Algorithm 7 Lazy k-best Extraction

Input :	$\langle\langle V, E\rangle, \preceq_E\rangle$, an ordered directed acyclic hypergraph
	W_D, a monotonic derivation weight function
	t, a target vertex
	k, an integer ≥ 1
Output :	k-best derivations of t

LAZY-K-BEST($\langle\langle V, E\rangle, W_D, t, k\rangle$)

1 **for** $v \in V$
2      $visited[v] = $ FALSE
3      $kbest[v] = cand[v] = \varnothing$
4 LAZY-J-BEST-VERTEX(t, k)
5 **return** $kbest[t]$

LAZY-J-BEST-VERTEX(v, j)

1 **if** $visited[v] = $ FALSE
2   **for** each incoming hyperedge e of v
3   PUSH($cand[v], \langle e, \mathbf{1}\rangle$)
4      $visited[v] = $ TRUE
5 **while** $\|kbest[v]\| < j$ **and** $\|cand[v]\| > 0$
6      $\langle e, \mathbf{x}\rangle = $ POP($cand[v]$)
7   append $\langle e, \mathbf{x}\rangle$ to $kbest[v]$
8   LAZY-PUSH-NEIGHBORS($cand[v], \langle e, \mathbf{x}\rangle$)

LAZY-PUSH-NEIGHBORS($cand, \langle e, \mathbf{x}\rangle$)

1 **for** $i = 1 \ldots |e|$
2      $v_i = \text{pred}(e, \preceq_e, i)$
3   LAZY-J-BEST-VERTEX($v_i, x_i + 1$)
4   **if** $x_i < \|kbest[v_i]\|$ **and** $\langle e, \mathbf{x} + \mathbf{b_i}\rangle \notin cand$
5   PUSH($cand, \langle e, \mathbf{x} + \mathbf{b_i}\rangle$)

derivation of v_1 will only be generated if a candidate that uses the 7-best derivation is popped at vertex v. Depending on how good the derivations of v_2 and v_3 are, this may never happen.

Pseudocode is given in Algorithm 7. Surprisingly, perhaps, very few changes are required to turn the eager bottom-up iterative algorithm into a lazy top-down recursive algorithm. It is worth comparing the pseudocode with that of Algorithm 6. The main differences are that instead of always popping k derivations, LAZY-J-BEST-VERTEX is given a parameter $j \leq k$ which controls how many derivations are popped. And in LAZY-PUSH-NEIGHBORS, a call is made to LAZY-J-BEST-VERTEX to create the jth subderivation only when it is certain that it is required.

3.3   HISTORICAL NOTES AND FURTHER READING

Our definitions of hypergraphs and derivations are based on those of Huang and Chiang [2005] (who build on the work of Klein and Manning [2001a] and Gallo et al. [1993]), but there are minor differences in details (for instance, we do not assume an ordering among tail vertices).

The Viterbi algorithm presented here belongs to a family of algorithms that bear the name. The common thread running through these algorithms is that they use dynamic programming to find the maximum probability solution to a problem. The algorithm family is named after Andrew Viterbi, who described a version of the algorithm for calculating error probability bounds for convolutional codes [Viterbi, 1967]. Variants were independently discovered by other researchers shortly after.

Similarly, variations of the CYK algorithm were found by multiple researchers working independently. The algorithm is named for three authors of early descriptions: the "C" is for John Cocke [Cocke and Schwartz, 1970], the "Y" is for Daniel Younger [Younger, 1967], and the "K" is for Tadao Kasami [Kasami, 1965]. It is also frequently referred to by the name CKY.

CHAPTER 4

Decoding II: Tree Decoding

This chapter describes tree decoding, a two-stage approach to decoding in which the input sentence is first parsed and then the resulting parse tree is translated. We will focus on the second stage, assuming that the input sentence has already been parsed. Tree decoding is the principal decoding method for tree-to-string and tree-to-tree models.

To make the discussion more concrete, we will assume throughout this chapter that the translation grammar is an STSG and that the probabilistic model is a log-linear model. Typically, a shared-category STSG is used for tree-to-string models and a distinct-category STSG is used for tree-to-tree models. Decoding with distinct-category STSGs is rare in practice and we will therefore focus on the simpler, common case.

We will begin by describing decoding for models with rule-local features. These models are a perfect fit for dynamic programming methods. Following common practice, we will make the max-derivation approximation (described in Section 1.3.2). It turns out that the maximally weighted derivation can be found using a combination of tree parsing and the Viterbi algorithm. We will then describe approximate methods for decoding with non-local features, such as a n-gram language model. In the final section, we discuss alternative rule matching algorithms and we sketch the extension to distinct-category STSGs (for use with tree-to-tree models).

Throughout the chapter we will use the following input parse tree and STSG grammar as part of a running example.

Example 4.1   Let τ be the following German parse tree:[1]

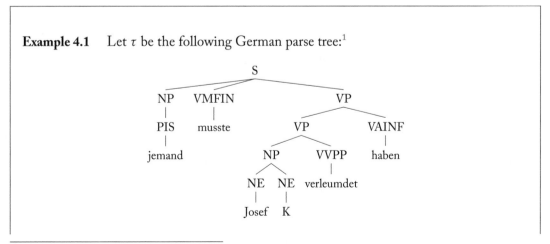

---

and let G be the STSG with the following rules.

$r_1 = $

```
      NP                    NP
      /\                    /\
   NE   NE              Josef  K.
    |    |
  Josef  K.
```

$r_2 = $

```
    VVPP                  VVPP
      |                     |
  verleumdet            slandered
```

$r_3 = $

```
    VVPP                  VVPP
      |                     |
  verleumdet            defamed
```

$r_4 = $

```
        VP                      VP
       /  \                    /  \
     NP   VVPP_2           VVPP_2  NE_1
      |
     NE_1
```

$r_5 = $

```
      VP                      VP
     /  \                    /  \
  VP_1   VAINF            have  VP_1
          |
        haben
```

$r_6 = $

```
         VP                          VP
        /  \                    /     |     \
      VP   VAINF             have  VVPP_2  NP_1
     /  \     |
  NP_1 VVPP_2 haben
```

$r_7 = $

```
              S                            S
          /   |    \                   /   |    \
        NP  VMFIN  VP_1         someone must  VP_1
         |    |
        PIS musste
         |
       jemand
```

$r_8 = $

```
               S                                     S
         /     |     \                    /   |     |     |     \
       NP   VMFIN     VP            someone must have VVPP_2 NP_1
        |     |      /  \
       PIS  musste  VP   VAINF
        |         /  \     |
     jemand    NP_1 VVPP_2 haben
```

$r_9 = $

```
               S                                          S
         /     |     \                    /    |    |    |    |    |    \
       NP   VMFIN     VP            NP_1 must have been VVPP_2 by someone
        |     |      /  \
       PIS  musste  VP   VAINF
        |         /  \     |
     jemand    NP_1 VVPP_2 haben
```

4.1   DECODING WITH LOCAL FEATURES

Initially, we will assume that all of the log-linear model's feature functions are rule-local. In other words, for any feature function h_i, the score of a derivation $h_i(d)$ can be expressed as a sum of scores of its component rules: $h_i(d) = \sum_{r \in d} h_i(r)$. In practice, this is usually true for all feature functions except the language model. Our first version of the string decoding problem can thus be expressed as follows.

Definition 4.2   (The Rule-Local String Decoding Problem).   Given a source sentence s with parse tree τ, a shared-category STSG G, and a conditional log-linear model $p(d|s)$ with M rule-local features, find the most probable synchronous derivation, d^*:

$$d^* \;=\; \arg\max_d \sum_{r \in d} \sum_{m=1}^{M} \lambda_m h_m(r),$$

where $d \in D(G, \tau)$ is any derivation with source derived tree τ.

4.1.1   A BASIC DECODING ALGORITHM

Decoding with a rule-local model is straightforward in principle: all we need to do is construct a hypergraph representation of the STSG translation forest and then apply the Viterbi max-derivation algorithm. To put this into practice we need to answer two questions: (i) how do we construct the hypergraph? and (ii) what is the derivation weight function for our rule-local STSG model?

The hypergraph can be constructed by several methods of varying complexity and efficiency. Perhaps the simplest method is to visit each node n of the tree and attempt to pattern match the source-side of every rule against the subtree rooted at n. For every rule that matches, a hyperedge is added to the hypergraph.

By pattern matching, we mean that the source-side fragment must be identical to the sub-tree, except at the fragment's non-terminals—a non-terminal indicates a gap in the form of an omitted subtree. Algorithm 8 gives a simple recursive method. The algorithm essentially per-forms a basic pre-order tree comparison, but with special handling of non-terminals. For each non-terminal in the fragment, line 4 inserts the corresponding subtree node into the *sites* set. As we will see shortly, this information will be used to construct the hyperedge corresponding to the rule match.

For a rule-local log-linear model, defining the derivation weight function is easy: the weight of a hyperedge e labeled with rule r is simply the weighted-sum of the feature function values for that rule, and the weight of a derivation $d = \langle e, S \rangle$ is the sum of the derivation's hyperedge and subderivation weights:

$$W_E(e) = \sum_{m=1}^{M} \lambda_m h_m(r) \qquad \text{and} \qquad W_D(d) = W_E(e) + \sum_{d' \in S} W_D(d'). \tag{4.1}$$

Algorithm 8 A Basic Rule Matching Algorithm

Input :	m	root node of rule fragment
	n	root node of subtree
	sites	output tree node set
Output :	*match*	Boolean flag indicating match

MATCH-RULE($m, n, sites$)

1 **if** label(m) $\neq$ label(n)
2   **return** FALSE
3 **if** $|$children(m)$| = 0$ **and** $|$children(n)$| > 0$
4   INSERT($sites$, m)
5   **return** TRUE
6 **if** $|$children(m)$| \neq |$children(n)$|$
7   **return** FALSE
8 **for** $i = 0$ **to** $|$children(m)$| - 1$
9   **if not** MATCH-RULE(children(m)[i], children(n)[i], $sites$)
10   **return** FALSE
11 **return** TRUE

The derivation weight function is equivalent to summing the weights of all the hyperedges along the derivation.

We now have everything we need. Algorithm 9 gives the pseudocode for a basic tree decoding algorithm. The function CONSTRUCT-HYPERGRAPH uses MATCH-RULE to determine every possible match of a grammar rule against the input parse tree. CONSTRUCT-HYPERGRAPH begins with an empty set of vertices, V, and hyperedges, E (lines 1 and 2). Lines 3–11 then perform a post-order traversal of the tree, which for each node, n, generates the corresponding vertex, $V[n]$, (line 4) and its incoming hyperedges (lines 5–11). While we have specified a post-order traversal, any bottom-up order would work equally well.

Once the hypergraph has been constructed, we apply the Viterbi max-derivation algorithm (line 2 of TREE-DECODE-1). Recall that VITERBI-DERIVATION (Algorithm 2 from Chapter 3) records the maximally weighted derivation of each vertex in a data structure called *best*. All that remains to do is to look-up the best derivation for the vertex corresponding to the root node of the input tree (line 3).

The algorithm can be modified to return the k-best derivations by substituting one of the k-best algorithms (Algorithm 6 or Algorithm 7) for the Viterbi algorithm and returning *kbest*$[V[root(\tau)]]$ at line 3.

Algorithm 9 A Basic Tree Decoding Algorithm

Input :	τ	a parse tree
	G	a shared-category STSG
	W_D	a monotonic derivation weight function
Output :	d^*	the maximally-weighted derivation of τ

TREE-DECODE-1(τ, G, W_D)

1 $\langle V, E \rangle = $ CONSTRUCT-HYPERGRAPH(τ, G)
2 VITERBI-DERIVATION$(\langle V, E \rangle, W_D)$
3 **return** $best[V[root(\tau)]]$

CONSTRUCT-HYPERGRAPH(τ, G)

1 $V = \varnothing$
2 $E = \varnothing$
3 **for** each node n of τ, visited in post-order
4   add vertex $V[n]$
5   **for** each source-side tree fragment α in $\text{proj}_s(G)$
6          $sites = \varnothing$
7   **if** MATCH-RULE$(\text{root}(\alpha), n, sites)$
8              $head = \{V[n]\}$
9              $tail = \{V[n'] : n' \in sites\}$
10   **for** each rule r in $\text{proj}'_s(\alpha)$
11   add hyperedge $\langle head, tail, r \rangle$ to E
12 **return** $\langle V, E \rangle$

Shortcomings of the Current Algorithm

As it stands, the tree decoding algorithm has a number of shortcomings (in addition to the limitation that the model must be rule-local).

- Hypergraph construction, while linear in the number of input tree nodes,[2] potentially has a very large constant factor: the algorithm tries to match every single source-side fragment in G at every single node of τ. For now, we will ignore this source of inefficiency, but we note that significantly better algorithms are known. We will return to this issue in Section 4.4.

- The algorithm will fail to produce a derivation if there is no combination of source-side fragments that fully covers the tree. In practice, this is a frequent occurrence: the input to a decoder often contains words that were not observed during training (and so do not

---

[2]Assuming a constant limit on the size of a rule's tree fragment.

occur in any grammar rule). A simple solution is to test, after the loop at lines 5–11 in CONSTRUCT-HYPERGRAPH, whether any hyperedges were produced and if not, to generate a glue rule that is guaranteed to match. For a tree node n, the simplest possible glue rule would have a 1-level source-side fragment with n's label at its root node and one child non-terminal for each of n's children. The target-side would simply duplicate the source-side, with a monotonic correspondence between source and target non-terminals. For instance, in our example grammar (Example 4.1), there is no rule that matches the input tree at the lower VP node. The monotonic 1-level glue rule for this node would be:

To allow the decoder to reorder the input, non-monotonic could also be generated. In practice, the use of non-monotonic glue rules has been shown to improve translation quality, although the improvements are usually modest (see, for example, Chung et al. [2011] or Li et al. [2013]). Additionally, a decoder may employ specialized routines to generate rules for certain classes of unseen word. For instance, to convert dates into the correct target-specific format or to transliterate named entities.

- For the max-derivation version of the algorithm, it is wasteful to construct the entire hypergraph: when a source-side fragment, α, has been matched, there is no need to add a hyperedge for every rule in $\text{proj}'_s(\alpha)$. Rule-locality means we need only add one (for the rule with the highest weighted sum, $\sum_{m=1}^{M} \lambda_m h_m(r)$). We could go further still and merge hypergraph construction with Viterbi search in an analogous fashion to the CYK max-derivation algorithm (Algorithm 4). This would not affect the time complexity of the algorithm (it still has to generate a candidate derivation for every hyperedge) but it would reduce the space complexity by eliminating the need to store most hyperedges.

- For the k-best version of the algorithm, we can also eliminate hyperedges, although not to the same extent as for the max-derivation version. When a source-side fragment, α, has been matched, we need to add a hyperedge for the k-best rules in $\text{proj}'_s(\alpha)$. By making a minor modification to the k-best algorithm, we can reduce this to a single hyperedge by treating the k rules as a group: instead of labeling hyperedges with a single rule identifier, we label them with a list of up to k identifiers, sorted by rule weight. We will describe this modification in detail in the next section.

4.1.2 HYPEREDGE BUNDLING

Figure 4.1 shows the STSG hypergraph that results from pattern matching the grammar rules of Example 4.1 against the parse tree. For clarity of presentation, where there are multiple hyper-

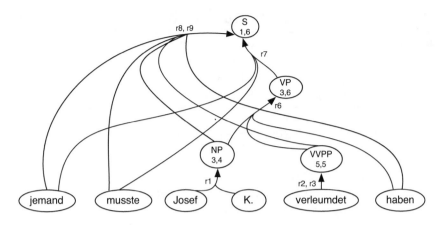

Figure 4.1: Hypergraph representation of the translation forest for the input parse tree and STSG grammar of Example 4.1 (we have omitted vertices with no incoming hyperedges). Hyperedges labeled with multiple rules represent multiple hyperedges (one per rule).

edges with the same head and tail, we have shown a single hyperedge and labeled it with a list of rules. These multi-labeled hyperedges should be understood to represent multiple distinct labeled hyperedges, with one per STSG rule. By modifying the hypergraph representation used by our algorithm, we can perform a similar merging of hyperedges. This is sometimes called *hyperedge bundling*. Since there is an ordering on rule weights, we can use this representation to improve the performance of the k-best algorithm for our particular application.

At this point, it may appear that we are indulging in an act of premature optimization: why complicate a simple, general algorithm by optimizing it for a particular application when it may already meet our needs? If we were to stop at a rule-local model then that would be a fair criticism. For now, keep in mind that we are working toward a model with non-local features. In that setting, the search hypergraphs become dramatically larger and any optimization of this kind is more likely to pay off. Most decoders do in fact perform hyperedge bundling of this sort and so it is worthwhile to introduce the method now in the simplified context of rule-local modeling. Ultimately, this approach will be applied not in k-best derivation extraction, but in its non-local, beam-search cousins.

To define the modified version of the k-best algorithm we first need to update our representations of hyperedges and hypergraph derivations. Instead of labeling a hyperedge with a rule identifier, r, we will label it with the identifier, q, of the source-side projection, $\text{proj}_s(r)$. For each source-side tree fragment, q, we will assume the existence of an array containing the rules of the inverse projection, $\text{proj}'_s(q)$, sorted by weight. To distinguish the two representations, we will refer to this form of hypergraph as a *bundled hypergraph*. The definition of a derivation with backpoint-

---

Algorithm 10 The Eager-Push-Neighbors Algorithm, Adapted for Bundled Hypergraphs

Input :	m	root node of rule fragment
	n	root node of subtree
	sites	output tree node set
Output :	*match*	Boolean flag indicating match

EAGER-PUSH-NEIGHBORS-BUNDLED($cand, \langle e, \mathbf{x}, y \rangle$)

1   **for** $i = 1 \ldots |e|$
2       $v_i = \text{pred}(e, \preceq_e, i)$
3   **if** $x_i < |kbest[v_i]|$ **and** $\langle e, \mathbf{x} + \mathbf{b_i}, y \rangle \notin cand$
4   PUSH($cand, \langle e, \mathbf{x} + \mathbf{b_i}, y \rangle$)
5   **if** $y < |\text{proj}'_s(e)|$ **and** $\langle e, \mathbf{x}, y + 1 \rangle \notin cand$
6   PUSH($cand, \langle e, \mathbf{x}, y + 1 \rangle$)

---

ers (Definition 3.16 in Chapter 3) is extended for bundled hypergraphs to include an index into one of these sorted rule arrays. The hyperedge e of a derivation with backpointers, is thus bound to a distinct STSG rule through the combination of the source-side fragment identifier and an array index:

Definition 4.3   (Bundled Derivation with Back-Pointers).   A *bundled derivation with back pointers* is a tuple $\langle e, \preceq_e, \mathbf{x}, y \rangle$, where $\langle e, \preceq_e \rangle$ is an ordered hyperedge in a bundled hypergraph, $\mathbf{x}$ is a coordinate vector in which each element x_i indicates the position of the ith subderivation in its respective k-best list, and y is an index into an array that contains the synchronous rules from $\text{proj}'_s(q)$, where q is the source-side rule projection corresponding to e.

The only substantive change required to the k-best algorithm is in PUSH-NEIGHBORS. Algorithm 10 shows the eager version (the changes required for the lazy version are identical). Lines 1–4 are the same as in the original EAGER-PUSH-NEIGHBORS (Algorithm 6) except for the presence of index y in the derivation tuples. Lines 5–6 create the neighbor that differs from the input derivation only in its translation. It is assumed that the array indexed by y is ordered best-first by rule weight.

4.2   STATE SPLITTING

In this section and the next, we discuss methods for decoding with non-local features. While all of the methods presented here were originally developed for n-gram language models, they can be (and have been) applied to other types of non-local feature. We begin by adding a bigram language model feature to our log-linear model.

4.2.1   ADDING A BIGRAM LANGUAGE MODEL FEATURE

As a running example, we will suppose that our log-linear model includes a bigram language model among its M feature functions. If the language model is the ith feature function and all other feature functions are rule-local then the objective function becomes

$$d^* \; = \; \arg\max_d \left(\lambda_i \log p_{\text{LM}}(d) + \sum_{r \in d} \sum_{m \neq i} \lambda_m h_m(r) \right), \tag{4.2}$$

where $d \in D(G, \tau)$ is any derivation with source-side derived tree τ and $p_{\text{LM}}(d)$ is the language model probability of d's target-side yield. The bigram language model probability for a sentence $s = w_1, w_2, \ldots, w_{|s|}$ is

$$p_{\text{LM}}(s) = \prod_{i=1}^{|s|+1} p_{\text{LM}}(w_i \mid w_{i-1}), \tag{4.3}$$

where $w_0 = \text{BOS}$ and $w_{|s|+1} = \text{EOS}$ are distinguished tokens that mark the beginning and end of a sentence.

Of course, the objective function as currently defined is not suitable for dynamic programming: the search algorithm cannot wait until it has produced a derivation of a complete sentence before scoring it with the language model feature. For search to be efficient, the algorithm must exploit the independence assumptions of the bigram language model. While our current algorithm fully exploits the independence assumptions of the rule-local features, it is incompatible with those of the language model. To demonstrate this, let us return to our example STSG hypergraph (Figure 4.1). Consider the two derivations of the vertex labeled (VP, 3, 6). Both derivations include the hyperedges labeled r_1 and r_6, but differ in whether they also include r_2 or r_3. The rules r_1, r_2, r_3, and r_6 have the following target-sides, respectively:

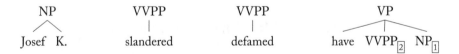

The two derivations therefore have the target yields "have slandered Josef K." and "have defamed Josef K." We will call these derivations d_1 and d_2, respectively. Now suppose that d_1 and d_2 become subderivations of some larger derivation, d_3. To calculate the weight of d_3, the derivation weight function must include one of the terms $p(\text{slandered} \mid \text{have})$ or $p(\text{defamed} \mid \text{have})$ and one of the terms $p(\text{Josef} \mid \text{slandered})$ or $p(\text{Josef} \mid \text{defamed})$. Without taking into account which of these terms the language model favors, and by how much, it is impossible to determine which of d_1 or d_2 will make the better subderivation. In general, it is not possible to define a decomposable derivation weight function over the hypergraph when the score of a derivation depends on the target yields of its subderivations.

4.2.2   THE STATE-SPLIT HYPERGRAPH

The impossibility of defining a monotonic derivation weight function over the translation hypergraph is the result of an incompatibility between the hypergraph structure and the independence assumptions of the bigram language model. By restructuring the hypergraph it is possible to remove this incompatibility. In fact, through a process of state splitting, it is always possible to construct a hypergraph that encodes a STSG translation forest while also respecting the independence assumptions of any non-local features (although, as we will see, the practicality of actually doing so is another matter).

In the context of incorporating a n-gram language model feature, this process is often referred to as *intersection*, since it is equivalent to Bar-Hillel et al. [1961]'s method for intersecting a context-free grammar with a finite-state automaton (the translation forest is context-free and the n-gram language model is a finite-state automaton[3]). For an n-gram language model of order N, the method involves grouping the derivations of a vertex according to the $N - 1$ left and right boundary words of their target yield, since it is variation in the boundary words that compromise the monotonicity of a potential derivation weight function. Each vertex is replaced by a set of vertices with finer-grained labels that encode the left and right boundary words.

For the bigram language model example, a minimally[4] expanded hypergraph encodes the leftmost and rightmost boundary words of a translation in each vertex label. Figure 4.2 shows part of the STSG hypergraph from Figure 4.1 after being expanded to include the boundary words of the translations. In order that the figure does not become unreadably cluttered, we have omitted the two hyperedges arising from the application of rule r_8 and we have omitted the vertex and two hyperedges arising from the application of rule r_9.

We can now define a monotonic derivation weight function, although doing so is a little fiddly. We will begin by defining a function to score a partial translation with the bigram language model. Our first version, $h_i'(d)$, takes a derivation d as input:

$$h_i'(d) = \log \prod_{i=2}^{|t|} p_{\mathrm{LM}}(w_i \mid w_{i-1}), \tag{4.4}$$

where $t = w_1, w_2, \ldots, w_{|t|}$ is the target-side yield of d. In order that $h_i'(d)$ assigns the correct language model score to a full sentence derivation, we require that the target yield is padded with a BOS symbol to the left and a EOS symbol to the right. We will assume that the grammar contains an additional rule,

---

[3]In practice, every target-side string of the translation grammar is usually also a valid string in the n-gram FSA. Although the name "intersection" might suggest otherwise, the n-gram language model should be thought of as weighting derivations rather than filtering them.

[4]This is minimal if we treat the language model as a black box and assume that every sequence of N target words is potentially a valid language model state. See Heafield [2011] for discussion of how the number of states can be minimized when knowledge of the language model's content is taken into account.

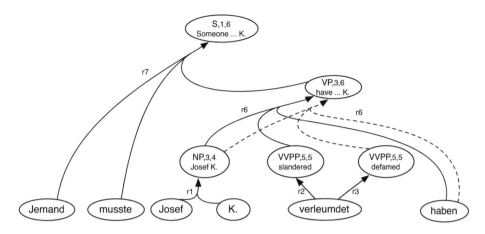

Figure 4.2: Partial STSG hypergraph for the input sentence and grammar of Example 4.1 after expansion to include boundary words. We have omitted the hyperedges for rules r_8 and r_9. (The dashed hyperedge line is for visual clarity only: there is no difference in meaning.)

The symbol $S^{\ddagger}$ replaces $S^{\dagger}$ as the grammar's start symbol. Now let us use h_i' to define a tentative pair of weight functions:

$$W_E(e) = \sum_{m \neq i} \lambda_m h_m(r) \tag{4.5}$$

and

$$W_D(d) = \lambda_i h_i'(d) + W_E(e) + \sum_{d' \in S} \left(W_D(d') - \lambda_i h_i'(d') \right). \tag{4.6}$$

As currently defined, $W_D(d)$ does not decompose the calculation of the language model score. Rather, it computes the score in full for each derivation and deducts the language model scores of subderivations. In practice, querying the language model in order to calculate scores incurs a significant computational cost and, since a derivation usually shares most of its bigrams with its subderivations, clearly the current method is wasteful. Instead, it is better to calculate for each derivation the score for bigrams that appear only in that derivation, and not in any subderivation. If we think of a derivation $d = \langle e, S \rangle$ in terms of bottom-up rule application, the bigrams of interest are those that are produced by the application of e's rule. These bigrams can be identified by considering the target-side of e's rule and the subderivations in S. They are: (i) pairs of

Hypergraph	Vertices	Hyperedges
Original	$O(|\tau|)$	$O(|G| \cdot |\tau|)$
State-split	$O(|\tau| \cdot |T_t|^{2(N-1)})$	$O(|G| \cdot |\tau| \cdot |T_t|^{2(N-1)\cdot\mathrm{rank}(G)})$

Table 4.1: Size of hypergraph for a translation forest (original) and the state-split version for a n-gram language model (state-split). $|G|$ is the number of grammar rules, $|\tau|$ is the number of input tree nodes, T_t is the set of target-side terminals, N is the order of the n-gram language model, and $\mathrm{rank}(G)$ is the grammar's rank.

consecutive terminals; (ii) the right and left border words of subderivations whose substitution sites are neighboring pairs of non-terminals; (iii) the left border word of a subderivation whose substitution site is a non-terminal that follows a terminal; and (iv) the right border word of a subderivation whose substitution site is a non-terminal that precedes a terminal.

Let us give the name new-bigrams to the function that, given a derivation $d = \langle e, S \rangle$, yields the set of freshly-produced bigrams, as enumerated above. Notice that new-bigrams does not need to know anything about the subderivations other than their boundary words. Since the boundary words are encoded in the vertices in e's tail, new-bigrams is a function of e. Let us revise our language model feature function:

$$h_i(e) = \log \prod_{(w_{j-1}, w_j)} p_{\mathrm{LM}}(w_j \mid w_{j-1}), \tag{4.7}$$

where $(w_{j-1}, w_j) \in$ new-bigrams(e). We can now express the weight functions in a form that matches the rule-local versions:

$$W_E(e) = \lambda_i h_i(e) + \sum_{m \neq i} \lambda_m h_m(r) \quad \text{and} \quad W_D(d) = W_E(e) + \sum_{d' \in S} W_D(d'). \tag{4.8}$$

4.2.3 COMPLEXITY

We now have a dynamic programming method for finding the best derivation, or k-best derivations, of a model with non-local features—at least in theory. Algorithmically, it would be straightforward to fully expand the original translation forest hypergraph into a state-split hypergraph and then apply standard max-derivation or k-best algorithms. Unfortunately, this approach is not feasible in practice since the state-split hypergraph is too large: whereas a translation forest can be represented as a hypergraph in $O(|G| \cdot |\tau|)$ space (where $|G|$ is the number of grammar rules and $|\tau|$ is the number of input tree nodes), with a n-gram language model, the state-split hypergraph is *much* larger (see Table 4.1). With the full state-split forest out of reach, we must instead rely on approximate methods that generate a manageable subhypergraph.

4.3   BEAM SEARCH

In this section, we present approximate methods for decoding with models that include non-local features. All approximate tree decoding methods make use of *beam search*, a strategy that has been widely-used elsewhere in natural language processing. In general terms, beam search is an approximate form of best-first search in which, at each step, partial solutions are ranked according to a heuristic measure of how promising they appear to be, and all but the most promising solutions are discarded. At a given step, the beam (or sometimes "stack") is the set of promising partial solutions that are deemed to be worth pursuing in a subsequent step.

In tree decoding, beams are used to confine search to the most promising areas of the state-split hypergraph. Decoding begins by constructing the basic translation forest hypergraph. Each vertex of this hypergraph can be thought of as a window onto a set of finer-grained vertices belonging to the state-split hypergraph. As we have seen, the numbers of state-split vertices can be unmanageably large and so a beam restricts the view to a manageable subset of state-split vertices.

4.3.1   THE BEAM

Figure 4.3 depicts the search structure used for beam search. The base hypergraph is the translation hypergraph from Figure 4.1, except that here we have labeled the hyperedges with source-side rule identifiers. Every non-leaf vertex has an associated beam, which is essentially a list of k-best lists. Additionally, every entry in the beam has an associated state value, which is equivalent to the fine-grained state in the state-split hypergraph.

There are various ways to constrain the size of the beam. Usually, it is the number of entries per beam (the number of rows in Figure 4.1) that is restricted and the maximum allowed size is referred to as the beam size. Note that since each beam entry can hold multiple derivations, the total number of derivations in the beam may be larger.

For a vertex v, we will write beam$[v]$ to refer to that vertex's beam; we will write beam$[v][i]$ and state$[v][i]$ to refer to the ith k-best list and state object, respectively; and we will write beam$[v][i][j]$ to refer to an individual derivation in the k-best list.

A derivation over the beam search hypergraph has the form $\langle e, \preceq_e, \mathbf{x}, \mathbf{x}', y \rangle$, closely resembling a bundled derivation with backpointers (Definition 4.3). The difference here is that a backpointer is a pair (x_i, x_i'), where x_i and x_i' are the ith elements of $\mathbf{x}$ and $\mathbf{x}'$, respectively. For a derivation $\langle e, \preceq_e, \mathbf{x}, \mathbf{x}', y \rangle$, each back pointer (x_i, x_i') refers to the subderivation beam$[u_i][x_i][x_i']$, where u_i is the ith vertex in tail(e) (ordered by $\preceq_e$). In other words, x_i points to a k-best list and x_i' points to a specific derivation within the list.

Notice that there is a direct correspondence between derivations in the beam search structure and derivations in the state-split hypergraph: every beam$[v][i][j]$ corresponds to exactly one state-split derivation. Of course, due to restrictions on the size of the beam, not every state-split derivation can be represented in the beam search structure. Since all the information required to calculate the state-split derivation weight function is also encoded in the beam-search structure,

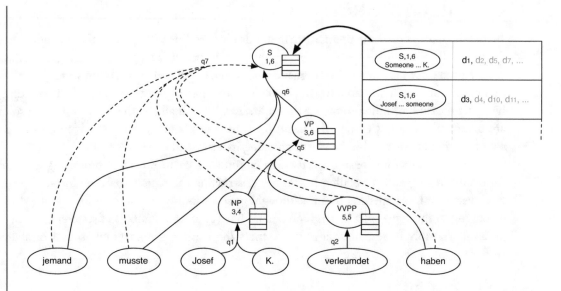

Figure 4.3: The beam-based search structure for the input parse tree and STSG grammar of Example 4.1. Each entry in the beam contains a representation of the search state (depicted as the equivalent vertex in the state-split hypergraph) along with the group of derivations that share that state, ordered by weight. We have depicted a larger number of derivations than are actually possible in the example grammar. The "grayed-out" entries are the recombined derivations. These are required for later k-best derivation extraction, but redundant in max-derivation search.

the weight function carries over to the beam search structure with only superficial differences. In a slight abuse of notation, we will apply the existing function, W_D, directly to derivations in the beam search structure.

If we are using beam search as an approximate max-derivation algorithm, then it is unnecessary for a beam entry to contain a k-best list. The beam need only record the single best derivation for each state value. In this case, we can discard the other items without any risk of increasing the search error.[5] However, if we are using beam search as (part of) an approximate k-best algorithm, then we should retain the items for later use. We will assume the latter case. To refer to the Viterbi derivation formed from combining the 1-best subderivations, we will write $\langle e, \preceq_e, \mathbf{x}, \mathbf{1}, y \rangle$.

4.3.2   REST COST ESTIMATION

One complication that arises from beam search is the requirement for a meaningful ordering between derivations with distinct search states. Recall that the current derivation weight function

---

[5]This is often called "recombination."

ignores the first $N - 1$ words of a derivation and ignores the fact that the last $N - 1$ words will become the context of n-grams that extend to the right in subsequent derivations. These simplifications are fine when comparing derivations that share the same $N - 1$ boundary words (such as those derivations inside a beam entry) since those derivations will all behave identically with respect to the language model. The problem arises when comparing derivations belonging to different entries. These comparisons are necessary because they are the basis for ordering the entries within the beam.

In order to make weight comparisons meaningful, a heuristic method is used to adjust the score. Here we will use the heuristic proposed by Heafield et al. [2012][6]: if the language model order is N, then the first word is scored with a separate unigram model (estimated from the same data); the second word is scored with a bigram model; and so on, up until the $N - 1^{th}$, which is scored with a language model of order $N - 1$. The remaining words are scored using the same method as previously (sub-N-grams are not scored for the $N - 1$ right boundary words). The adjusted bigram language model feature function is

$$h_i''(e) = \log \left(p_{\text{LM}_1}(w_1) \times \prod_{(w_{j-1}, w_j)} p_{\text{LM}_2}(w_j \mid w_{j-1}) \right), \tag{4.9}$$

where w_1 is the left-most word (yielded by any derivation $d = \langle e, S \rangle$), $(w_{j-1}, w_j) \in$ new-bigrams(e) and LM_1 and LM_2 are the unigram and bigram language models, respectively. The adjusted hyperedge and derivation weight functions are

$$W_E'(e) = \lambda_i h_i''(e) + \sum_{m \neq i} \lambda_m h_m(r) \quad \text{and} \quad W_D'(d) = W_E'(e) + \sum_{d' \in S} W_D(d'). \tag{4.10}$$

Note that the standard derivation weight function, W_D, is used for scoring subderivations. It is therefore necessary to calculate both the standard and adjusted derivation weights, $W_D(d)$ and $W_D'(d)$, for every derivation d. The adjusted derivation weight is used only for ordering derivations within the beam.

4.3.3 MONOTONICITY REDUX

We are now almost ready to describe the beam search algorithms. Before we do, let us recap the (somewhat complicated) situation regarding search structures, derivations, and monotonicity.

1. For a model with non-local features, we cannot define a monotonic weight function over derivations of the translation hypergraph.

---

[6]The estimation of the language model cost of the left-side boundary words has long been common practice [Li and Khudanpur, 2008]. However, these costs were usually obtained using probabilities from lower-order estimates of higher-order n-gram models. Heafield et al. [2012] noted that these estimates were meant to be consulted in the context of a language model backoff routine, and showed that using separately trained lower order models resulted in better search.

2. Through state-splitting, it is possible (at least in theory) to construct a finer-grained hypergraph over which we *can* define a monotonic derivation weight function (Section 4.2). For this to be practical, the crucial question is the size of the hypergraph. If it is computationally feasible to construct the hypergraph, then we can determine exactly the max-derivation or k-best derivations using standard hypergraph algorithms from the previous chapter. This is generally not possible when the model includes an n-gram language model.

3. For beam search, we take a different tack: we perform search over the original hypergraph, but we define a heuristic weight function that indicates how promising we believe a derivation to be for subsequent use as a subderivation. We hedge our bets by proposing multiple promising derivations at each vertex (and storing them in a beam). Although the derivation weight function carries over essentially unchanged from the state-split hypergraph, the change in hypergraph structure breaks the function's monotonicity. In a nutshell, since a vertex no longer distinguishes fine-grained state values (with the distinction being made within the beam instead), the maximally weighted derivation of a vertex is no longer guaranteed to be an optimal subderivation.

While non-monotonicty makes exact max-derivation and k-best derivation algorithms prohibitively expensive, beam search allows us to approximate them.

- Beam search is an approximate max-derivation algorithm: after the algorithm has run, the approximate best derivation is the highest scoring search item in the target vertex's beam.

- Beam search combined with a standard k-best derivation algorithm gives an approximate k-best algorithm: after beam search, the search structure can be converted into a state-split hypergraph (which is a subhypergraph of the full state-split hypergraph) and standard k-best extraction can be applied.

In the remainder of this section, we will describe four beam-filling algorithms. To help illustrate how they work, we will use the following example.

Example 4.4   Consider the following hypergraph fragment:

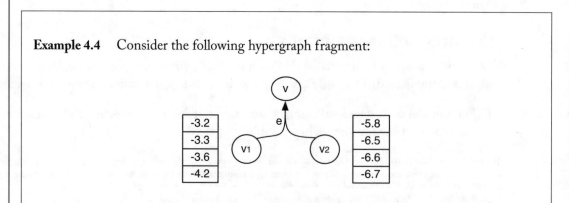

The values shown in the two beams indicate the weight of the 1-best derivation for each beam entry. Suppose that there are two derivation weight functions, one is monotonic and the other not:

$$W_{D_1}(d) = W_E(e) + \sum_{d' \in S} W_{D_1}(d') \quad \text{and} \quad W_{D_2}(d) = W_{D_1}(d) + \text{noise}(d).$$

The first, $W_{D_1}(d)$, simply sums the hyperedge weight and the subitem weights; the second, $W_{D_2}(d)$, calculates the same sum but adds a small amount of "noise"—a value between 0 and -1.5 that can be determined given the derivation, but not from the subderivation weights. Assume that $W_E(e)$ returns the value -0.7.

We can depict the weights of all 16 possible subderivations in a 4 x 4 grid, where the input weights for v_1's subderivations run along the vertical axis and the input weights for v_2's subderivations run along the horizontal axis. The top-left corner represents the weight of the derivation formed from the two best input subderivations and the bottom-right, the derivation formed from the two worst input subderivations. The grids for the two weight functions are:

	-5.8	-6.5	-6.6	-6.7
-3.2	-9.7	-10.4	-10.5	-10.6
-3.3	-9.8	-10.5	-10.6	-10.7
-3.6	-10.1	-10.8	-10.9	-11.0
-4.2	-10.7	-11.4	-11.5	-11.6

and

	-5.8	-6.5	-6.6	-6.7
-3.2	-10.6	-11.6	-11.6	-11.5
-3.3	-10.8	-10.5	-11.1	-11.5
-3.6	-10.7	-11.4	-11.2	-11.6
-4.2	-12.1	-11.9	-12.0	-11.7

Notice that in the first grid, every weight is greater than its neighbor to the right or below. This follows immediately from the definition of monotonicity. We can enumerate the derivations in order by applying the priority-queue based search strategy used in the k-best algorithms (Algorithms 6 and 7). This is not the case for the second, non-monotonic weight function.

4.3.4 EXHAUSTIVE BEAM FILLING

Exhaustive beam filling solves the problem of non-monotonicity by brute-force: at each vertex, it enumerates *every* derivation (subject to the contents of the beams in predecessor vertices) then sorts them by weight (including the rest cost estimate) and fills the beam with the most promising k derivations. In Example 4.2, this method enumerates all 16 derivations. In practice, there will usually be many more subderivations in each incoming beam, and there may be more than two incoming beams. For instance, if $k = 50$ and some hyperedge has a tail with five vertices, then that makes $50^5 = 312{,}500{,}000$ derivations (just for that one hyperedge). Although still too expensive

---

Algorithm 11 A Beam Search-based Tree Decoding Algorithm

Input :	τ	a parse tree
	G	a shared-category STSG
	W_D	a monotonic derivation weight function
	k	the maximum beam size (an integer ≥ 1)
Output :	d^*	approximation to maximally-weighted derivation of τ

TREE-DECODE-2(τ, G, W_D, k)

1 $\langle V, E \rangle$ = CONSTRUCT-HYPERGRAPH(τ, G)   **//** See Algorithm 9 (page 73)
2 **for** $v \in V$
3      $visited[v]$ = FALSE
4 $t = V[\text{root}(\tau)]$
5 VISIT(t, EXHAUSTIVE-BEAM-FILL)   **//** See Algorithm 1 (page 56)
6 **return** HEAD($beam[t]$)

EXHAUSTIVE-BEAM-FILL(v)

1 $beam[v] = buffer = \varnothing$
2 **for** each incoming hyperedge e of v
3   **for** $\mathbf{x} \in \{(x_1, \ldots, x_{|\text{tail}(e)|}) : x_i \in \text{range}(|beam[\text{pred}(e, \preceq_e, i)]|\}$
4   **for** $y \in \text{range}(|\text{proj'}_s(e)|)$
5   append $\langle e, \mathbf{x}, \mathbf{1}, y \rangle$ to $buffer$
6 RECOMBINE-SORT-PRUNE($buffer, beam[v]$)

RECOMBINE-SORT-PRUNE($buffer, beam$)

1 group $buffer$'s derivations according to state value
2 **for** each group g
3   sort g's derivations by weight
4 $beam$ = list of k best groups ordered by weight of group's best derivation

---

to be practical, this is the simplest beam-filling method and will bring us within reach of a usable search algorithm.

Algorithm 11 shows the pseudocode. The top-level function, TREE-DECODE-2, begins by constructing the translation forest hypergraph. The VISIT procedure calls EXHAUSTIVE-BEAM-FILL on vertex t, the target vertex, but only after calling EXHAUSTIVE-BEAM-FILL on every predecessor of t (in topological order).

At line 3 of EXHAUSTIVE-BEAM-FILL, every valid value of $\mathbf{x}$ is enumerated: this is the Cartesian product of subderivation index sets (one index set for each predecessor vertex $u_i \in$

tail(e)). The function pred($e, \preceq_e, i$) returns the ith predecessor vertex $u_i \in$ tail(e), subject to the tail ordering, $\preceq_e$, implicit in the translation forest. The function range(n) returns the set of integers in the range $1 \ldots n$. (Note in line 3 that the range calculations take account of the possibility that a predecessor beam contains fewer than k entries.) At line 4, the STSG rule indices are enumerated for the source-side rule specified by e. All derivations are collected in a list, called *buffer*. The function RECOMBINE-SORT-PRUNE takes care of organizing the derivations into beam entries, and then pruning the beam to k entries (the size of *buffer* is likely to far exceed the maximum beam size, k).

If we are only interested in finding a single derivation (i.e., we are using beam search as an approximate max-derivation algorithm), then the beam only needs to retain the maximally-weighted subderivation for each distinct state and RECOMBINE-SORT-PRUNE can discard the sub-optimal derivation. If we want to generate a k-best list from the (partial) state-split hypergraph then the suboptimal derivations must be retained. In the pseudocode we assume the latter case.

4.3.5 CUBE PRUNING

Cube pruning is a heuristic beam-filling strategy. It is based on the assumption that the weight function is approximately monotonic. In other words, it is based on the assumption that combining high-scoring subderivations makes a better strategy than combining low-scoring subderivations (while not guaranteeing the best result). In practice, this near monotonicity is a reasonable assumption. The artificially generated grid in Example 4.2 exhibits the kind of near monotonicity that is common in log-linear models with a n-gram language model. The noise factor (which resembles the language model weight) is unpredictable, but it is only one component of the weight function and has a limited ability to disorder the grid. On average, the items near the top-left will be better than the items near the bottom-right.

The "cube" in the name "cube pruning" refers to the search grid that notionally contains the derivations along a Hiero hyperedge. For the hyperedge corresponding to binary rule application, the grid has three dimensions: the two incoming beams plus the translation dimension that results from hyperedge bundling.

The cube pruning algorithm closely resembles the eager k-best algorithm (Algorithm 6). It begins by generating the "corner" derivation and adding it to a priority queue. As each derivation is popped from the queue, its neighbors are constructed, weighted, and pushed. The crucial difference is that when derivations are popped from the candidate queue, they do not arrive in true best-first order (because of the non-monotonicity). To compensate for this, the beam size is typically increased, meaning that a larger number of derivations are popped for each vertex.

Figure 4.4 depicts the cube corresponding to the second, non-monotonic grid in Example 4.2. As each derivation is popped from the candidate queue, its neighbors are pushed. The popped derivations are gathered in a buffer, which will later be sorted before the derivations are added to the beam.

Algorithm 12 The Cube Pruning Algorithm for STSG Derivations

Input :	τ	a parse tree
	G	a shared-category STSG
	W_D	a monotonic derivation weight function
	k	the maximum beam size (an integer ≥ 1)
Output :	d^*	approximation to maximally-weighted derivation of τ

TREE-DECODE-3(τ, G, W_D, k)

1   $\langle V, E \rangle = $ CONSTRUCT-HYPERGRAPH(τ, G) // See Algorithm 9 (page 73)
2   **for** $v \in V$
3       $visited[v] = $ FALSE
4   $t = V[\text{root}(\tau)]$
5   VISIT$(t, $ CP-BEAM-FILL$)$ // See Algorithm 1 (page 56)
6   **return** HEAD$(beam[t])$

CP-BEAM-FILL(v)

1   $beam[v] = cand = seen = buffer = \varnothing$
2   **for** each incoming hyperedge e of v
3   PUSH$(cand, \langle e, \mathbf{1}, \mathbf{1}, 1 \rangle)$
4   **while** $|buffer| < k$ **and** $|cand| > 0$
5       $\langle e, \mathbf{x}, \mathbf{1}, y \rangle = $ POP-MAX$(cand)$
6   append $\langle e, \mathbf{x}, \mathbf{1}, y \rangle$ to $buffer$
7   CP-PUSH-NEIGHBORS$(cand, seen, \langle e, \mathbf{x}, \mathbf{1}, y \rangle)$
8   RECOMBINE-SORT-PRUNE$(buffer, beam[v])$ // See Algorithm 11 (page 86)

CP-PUSH-NEIGHBORS$(cand, seen, \langle e, \mathbf{x}, \mathbf{1}, y \rangle)$

1   **for** $i = 1 \ldots |e|$
2       $v_i = \text{pred}(e, \preceq_e, i)$
3   **if** $x_i < |kbest[v_i]|$
4   CP-PUSH-IF-NEW$(cand, seen, \langle e, \mathbf{x} + \mathbf{b_i}, \mathbf{1}, y \rangle)$
5   **if** $y < |\text{proj}'_s(e)|$
6   CP-PUSH-IF-NEW$(cand, seen, \langle e, \mathbf{x}, \mathbf{1}, y + 1 \rangle)$

CP-PUSH-IF-NEW$(cand, seen, d)$

1   **if** $d \notin seen$
2   PUSH$(cand, d)$
3   PUSH$(seen, d)$

(a)

−10.6	−11.6	−11.6	−11.5
−10.8	−10.5	−11.1	−11.5
−10.7	−11.4	−11.2	−11.6
−12.1	−11.9	−12.0	−11.7

(b)

−10.6	−11.6	−11.6	−11.5
−10.8	−10.5	−11.1	−11.5
−10.7	−11.4	−11.2	−11.6
−12.1	−11.9	−12.0	−11.7

(c)

−10.6	−11.6	−11.6	−11.5
−10.8	−10.5	−11.1	−11.5
−10.7	−11.4	−11.2	−11.6
−12.1	−11.9	−12.0	−11.7

(d)

−10.6	−11.6	−11.6	−11.5
−10.8	−10.5	−11.1	−11.5
−10.7	−11.4	−11.2	−11.6
−12.1	−11.9	−12.0	−11.7

Figure 4.4: The cube after one (a), two (b), three (c), and four (d) derivations have been popped from the priority queue and their neighbors pushed. The white boxes indicate the derivations that have been popped, the light gray boxes indicate the contents of the candidate queue, and the dark gray boxes indicate the derivations that have yet to be reached. Notice that the order in which derivations are popped is approximately, but not exactly, monotonic.

Pseudocode for the cube pruning algorithm is given in Algorithm 12. CP-Beam-Fill is the counterpart of Eager-K-Best-Vertex from Algorithm 6. As derivations are popped from the priority queue they are collected in a buffer and then sorted after the pop derivation/push neighbors loop (lines 4–7) has completed.

The function CP-Push-Neighbors is identical to Eager-Push-Neighbors-Bundled (from Section 4.1.2) except that the check for duplicate derivations is extended to allow for the possibility that a derivation that was previously added to *cand* is popped before it is generated a second time (an impossibility in the monotonic case). This is achieved through the use of a set (called *seen* in the pseudocode) that records all of the derivations that have been generated for a vertex. The function CP-Push-If-Seen tests for the existence of a derivation in this set before pushing it to the candidate queue.

4.3.6 CUBE GROWING

Cube growing [Huang and Chiang, 2007] is a beam-filling version of the lazy k-best algorithm (Algorithm 7). Like its k-best counterpart, cube growing generates derivations on-demand—if and when they are required as a subderivation of a larger derivation—instead of eagerly filling every beam with k derivations.

Non-monotonicity makes lazily filling beams a more challenging problem than lazily filling k-best lists. The difficulty in generating the jth derivation of a vertex on-demand is of course that cube-based generation does not yield derivations in true best-first order. Like in cube pruning, the algorithm must over-generate derivations and store them in a buffer. The challenge is restricting

-10.6	-11.6	-11.6	-11.5
-10.8	-10.5	-11.1	-11.5
-10.7	-11.4	-11.2	-11.6
-12.1	-11.9	-12.0	-11.7

$-9.7 - 0.9$	$-10.4 - 1.2$	$-10.5-?$	$-10.6-?$
$-9.8 - 1.0$	$-10.5-?$	$-10.6-?$	$-10.7-?$
$-10.1-?$	$-10.8-?$	$-10.9-?$	$-11.0-?$
$-10.7-?$	$-11.4-?$	$-11.5-?$	$-11.6-?$

Figure 4.5: Left: the cube after the first candidate has been popped from the priority queue. The cell colors have the same meaning as in Figure 4.4. Right: the same cube with scores broken down into their two components: the additive part and the noise part (if known). The white cells are those in which the additive weight exceeds -10.6. These are the cells that potentially hold a better derivation than the first candidate.

the growth of this buffer: if the buffer size reaches k, then the algorithm ceases to be any more efficient than cube pruning.

Huang and Chiang [2007] present cube growing in the context of language model integration. They assume that the derivation weight function has two components: a monotonic, rule-local part and a non-monotonic language model part. The language model always decreases[7] the weight. This resembles the behavior of our artificial noise function from Example 4.4. Returning to that example, suppose that we want to lazily generate the 1-best derivation. If we pop the first derivation from the priority queue, then we arrive at the cube shown on the left in Figure 4.5. At this point, we have no way of knowing if we have popped the true 1-best derivation. However, we do have some knowledge about the weights of the unreached derivations: we know the additive component of their weights and we know that this is an upper bound on the true weight (since adding the noise component can only reduce the weight or leave it unchanged). From this we can infer the region of the cube where better derivations potentially lie—and conversely we can safely eliminate the remaining derivations from consideration. This information is summarized in the right-hand cube of Figure 4.5.

Whereas our noise function has a minimum value of zero, potentially leaving the additive weight unchanged, cube growing assumes that the language model will always reduce the weight by some minimum value, δ. Huang and Chiang used a heuristic method to estimate a separate value of δ for every hyperedge. They do this as follows. First, they decode the input without the language model to generate the k-best distinct derivations ($k = 100$ in their experiments). They then use the language model to compute the full hyperedge weights for all hyperedges occurring in the k derivations. For each distinct hyperedge, they take the minimum observed weight difference (with and without the language model) as the δ value. If a hyperedge is not represented in the k-best derivations, they calculate the weight—with and without the language model—of the 1-best derivation along that hyperedge and use that single weight difference as the δ value.[8]

---

[7]Huang and Chiang [2007] actually used derivation costs, where lower costs are better. We assume here that higher weights are better.

[8]For further discussion of these heuristics, see also Vilar and Ney [2009] and Xu and Koehn [2012], who implemented cube growing for hierarchical phrase-based models.

Algorithm 13 The Cube Growing Algorithm for STSG Derivations

Input :	τ	a parse tree
	G	a shared-category STSG
	W_D	a monotonic derivation weight function
	k	the maximum beam size (an integer ≥ 1)
Output :	d^*	approximation to maximally-weighted derivation of τ

TREE-DECODE-4(τ, G, W_D, k)

1   $\langle V, E \rangle$ = CONSTRUCT-HYPERGRAPH(τ, G) // See Algorithm 9 (page 73)
2   **for** $v \in V$
3       $visited[v]$ = FALSE
4       $beam[v] = cand[v] = seen[v] = buffer[v] = \varnothing$
5   CG-BEAM-FILL$(V[\text{root}(\tau)], k)$
6   **return** HEAD$(beam[V[\text{root}(\tau)]])$

CG-BEAM-FILL(v, j)

1   **if** $visited[v]$ = FALSE
2   **for** each incoming hyperedge e of v
3   CG-PUSH-IF-NEW$(cand[v], seen[v], \langle e, \mathbf{1}, \mathbf{1}, 1 \rangle)$
4       $visited[v]$ = TRUE
5   **while** $|beam[v]| < j$ **and** $|beam[v]| + |buffer| < k$ **and** $|cand| > 0$
6       $\langle e, \mathbf{x}, \mathbf{1}, y \rangle$ = POP-MAX$(cand[v])$
7   append $\langle e, \mathbf{x}, \mathbf{1}, y \rangle$ to $buffer[v]$
8   CG-PUSH-NEIGHBORS$(cand[v], seen[v], \langle e, \mathbf{x}, \mathbf{1}, y \rangle)$
9       $bound$ = max $\{$CG-ESTIMATE-UPPER-BOUND$(d) : d \in cand[v]\}$
10   CG-RECOMBINE$(buffer[v], beam[v], bound)$
11 CG-RECOMBINE$(buffer[v], beam[v], -\infty)$

CG-PUSH-IF-NEW$(cand, seen, \langle e, \mathbf{x}, \mathbf{1}, y \rangle)$

1   **return if** $\langle e, \mathbf{x}, \mathbf{1}, y \rangle \in seen$ **or** $y > |\text{proj}'_s(e)|$
2   **for** $i = 1 \ldots |e|$
3       $v_i = \text{pred}(e, \preceq_e, i)$
4   CG-BEAM-FILL(v_i, x_i)
5   **return if** $x_i > |beam[v_i]|$
6   PUSH$(cand, \langle e, \mathbf{x}, \mathbf{1}, y \rangle)$
7   PUSH$(seen, \langle e, \mathbf{x}, \mathbf{1}, y \rangle)$

CG-RECOMBINE$(buffer, beam, bound)$

1   **while** $|buffer| > 0$ **and** MAX$(buffer) \geq bound$
2   add POP-MAX$(buffer)$ to $beam$

Pseudocode for the cube growing algorithm is given in Algorithm 13. Broadly, the algorithmic changes compared with cube pruning resemble the algorithmic changes from eager to lazy k-best extraction: most notably in the single top-level call to CG-BEAM-FILL at the root vertex (line 5), which initiates a top-down recursive sequence of calls to CG-BEAM-FILL with varying values of the parameter j.

Let us examine the individual functions.

- CG-PUSH-IF-NEW pushes a (previously unseen) derivation onto a candidate priority queue, but only after making calls to CG-BEAM-FILL to ensure that the subderivations have been created.

- CG-RECOMBINE shifts items from the buffer to the beam, but only if they have a weight that matches or exceeds a threshold value. It is assumed that the derivation is added at the correct position in the beam and is recombined if necessary.

- CG-ESTIMATE-UPPER-BOUND (not shown) computes an estimate of the maximum possible weight of a derivation. It does this by adding δ to the monotonic component of the weight.

- CG-PUSH-NEIGHBORS (not shown) generates the neighbors of the given derivation and pushes them to the priority queue. The function is identical to the cube pruning version (CP-PUSH-NEIGHBORS in Algorithm 12) except that CG-PUSH-IF-NEW is used in place of CP-PUSH-IF-NEW.

In experiments, Huang and Chiang demonstrate that cube growing can provide a better speed-accuracy trade-off than cube pruning. While it provides an algorithmically interesting alternative to cube pruning, cube growing is yet to see wide adoption.

4.3.7 STATE REFINEMENT

So far, all of the beam-filling algorithms have treated search state as atomic: two derivations either have the same state value or they do not. Heafield et al. [2013] observed that states can have varying degrees of similarity and that commonalities can be exploited to improve the accuracy of beam search. They focus on n-gram language model state, developing a bottom-up beam-filling algorithm that takes into account the tendency for the language model to weight derivations more similarly if they share boundary words. The algorithm begins with a coarse representation of state in which all of the subderivations in a predecessor beam share the same state. As the algorithm progresses, subderivation states are selectively refined according to how promising a candidate derivation appears to be.

As an example, imagine that we are applying rule r_5 from the grammar in Example 4.1:

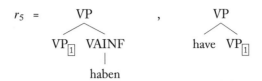

The VP subderivation translates "Josef K. verleumdet," which according to our grammar yields "slandered Josef K." or "defamed Josef K." In a grammar learned from data, it is likely that the translations include many alternatives:

"slandered K.," "slandered him," "defamed K.," "defamed him," "traduced Josef K.," "traduced K.," …

Suppose that a 4-gram language model has been trained on data that contains many instance of n-grams starting "have slandered" and "have defamed"

"have slandered Josef K.," "have slandered K.," "have defamed Josef K.," …

but never containing the bigram "have traduced" (let alone "have traduced him" or "have traduced Josef K."). Conceivably, the model could have a strong enough preference for choosing one of the translations beginning "slandered" or "defamed" that any translation beginning "traduced" is barely worth considering. This kind of sub-state similarity can be used to prioritize *groups* of subderivations during search.

Heafield et al.'s method groups subderivations at multiple levels of granularity. In effect, it transforms the structure of a beam from a flat list into a tree. This tree is called a *state tree*, since its nodes correspond to (language model) states and *partial states*, which are states with hidden words. At the top of the tree, the root node corresponds to an empty state value (a partial state where all words are hidden). Following a branch uncovers a single boundary word, with the leaves corresponding to full state values. Thus, a state value becomes progressively refined as one traces a path from the tree's root to a leaf. Figure 4.6 shows an example state tree. We have simplified it by showing only right boundary words. A full state tree alternately adds left and right boundary words (from outermost to innermost) as the tree grows from top to bottom.

The nodes of a state tree are given weights, which they inherit from their underlying derivations. Weights are assigned to nodes as follows.

- The weight of a leaf node is the weight of its best derivation. In Figure 4.6, the weight of n_{10} is $W_D(d_1)$, the weight of n_{11} is $W_D(d_3)$, and so on.

- The weight of a non-leaf node is the weight of its best child. In Figure 4.6, the weight of n_5 is $W_D(d_1)$, the weight of n_6 is $W_D(d_6)$, and so on.

Child nodes are ordered by weight, where the left child has the highest weight and the right child has the lowest.

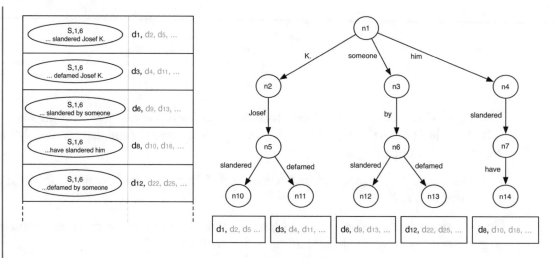

Figure 4.6: A beam (left) and the corresponding state tree (right). We assume the language model has order four and so the state comprises (up to) three left and right boundary words. As a simplification, we show only right boundary words. We do not use state tree minimization.

The purpose of a state tree is to guide search. When a candidate derivation is being generated during bottom-up search, every predecessor beam has an associated state tree and these trees determine the order in which subderivations are selected. To see how this works, we first need to define a couple of concepts. The first is the *breadcrumb*.

Definition 4.5 (Breadcrumb). A *breadcrumb* is a pair $\langle n, c \rangle$, where n is a state tree node and c is a counter that tracks how many of n's children have been visited. The weight of a breadcrumb $\langle n, c \rangle$ is defined as the weight of the state tree node n.

As we will see shortly, breadcrumbs are used to implement a form of backtracking.

Definition 4.6 (Partial Derivation). A *partial derivation* is a tuple $\langle e, \preceq_e, \mathbf{B}, y \rangle$, where $\langle e, \preceq_e \rangle$ is an ordered hyperedge in a bundled[9] hypergraph, $\mathbf{B}$ is a vector of breadcrumbs indicating the positions of subderivation groups in their respective state trees, and y is an index into an array that contains the synchronous rules from $\text{proj}'_s(q)$, where q is the source-side rule projection corresponding to e. As for derivations with backpointers, we will drop the ordering relation and write $\langle e, \mathbf{B}, y \rangle$ when the relation can be unambiguously inferred from context.

---

[9]In Heafield et al.'s original presentation, the hypergraph is not bundled. For consistency with the other beam-filling algorithms, we will assume a bundled hypergraph, but will "unbundle" the partial derivations in the course of the search algorithm to avoid changing the behavior of the original algorithm.

Notice the similarity of a partial derivation to a derivation with backpointers. In general, a partial derivation does not represent a single derivation; rather, it represents a set of potential derivations, each of which is reachable through state refinement. Only at the maximum level of refinement (when all breadcrumbs point to state tree leaves) does a partial derivation correspond uniquely to a derivation.

Like cube pruning and cube growing, Heafield et al.'s search algorithm uses a priority queue to fill beams. In this case, the queue holds partial derivations. Of course, to be used in a priority queue, a partial derivation must have a priority. This is calculated by summing the hyperedge weight $W_E(e)$ and the weights of the breadcrumbs, $\sum_i W_D(B_i)$. Recall from Section 4.2.2 that the hyperedge weight function takes into account the cost of newly-produced n-grams. In our bigram example, we defined a function called new-bigrams that yielded this set. Here, the equivalent function uses the breadcrumbs' partial state to determine the set of newly produced n-grams. The weight of a partial derivation therefore depends on how refined the breadcrumbs are: the more they are refined, the better the estimated weights.

The queue is initialized with partial derivations in which all breadcrumbs pointing to root state tree nodes and have a counter value of zero. As search progresses, the partial derivations are refined. When a fully-refined derivation is popped it is added to a buffer for subsequent recombination and insertion into the beam. When a partial derivation is popped from the queue, (up to) two new partial derivations are pushed.

Algorithm 14 gives the pseudocode for the decoding algorithm. Let us examine the main functions.

- SR-Beam-Fill has a similar structure to the cube pruning and cube growing beam-filling functions. Line 1 initializes some vertex-specific variables. Lines 2–7 initialize the priority queue by pushing the initial partial derivations. Note that we add one partial derivation for each rule right-hand side (lines 6–7). This is for consistency with Heafield et al.'s presentation, which does not use hyperedge bundling. Lines 8–14 pop partial derivations, either adding them to the buffer if they are fully refined (line 12) or partitioning them otherwise (line 14). Line 15 moves items from the buffer to the beam. Finally, line 16 constructs the state tree corresponding to the beam.

- SR-Partition attempts to expand the partial derivation $\langle e, \mathbf{B}, y \rangle$, generating (up to) two new partial derivations for each breadcrumb B_i in $\mathbf{B}$. The first is produced by refining B_i by following the leftmost branch in the state tree (lines 4 and 5). The second is produced by advancing the breadcrumb counter, opening up a new region of the state tree for exploration (lines 6–8).

- SR-Choose-Node chooses the next state tree node to refine from a vector of breadcrumbs. Heafield et al. use the heuristic of picking the node with the fewest revealed words or in the case of a tie, the left-most such node.

Algorithm 14 Heafield et al. [2013]'s State Refinement Algorithm for STSGs

---

Input :	τ	a parse tree
	G	a shared-category STSG
	W_D	a monotonic derivation weight function
	k	the maximum beam size (an integer ≥ 1)
Output :	d^*	approximation to maximally-weighted derivation of τ

TREE-DECODE-5(τ, G, W_D, k)

1   $\langle V, E \rangle$ = CONSTRUCT-HYPERGRAPH(τ, G) // See Algorithm 9 (page 73)
2   **for** $v \in V$
3       $visited[v]$ = FALSE
4   $t = V[\text{root}(\tau)]$
5   VISIT$(t, \text{SR-BEAM-FILL})$ // See Algorithm 1 (page 56)
6   **return** HEAD$(beam[t])$

SR-BEAM-FILL(v)

1   $beam[v] = state\text{-}tree[v] = queue = buffer = \varnothing$
2   **for** each incoming hyperedge e of v
3       $\mathbf{B} = \varnothing$
4   **for** $i = 1 \ldots |e|$
5   append $\langle \text{root}(state\text{-}tree[\text{pred}(e, \preceq_e, i)], 0 \rangle$ to $\mathbf{B}$
6   **for** $y = 1 \ldots |\text{proj}'_s(e)|$
7   PUSH$(queue, \langle e, \mathbf{B}, y \rangle)$
8   **while** $|buffer| < k$ **and** $|queue| > 0$
9       $\langle e, \mathbf{B}, y \rangle$ = POP-MAX$(queue)$
10   **if** every breadcrumb in $\mathbf{B}$ points to a leaf node
11          $\mathbf{x} = \langle x_1, \ldots, x_{|\mathbf{B}|} \rangle$, where x_i is the index of the beam entry for B_i's node.
12   append $\langle e, \mathbf{x}, \mathbf{1}, y \rangle$ to $buffer$
13   **else**
14   SR-PARTITION$(queue, \langle e, \mathbf{B}, y \rangle)$
15   RECOMBINE-SORT-PRUNE$(buffer, beam[v])$ // See Alg. 11 (page 86)
16   SR-BUILD-STATE-TREE$(beam[v], state\text{-}tree[v])$

---

continued…

Algorithm 15 Heafield et al. [2013]'s State Refinement Algorithm for STSGs (continued)

SR-PARTITION($queue, \langle e, \mathbf{B}, y \rangle$)

1   $i = $ SR-CHOOSE-NODE($\mathbf{B}$)
2   $\langle n, c \rangle = B_i$
3   $\mathbf{B}' = \mathbf{B}$
4   $B_i' = \langle$ LEFT-CHILD$(n), 0 \rangle$
5   PUSH($queue, \langle e, \mathbf{B}', y \rangle$)
6   **if** $c < $ NUM-CHILDREN(n)
7       $B_i' = \langle n, c + 1 \rangle$
8   PUSH($queue, \langle e, \mathbf{B}', y \rangle$)

SR-CHOOSE-NODE($\mathbf{B}$)

1   $min = \infty$
2   $i_{min} = 0$
3   **for** $i = 1 \ldots |\mathbf{B}|$
4       $\langle n, c \rangle = B_i$
5       $num = $ number of unrevealed words at node n
6   **if** $num < min$
7           $min = num$
8           $i_{min} = i$
9   **return** i_{min}

- SR-BUILD-STATE-TREE (not shown) builds a state tree for a given beam. One possibility is to construct the state tree in one go, as this function suggests. For efficiency, Heafield et al. instead constructed the state tree lazily. The "tree" begins as a flat list that is progressively transformed into a tree as branch points are reached (i.e., at calls to LEFT-CHILD in SR-PARTITION). We refer the reader to the original presentation for further details.

In experiments, the speed vs. accuracy trade-off is shown to be better than that of cube pruning for Hiero and string-to-tree systems. For details, see the original paper.

4.4   EFFICIENT TREE PARSING

In Section 4.1.1, we described a simple algorithm for constructing a STSG forest hypergraph. For an input tree τ and grammar G, the algorithm has complexity $\mathcal{O}(|G| \cdot \tau)$. For the grammars used in state-of-the-art translation systems, the $|G|$ term makes this algorithm prohibitively slow. Fortunately, there are better algorithms.

Recall that in Section 1.2 we noted that, apart from superficial differences, STSG rules are equivalent to tree transducer rules of a specific, restricted form (namely, linear and non-deleting[10]). This equivalence immediately opens up one method of hypergraph construction, since we can compile the grammar into a tree transducer. There are standard algorithms for transducing an input tree and the resulting structure is equivalent to the desired translation forest hypergraph. Matthews et al. [2014] present an efficient version of this method that determinizes the transducer, resulting in a compact deterministic finite-state automaton (DFSA). The input tree is converted to a DFSA of the same form and transduction is performed using a standard DFSA intersection algorithm.

An alternative hypergraph construction algorithm is given by Zhang et al. [2009]. Their algorithm follows similar principles. In particular, it involves a similar compilation of the rule set into a compact trie-style structure. However, Zhang et al. [2009] did not use standard DFSA intersection. Instead, they design a specialized algorithm that accepts a parse forest hypergraph as input. This makes the algorithm suitable for use in both tree-to-string and forest-to-string models (we will introduce forest-to-string models in Chapter 6).

4.5   TREE-TO-TREE DECODING

So far, we have assumed that our model uses a shared-category STSG, which is the typical case for a tree-to-string model. For a tree-to-tree model, the grammar would usually be a distinct-category STSG (although, as we noted in Chapters 1 and 2, tree-to-tree models are rare in practice due to the difficulty of learning grammars from data).

Decoding for tree-to-tree models differs in the tree parsing step, but is otherwise essentially the same as tree-to-string decoding. Recall from Section 3.1.3 that for a distinct-category synchronous grammar, the translation hypergraph encodes both source and target non-terminal symbols in the vertex labels. Tree parsing must therefore take account of the target-side tree structure. For a tree-to-tree model, a STSG rule $\langle \alpha, \beta \rangle$ can only be applied if:

1. the source-side tree fragment can be matched against the input parse tree (just as in shared-category tree parsing); and

2. for each input parse tree node, v, where a leaf non-terminal of α is matched,

$$A, B \overset{*}{\Rightarrow} s_i \ldots s_j, t_m \ldots t_n,$$

where $A = \text{root}(\alpha)$, $B = \text{root}(\beta)$, $s_i \ldots s_j$ is the subspan of source words covered by v, and $t_m \ldots t_n$ is any derivable sequence of target words.

---

[10]See Knight and Graehl [2005] for an excellent overview of tree transducers for natural language processing.

Example 4.7 Consider the following STSG rule, which is a distinct-category variant of rule r_6 from the grammar in Example 4.1.

Suppose that we are parsing the tree τ (from that same example) and we want to apply rule r_6'. The rule can only be applied if the source-side tree fragment can be matched against the input parse tree and the following two conditions apply:

1. NP, NP $\overset{*}{\Rightarrow}$ Josef K, …

2. VVPP, VBN $\overset{*}{\Rightarrow}$ verleumdet, …

(The derived target strings can be any derivable word sequences.) In bottom-up tree parsing, these two conditions can be tested by checking for the existence of vertices (NP,NP,3,4) and (VVPP,VBN,5,5). For our example parse tree, applying rule r_6' results in the generation of the following hyperedge, but only if we assume the existence of rules that produce the (NP,NP,3,4) and (VVPP,VBN,5,5) vertices:

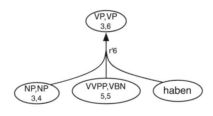

It is straightforward to modify the simple shared-category tree parsing algorithm from Section 4.1.1 to check for target-side non-terminal matches in the manner outlined above. More efficiently, standard finite-state tree transducer methods could be used (similarly to tree-to-string tree parsing—Section 4.4). Eisner [2003] also gives a simple algorithm that is efficient provided that there are tight limits on the number of nodes in a source-side tree fragment.

Once a distinct-category hypergraph has been constructed, beam-search can proceed as before, giving a complete tree-to-tree decoding algorithm.

4.6 HISTORICAL NOTES AND FURTHER READING

Tree decoding, in various forms, was first proposed for dependency-based translation models [Ding and Palmer, 2005, Lin, 2004, Quirk et al., 2004, 2005] and shortly after for constituency-based models [Huang et al., 2006, Liu et al., 2006]. The approach described here is closest to Huang et al.'s, which was originally (and often still is) referred to as *syntax-directed translation* in reference to its formal origins in compiler theory. Huang et al.'s approach was later extended by Mi et al. [2008] to use *forest decoding*, which we will cover in Section 6.1.4.

The state-splitting approach to string decoding with a language model was used by Wu [1996] to integrate a bigram language model into an ITG decoder.

The cube pruning algorithm was originally designed to solve the problem of integrating a n-gram language model into the SCFG-based Hiero decoder [Chiang, 2007]. It was subsequently generalized and applied to phrase-based and STSG-based decoding [Huang and Chiang, 2007], as well as to reranking for statistical parsing [Huang, 2008]. Hopkins and Langmead [2009] showed that the algorithm is equivalent to A* search using specific (inadmissible) heuristics.

CHAPTER 5

Decoding III: String Decoding

String decoding has a lot in common with tree decoding. Almost all of the search machinery from the previous chapter can be redeployed here (in fact, the methods were originally developed for string decoding). So, how is string decoding different? The answer depends on the grammar. For some types of model—most notably Hiero—the only substantive difference is in the construction of the translation hypergraph: whereas tree decoding matches rules against a tree, string decoding employs monolingual string parsing. The hypergraph search techniques—beam search and the beam filling algorithms—carry over unchanged.

For models with richer grammars, string decoding presents some additional challenges for efficient implementation. We will cover two prominent issues in this chapter, both of which can be understood in terms of parse forest complexity. The first challenge is decoding with large non-terminal sets, such as those used in SAMT grammars. The second challenge is decoding with non-binary grammars, such as GHKM grammars.

As in the previous chapter, we will assume a fixed grammar and model form in order to keep the discussion concrete. Specifically, we will assume that our grammar is a shared-category SCFG and our statistical model is a log-linear model. Since we have already covered beam search, we will assume from the outset that our model includes non-local features. Given this configuration, we will begin with the simplest possible decoding algorithm. We will then examine worst-case parse forest complexity before discussing strategies for handling problematic cases. For most of the chapter, we will treat the monolingual parser as a black box (if you keep in mind the CYK parsing algorithm from Chapter 3 then this will not be too far wide of the mark). In Section 5.5, we will open the box and study two parsing algorithms that are particularly well-suited for use in decoding. Finally, in Section 5.6, we will discuss methods for decoding with STSGs and distinct-category SCFGs.

As in the last chapter, we will use an input sentence and grammar in a running example.

Example 5.1 Let s be the following German sentence:

Jemand musste Josef K. verleumdet haben
Someone must Josef K. slandered have

and let G be the SCFG with the following rules:

r_1	NP	→Jemand	,	Someone
r_2	NP	→Josef K.	,	Josef K.
r_3	VBN	→verleumdet	,	slandered
r_4	VBN	→verleumdet	,	defamed
r_5	VP	→NP_1 VBN_2 haben	,	have VBN_2 NP_1
r_6	S	→NP_1 musste VP_2	,	NP_1 must VP_2
r_7	S	→NP_1 musste NP_2 VBN_3 haben	,	NP_1 must have VBN_3 NP_2
r_8	S	→NP_1 musste NP_2 VBN_3 haben	,	NP_2 must have been VBN_3 by NP_1

The grammar rules in Example 5.1 are consistent with GHKM-style string-to-tree extraction, where STSG rules are extracted and then converted to SCFG through the removal of internal tree structure.

5.1   BASIC BEAM SEARCH

For an arbitrary input string s and a shared-category SCFG grammar G, the translation hypergraph $\langle V, E \rangle$ can be constructed using little more than standard CFG parsing. The method is analogous to the tree parsing-based method of the previous chapter: first a monolingual parse forest hypergraph is constructed by parsing s with the source-side CFG projection of G; then the parse hypergraph is converted to a translation hypergraph by replacing hyperedges. Algorithm 16 shows the construction algorithm in pseudocode form.

Algorithm 16 Algorithm for constructing a shared-category SCFG hypergraph

Input :	s	a source string
	G	a shared-category SCFG
Output :	$\langle V_s, E \rangle$	translation hypergraph

CONSTRUCT-HYPERGRAPH(s, G)

1   $\langle V_s, E_s \rangle = \text{PARSE}(s, \text{proj}_s(G))$
2   $E = \varnothing$
3   **for** $e_s \in E_s$
4   **for** $r \in \text{proj}'_s(\text{rule}(e_s))$
5   add labeled hyperedge $\langle \text{head}(e_s), \text{tail}(e_s), r \rangle$ to E
6   **return** $\langle V_s, E \rangle$

The PARSE function (line 1) can be any CFG parsing algorithm that returns a hypergraph representation of the parse forest. Lines 2–5 construct the corresponding translation hypergraph by using the inverse projection to map source-side CFG rules to SCFG rules. In practice, the constructed hypergraph will usually be in the compact bundled form that we saw in Section 4.1.2. Figure 5.1 shows the resulting SCFG hypergraph for the input sentence and grammar of Example 5.1.

Algorithm 17 gives pseudocode for a basic string decoding algorithm that combines hypergraph construction with bottom-up beam search. We have left the BEAM-FILL function unspecified. The most widely used beam-filling algorithm is cube pruning, but any of the bottom-up beam-filling algorithms from the previous chapter could be used. Notice that the function STRING-DECODE-1 is almost identical to TREE-DECODE-2 (Algorithm 11 on page 86).

As given, the algorithm does not handle parse failures. In practice, this is often unnecessary since a secondary glue grammar can specify rules to ensure that parsing will always succeed. Alternatively, the algorithm could dynamically generate its own glue rules.

5.1.1 PARSE FOREST COMPLEXITY

In theory, STRING-DECODE-1 works for any shared-category SCFG. However, the practicality of the algorithm depends on the size of the parse forest hypergraph, which in turn depends on the length of the input string, $|s|$, and on certain properties of the grammar, including the number of rules, $|G|$.

The simplest grammar we are likely to encounter is a Hiero grammar. Recall from Chapter 2 that Hiero grammars are binary and have two distinct non-terminal symbols, X and S. Table 5.1 gives worst-case bounds for the numbers of vertices and hyperedges in a Hiero parse forest. How did we arrive at these values? The vertex bound is simple: there are potentially two vertices for every subspan of s, one for the X symbol and one for the S symbol, giving a maximum of $2 \times |s|^2 = \mathcal{O}(|s|^2)$ vertices.

For the hyperedge bound, consider the potential hyperedges arriving at a particular vertex v and labeled with a particular rule identifier r. By definition, there is one such hyperedge for every possible application of rule r over the span corresponding to vertex v. Each distinct application of a rule over a span of words $w_i \ldots w_j$ can be described by listing the subspans covered by its subderivations. For example, consider the rule with the following source right-hand side:

Grammar Type	Vertices	Hyperedges
Hiero	$\mathcal{O}(|s|^2)$	$\mathcal{O}(|G| \cdot |s|^3)$
SAMT	$\mathcal{O}(|N| \cdot |s|^2)$	$\mathcal{O}(|G| \cdot |N| \cdot |s|^3)$
Arbitrary SCFG	$\mathcal{O}(|N| \cdot |s|^2)$	$\mathcal{O}(|G| \cdot |N| \cdot |s|^{\mathrm{rank}(G)+1})$

Table 5.1: Worst-case sizes of parse forest hypergraphs for Hiero, SAMT, and arbitrary SCFG grammars. The input parameters are the source sentence length, $|s|$, the number of grammar rules, $|G|$, the number of distinct non-terminal symbols, $|N|$, and the rank of the grammar, $\mathrm{rank}(G)$.

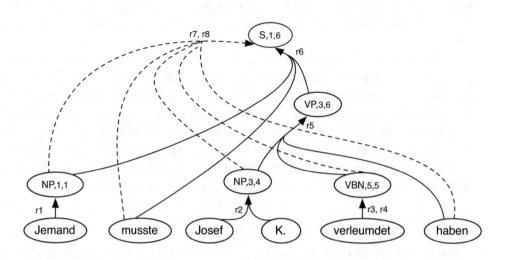

Figure 5.1: SCFG hypergraph for the input sentence and grammar of Example 5.1. Hyperedges labeled with multiple rules represent multiple hyperedges (one per rule).

Algorithm 17 A Beam Search-based String Decoding Algorithm

Input :	s	a source string
	G	a shared-category SCFG
	W_D	a monotonic derivation weight function
	k	the maximum beam size (an integer ≥ 1)
Output :	d^*	approximation to maximally-weighted derivation of s

---

STRING-DECODE-1(s, G, W_D, k)

1   $\langle V, E \rangle = $ CONSTRUCT-HYPERGRAPH(s, G)
2   **for** $v \in V$
3       $visited[v] = $ FALSE
4   $t = V[1, |s|, S^\dagger]$
5   VISIT$(t, $ BEAM-FILL$)$ // See Algorithm 1 (page 56)
6   **return** HEAD$(beam[t])$

a b X c X.

Suppose that we want to enumerate rule applications over the span $w_5 \ldots w_{13}$. One possible rule application could have subderivations over $w_7 \ldots w_8$ and $w_{10} \ldots w_{13}$, while another could have subderivations over $w_7 \ldots w_{10}$ and $w_{12} \ldots w_{13}$.[1] For a given span, we can summarize a binary rule application with a single value: the number of words covered by the first non-terminal (which has $\mathcal{O}(|s|)$ possible values). Once that value is known, the position of every other symbol is fixed and there is only one possible way of applying the rule—and one hyperedge. For example, if the width of the first subspan is three words, then that determines the position of w_3, which must be 10. The second non-terminal therefore covers words 11, 12, and 13.

To get the total number of hyperedges, we must multiply $\mathcal{O}(|s|)$ by the number of rules and by the number of vertices at which they can be applied. If we assume that every S rule applies at every S vertex and every X rule applies at every X vertex, then we arrive at a total of $|G| \times |s|^2$ possible head vertex and rule pairs. Multiplying by $\mathcal{O}(|s|)$ gives a total of $\mathcal{O}(|G| \cdot |s|^3)$ hyperedges.

For SAMT grammars, the analysis is identical except that we must take into account $|N|$, the number of distinct non-terminal symbols. As we saw in Chapter 2, this number can run into hundreds or even thousands.

For arbitrary SCFGs, the number of possible rule applications, and thus the number of hyperedges, increases polynomially with rule rank: whereas for a fixed binary rule and head vertex there was one $\mathcal{O}(|s|)$ choice (the width of the first subspan) that uniquely determined a rule application, there are two choices for a ternary rule, three for a quarternary rule, and so on. Unless we take steps to address this issue, it effectively rules out decoding with arbitrary SCFGs of rank greater than two: a super-cubic number of hyperedges is likely to make decoding prohibitively slow for all but the shortest sentences. We will return to this issue shortly.

5.2   FASTER BEAM SEARCH

Even for binary grammars with small non-terminal sets, string decoding is usually slow in comparison to tree decoding or phrase-based decoding. Most decoders therefore do not implement the basic form of beam search outlined in the previous section, but make further approximations, trading off search accuracy for performance. Two such measures are constrained width parsing (typically used with Hiero and SAMT) and per-subspan beam search (typically used with SAMT or GHKM models).

5.2.1   CONSTRAINED WIDTH PARSING

For Hiero and SAMT models it is standard to constrain parsing so that non-glue rules are only applied over spans up to a constant length (typically 10 or 15 words). For longer spans, glue rules

---

[1]Of course, we are ignoring the fact that most words in a typical source sentence are distinct. In a sentence with few (or no) repeated words, the rule's terminals are anchored to words, limiting the number of possible applications. We will discuss the implications of this observation in Section 5.3.2.

Grammar Type	Vertices	Hyperedges
Hiero	$\mathcal{O}(|s|)$	$\mathcal{O}(|G| \cdot |s|)$
SAMT	$\mathcal{O}(|N| \cdot |s|)$	$\mathcal{O}(|G| \cdot |N| \cdot |s|)$
Arbitrary SCFG	$\mathcal{O}(|N| \cdot |s|)$	$\mathcal{O}(|G| \cdot |N| \cdot |s|^{\mathrm{rank}(G)-1})$

Table 5.2: Worst-case sizes of parse forest hypergraphs for Hiero, SAMT, and arbitrary SCFG grammars assuming a constant limit on span width for non-glue rule application. The input parameters are as in Table 5.1. The rank of the grammar, $\mathrm{rank}(G)$, is assumed to be greater than zero.

are used to combine suderivations from left-to-right (or sometimes allowing reordering). Part of the motivation for this constraint is consistency with training: there is a constraint on the width of initial phrases from which rules are extracted. If the source-side of a rule is extracted from an initial phrase of length 10 then does it make sense to apply it over a span of length 30?

The second motivation is of course performance: for long sentences, constraining parsing in this way dramatically reduces the size of the parse forest hypergraph. Table 5.2 gives worst-case bounds if we assume a constant limit on subspan width for non-glue rule application.

While this restriction is well motivated (and borne out empirically) for string-to-string models, it cannot be applied to string-to-tree models (recall that we defined these as models that are capable of producing trees of the same form as in the training data). Nor is it a panacea for efficiency issues: if $|N|$ or $\mathrm{rank}(G)$ is too large, then decoding is still likely to be prohibitively slow.

5.2.2   PER-SUBSPAN BEAM SEARCH

For grammars with large non-terminal sets, search complexity can be reduced by modifying the beam filling algorithm so that instead of generating k derivations for every vertex, it generates k derivations for every subspan. The modified beam-filling algorithm is called once per subspan instead of once per vertex. The result is that instead of adding k derivations to a single beam, the algorithm potentially distributes its k derivations to multiple beams, each ending up with less than k derivations at the end.

This strategy is most effective if running the per-subspan beam filling algorithm is faster than running multiple instances of the per-vertex version (where there will be one instance for every vertex over a particular subspan). This is easy to achieve for the non-exhaustive beam-filling algorithms of the previous chapter. We will use cube pruning as an example.

To see how the beam-filling algorithm is extended to work over subspans, think back to the discussion of the eager k-best algorithm (Section 3.2.4). The search procedure was first presented at the hyperedge level, with one priority queue used to enumerate the derivations for a single hyperedge. The procedure was then extended to share a priority queue across all incoming hyperedges of a vertex. Here we extend the priority queue's range further, initializing it with the

---

Algorithm 18 A String Decoding Algorithm with Per-span Cube Pruning

---

Input:	*s*	a source string
	G	a shared-category SCFG
	W_D	a monotonic derivation weight function
	k	the maximum beam size (an integer ≥ 1)
Output:	d^*	approximation to maximally-weighted derivation of *s*

STRING-DECODE-2(s, G, W_D, k)

1   $\langle V, E \rangle = $ CONSTRUCT-HYPERGRAPH(s, G)
2   **for** $w = 1 \ldots |s|$
3   **for** each subspan $[i, j]$ of s with width w
4           $V_{i,j} = \{v : v \in V \wedge \text{span}(v) = [i, j]\}$
5   MULTI-CP-BEAM-FILL$(V_{i,j})$
6   $t = V[1, |s|, S^{\dagger}]$
7   **return** HEAD$(beam[t])$

MULTI-CP-BEAM-FILL$(V_{i,j})$

1   $cand = seen = buffer = \varnothing$
2   **for** $v \in V_{i,j}$
3   **for** each incoming hyperedge e of v
4   PUSH$(cand, \langle e, \mathbf{1}, \mathbf{1}, 1 \rangle)$
5       $beam[v] = \varnothing$
6   **while** $|buffer| < k$ **and** $|cand| > 0$
7       $\langle e, \mathbf{x}, \mathbf{1}, y \rangle = $ POP-MAX$(cand)$
8   append $\langle e, \mathbf{x}, \mathbf{1}, y \rangle$ to $buffer$
9   CP-PUSH-NEIGHBOURS$(cand, seen, \langle e, \mathbf{x}, \mathbf{1}, y \rangle)$ **//** See Alg. 12 (page 88)
10 **for** $v \in V_{i,j}$
11      $buffer_v = \{d : d = \langle e, \mathbf{x}, \mathbf{1}, y \rangle \in buffer \wedge \text{head}(e) = v\}$
12   RECOMBINE-SORT-PRUNE$(buffer_v, beam[v], k)$ **//** See Alg. 11 (page 86)

$\langle e, \mathbf{1}, \mathbf{1}, 1 \rangle$ derivations from all incoming hyperedges of all vertices over a given subspan. A pop from the queue can potentially yield a derivation for any of the input vertices.

Algorithm 18 gives the pseudocode. In STRING-DECODE-2, lines 2–5 iterate over every subspan of s. Line 4 constructs the set of all vertices, $V_{i,j}$, over subspan i, j and line 5 passes this vertex set to MULTI-CP-BEAM-FILL, the multiple-vertex version of the cube pruning beam filling algorithm (Section 4.3.5).

MULTI-CP-BEAM-FILL differs from the single-vertex version in two ways. First, the priority queue, *cand*, is initialized with $\langle e, \preceq e, \mathbf{1}, 1 \rangle$ derivations from multiple vertices (lines 2–5). Second, at lines 10–12, the buffer is separated into sub-buffers, with one for each vertex.

Using per-subspan beam filling can substantially reduce the cost of decoding. If constrained width parsing is used, the beam filling algorithm is called $\mathcal{O}(|s|)$ times instead of $\mathcal{O}(|N| \cdot |s|)$. If parsing is unrestricted, the beam filling algorithm is called $\mathcal{O}(|s|^2)$ times instead of $\mathcal{O}(|N| \cdot |s|^2)$.

Note that this adjustment to the beam filling algorithm does not come with any guarantees about the distribution of derivations to beams. In fact, it is likely that many vertices' beams will not receive any derivations at all, since typical values of $|N|$ can be similar to (or, in the case of SAMT, much greater than) common values for k (a value somewhere between 30 and 1000 would not be surprising for either $|N|$ or k). A minor adjustment to MULTI-CP-BEAM-FILL could ensure that at least one derivation was popped for each incoming hyperedge, although this may not be desirable, especially if $|N|$ is very large. Treating vertices over a common subspan as roughly equivalent and allowing derivations to compete within those spans, irrespective of the vertex label, is an effective way to control computational complexity and is often used in practice.

5.3   HANDLING NON-BINARY GRAMMARS

Neither of the techniques in the previous section addresses the polynomial multiplication of hyperedges that results from increasing rule rank. In GHKM grammars, rules with five or six nonterminals are not uncommon and the problem must be addressed somehow. The most obvious strategy is grammar binarization. As we will see, perfect binarization is generally not possible—some SCFG (and STSG) grammar rules simply cannot be binarized—but this turns out not to be a big problem in practice, since non-binarizable rules can be discarded with little or no impact on translation quality. However, binarization has other, more serious drawbacks, which has led researchers to consider alternative approaches. By developing a more nuanced analysis of parse forest complexity, it has been demonstrated that not all non-binary rules are equally problematic. For a high proportion of non-binary rules, it turns out that binarization is unnecessary. In the simplest approach, *scope pruning*, problematic rules are simply discarded.

5.3.1   BINARIZATION

Before we discuss binarization for SCFGs, let us review how binarization works for CFGs.

CFG Binarization

CFG binarization replaces every super-binary rule with a set of rules of rank two or less, while maintaining weak equivalence between the original grammar and the binarized grammar. The exact details depend on the desired rule form for the output grammar, but generally speaking, each individual rule $A \rightarrow \alpha$ of rank three or more is replaced according to a recursive process. First, the right-hand side, α, is split into two substrings, α_1 and α_2, where each substring contains at least one non-terminal. The original rule is then replaced by one of three possible pairs of rules (the left pair if α_1 contains a single non-terminal, the middle pair if α_2 contains a single non-terminal, or the right pair otherwise):

$$
\begin{array}{ccc}
A & \rightarrow & \alpha_1 \; Vx \\
Vx & \rightarrow & \alpha_2
\end{array}
\quad \text{or} \quad
\begin{array}{ccc}
A & \rightarrow & Vx \; \alpha_2 \\
Vx & \rightarrow & \alpha_1
\end{array}
\quad \text{or} \quad
\begin{array}{ccc}
A & \rightarrow & Vx \; Vy \\
Vx & \rightarrow & \alpha_1 \\
Vy & \rightarrow & \alpha_2
\end{array}
$$

If a resulting Vx or Vy rule is super-binary then that rule is split and the process continues recursively.

The non-terminals Vx and Vy are called *virtual* non-terminals. These are symbols that are introduced through the binarization process. The set of virtual non-terminals must be disjoint from the original grammar's non-terminal set. Although formally the choice of symbol is arbitrary, by convention the symbol is usually a V followed by an integer (V1, V8721, etc.). A rule $Vx \rightarrow \alpha$ is called a virtual rule.

In terms of grammatical equivalence, it makes no difference whether a terminal ends up on the left or right of a split point. There may, however, be reasons for taking terminals into account when deciding where to split the rule (for instance, to maximize the sharing of virtual rules). Here we will adopt a convention of always placing a split point immediately before a non-terminal.

Example 5.2   The grammar in Example 5.1 contains two ternary rules, r_7 and r_8. We will use the source-side projection of r_7 as an example:

$$ S \quad \rightarrow \quad NP \; musste \; NP \; VBN \; haben $$

There are two ways to split the right-hand side. The split point can occur either before or after the second NP, resulting in one of the following two pairs of rules:

$$
\begin{array}{ccl}
S & \rightarrow & NP \; musste \; V1 \\
V1 & \rightarrow & NP \; VBN \; haben
\end{array}
\quad \text{and} \quad
\begin{array}{ccl}
S & \rightarrow & V2 \; VBN \; haben \\
V2 & \rightarrow & NP \; musste \; NP
\end{array}
$$

All of the resulting rules are binary, so the process terminates.

Synchronous Binarization

Now consider the SCFG rule r_7:

$$ S \quad \rightarrow \quad NP_1 \; musste \; NP_2 \; VBN_3 \; haben \quad , \quad NP_1 \; must \; have \; VBN_3 \; NP_2 $$

To binarize a SCFG rule, we must split both the source and the target right-hand side, while respecting the non-terminal alignments. This is referred to as *synchronous binarization*. For rule r_7, we can do this by splitting the source side and the target side after their first non-terminal:

$$S \rightarrow NP_1 \text{ musste } V3_2 \quad , \quad NP_1 \text{ must have } V3_2$$
$$V3 \rightarrow NP_1 \text{ VBN}_2 \text{ haben} \quad , \quad VBN_2 \text{ } NP_1$$

But unlike the CFG case, we cannot split the source-side after its second non-terminal:

$$S \rightarrow V4_1 \text{ VBN}_2 \text{ haben} \quad , \quad \text{???}$$
$$V4 \rightarrow NP_1 \text{ musste } NP_2 \quad , \quad \text{???}$$

The reason is that the two source-side NPs are aligned to the first and third target-side non-terminals and there is no way to split the target right-hand side without separating those two non-terminals.[2]

It turns out that there is always at least one way to split a ternary SCFG rule. For rules of rank four or higher, this is not the case—it depends on the rule's non-terminal alignments. For instance, there is no way to binarize the following rule:

$$S \rightarrow A_1 \text{ } B_2 \text{ } C_3 \text{ } D_4 \quad , \quad B_2 \text{ } D_4 \text{ } A_1 \text{ } C_3$$

Wherever you try to make a split point on the source-side, it is impossible to find a split point on the target side that correctly separates the corresponding non-terminals.

Clearly, the example above is artificial, but non-binarizable rules do occur in grammars extracted from real data. Fortunately, they appear to be rare: Zhang et al. [2006] find that only 0.3% of rules in a Chinese-English GHKM grammar are non-binarizable, and human analysis suggests that most of those result from errors in the underlying machine-learned word alignments. Using hand-aligned data, Huang et al. [2009] find non-binarizable rules at rates of 0.3%, 0.1%, and 0.6% for Chinese-English, French-English, German-English, respectively. Wu [1997] warns that while non-binarizable reordering patterns are unusual for fixed word-order language pairs, this should not be expected to hold for pairs that involve free word-order languages.

Zhang et al. [2006] give an algorithm for synchronous binarization. For each input rule in turn, the algorithm deterministically generates a *binarization tree* if the rule is binarizable or returns a failure status otherwise. The binarization tree represents the recursive splitting process that is necessary to produce an equivalent set of binary rules. The binarization tree is generated solely from the rule's non-terminal alignment pattern. The algorithm takes no account of the rule's terminals or its non-terminal labels. For instance, rule r_7 is reduced to the sequence $(1, 3, 2)$, which represents the target-side permutation of the non-terminals. The algorithm then generates the tree

$$(1\ 3\ 2)$$
$$(1) \quad (3\ 2)$$

---

[2]Such a split becomes possible if we express our rules in a richer grammar formalism than SCFG. Specifically, Multitext Grammar [Melamed, 2003] allows such discontinuities and there is a string decoding algorithm for it (albeit an exponential one). See Zhang et al. [2006] for details.

The tree generation part of the algorithm is a shift-reduce algorithm and runs in time linear with respect to the rule rank. Having generated a binarization tree, the binarization algorithm then splits the rule, as prescribed by the tree, and adds the newly generated rules to the output grammar.

Synchronous binarization reduces the parse forest complexity, making it cubic with respect to the input sentence length (or linear if constrained width parsing is used). However, this comes at a cost.

- The introduction of virtual non-terminals can greatly increase the $|N|$ term (Section 5.1.1), which multiplies the worst-case number of vertices and hyperedges.

- Since the target-side of a rule in the original grammar is distributed across multiple binarized rules, beam search must make pruning decisions having seen only a fragment of the full target side. This can lead to search errors (this problem can be ameliorated through the use of terminal-aware synchronous binarization [Fang et al., 2011]).

Asynchronous Binarization

One alternative to synchronous binarization, proposed by DeNero et al. [2009b], is to perform monolingual binarization twice. This results in a three-stage decoding process. For an input sentence s and shared-category SCFG G we have the following.

1. The source sentence s is parsed using a binarized version of $\text{proj}_s(G)$. The target-side of the grammar is ignored, so any CFG binarization technique can be used.

2. The resulting parse forest is converted back into n-ary form by "undoing" the binarization. Of course, to maintain cubic complexity, the forest must be pruned. DeNero et al. [2009b] use a method in which derivations are weighted according to a rule-local version of the statistical model. Vertices are pruned based on max-marginal thresholds.

3. (Optionally) the n-ary forest is re-binarized, this time using a binarization strategy that takes into account the target-side only, and is tailored to beam search.

5.3.2   ALTERNATIVES TO BINARIZATION

DeNero et al. [2009a] and Hopkins and Langmead [2010] both examine the relationship between parsing complexity and the highly-lexicalized nature of translation grammars. They point out that the source-side terminals of a grammar rule effectively anchor the rule to a sentence, reducing the number of distinct ways in which the rule can be applied. For instance, consider again the source-side projection of r_7:

$$S \quad \rightarrow \quad \text{NP musste NP VBN haben}$$

For an arbitrary input sentence, an application of this rule is uniquely defined by four values.

1. The start position of the first NP.

2. The width of the subspan covered by the first NP.

3. The width of the subspan covered by the second NP.

4. The width of the subspan covered by the VBN.

Now suppose that the input sentence contains one occurrence each of the words *musste* and *haben*, at least two words apart. These words fix two out of the four values. Now all we need to know to uniquely determine a rule application is:

1. the start position of the first NP and

2. the width of the subspan covered by the second NP.

Despite having three non-terminals, the parsing complexity of this rule is only quadratic—under the assumption that each of the rule's terminals matches only one word in the input sentence. In most instances, this assumption is realistic. When the input sentence contains repeated words and this assumption does not hold, the analysis is a little more involved, but a lexicalized rule will usually have better parsing complexity than a non-lexical rule with the same number of non-terminals.

Lexical Normal Form

Based on this observation, DeNero et al. [2009a] propose Lexical Normal Form (LNF), a grammar transform that allows rules to contain more than two non-terminals provided that there are no adjacent non-terminals. Binarization is employed to handle non-terminal sequences. Compared with binary transforms, such as as Chomsky Normal Form or Greibach Normal Form, LNF generates far fewer virtual rules and virtual non-terminals.

Scope Pruning

A simpler approach to managing problematic rules is to remove them from the grammar altogether. This is the approach proposed by Hopkins and Langmead [2010].

Hopkins and Langmead analyze parsing complexity in terms of *scope*. Intuitively, a rule's scope is the number of decisions that must be made to determine how to fit the rule over the input sentence under the assumption that every word of the input sentence is unique. For a non-terminal, we must determine its start and end position. For a pair of non-terminals A B, we must determine the start point of A, the end point of B, and the split point between them. The important observation is that lexical items serve as anchors that remove the ambiguity of one or more of these positions.

The scope of a SCFG rule r can be computed by examining the source-side CFG projection, $q = \text{proj}'_s(r)$, and summing:

1. the number of non-terminals at the start of q's right-hand side (0 or 1);

2. the number of non-terminals at the end of q's right-hand side (0 or 1); and

3. the number of pairs of adjacent non-terminals in q's right-hand side (0 or more).

The scope of a grammar G is the maximum scope of any rule in G.

Example 5.3   The following tables show a number of rule right-hand sides and their corresponding scope values (we have used the symbol $\diamond$ to represent a generic non-terminal symbol).

Rule RHS	Scope
a b c d e	0
a $\diamond$ c $\diamond$ e	0
a $\diamond$ $\diamond$ d e	1
$\diamond$ b c d e	1

Rule RHS	Scope
a $\diamond$ $\diamond$ $\diamond$ e	2
$\diamond$ b c d $\diamond$	2
$\diamond$ $\diamond$ c d $\diamond$	3
$\diamond$ $\diamond$ $\diamond$ $\diamond$ $\diamond$	6

Hopkins and Langmead prove[3] that a grammar with scope k can be used to parse a sentence of length $|s|$ in $\mathcal{O}(|s|^k)$ chart updates without binarization (either explicit or implicit). In terms of parse forest complexity, using a scope-k grammar guarantees that the hyperedge bound will be $\mathcal{O}(|G| \cdot |N| \cdot |s|^k)$. Scope thus effectively replaces the concept of rank in determining the parsing complexity of a grammar.

In experiments, Hopkins and Langmead demonstrate that reducing a GHKM grammar to scope-3 by pruning does not harm translation quality (as measured by BLEU) compared to synchronous binarization.

5.4   INTERIM SUMMARY

This chapter began by describing the most basic possible approach to string decoding: hypergraph construction through string parsing, combined with beam search. While this approach will work reasonably well for some models, for others it will be prohibitively slow. For instance, the large non-terminal vocabularies of SAMT grammars and the super-binary grammars of GHKM are both problematic. We introduced a number of strategies to improve efficiency, but the efficacy of a strategy depends on the model. For Hiero, SAMT, and GHKM models, typical combinations of strategies would be as follows:

Hiero	Constrained width parsing.
SAMT	Constrained width parsing; per-subspan beam search.
GHKM	Binarization or scope pruning; per-subspan beam search.

---

[3]Under the assumption that there are constant limits on (i) the multiplicity of a symbol in the input sentence and (ii) the length of a rule right-hand side.

Grammar Type	Vertices	Hyperedges
Hiero	$\mathcal{O}(|s|)$	$\mathcal{O}(|G| \cdot |s|)$
SAMT	$\mathcal{O}(|N| \cdot |s|)$	$\mathcal{O}(|G| \cdot |N| \cdot |s|)$
GHKM (binarization)	$\mathcal{O}(|N'| \cdot |s|^2)$	$\mathcal{O}(|G'| \cdot |N'| \cdot |s|^3)$
GHKM (scope pruning)	$\mathcal{O}(|N| \cdot |s|^2)$	$\mathcal{O}(|G| \cdot |N| \cdot |s|^{\text{scope}(G)})$

Table 5.3: Worst-case sizes of parse forest hypergraphs for Hiero, SAMT, and GHKM grammars using recommended search strategies. The input parameters are as in Table 5.1. In the third row, G' is the binarized grammar and N' is its non-terminal set. Typically, these are much larger than the original grammar and non-terminal set.

The computational cost of string decoding can be largely understood in terms of parse forest complexity. Table 5.3 gives the worst-case bounds if we assume the combinations of strategies just given. On top of the cost of parse forest construction, we must also account for the cost of beam search. This cost depends on the beam-filling algorithm, but typically is proportional to the beam width, k, times the number of calls to the beam-filling function (which is either one per vertex or one per subspan, depending on whether per-subspan beam search is used).

In the following two sections, we return to hypergraph construction, examining two aspects of string decoding that we have so far ignored: algorithms for string parsing and methods for decoding with STSGs and distinct-category SCFGs.

5.5   PARSING ALGORITHMS

So far we have treated the parsing component of a decoder as a black box. One way to implement this component is to modify the CYK algorithm from Section 3.2.3 to construct a parse forest hypergraph. CYK requires that the grammar is in Chomsky Normal form and so we must perform conversion before and after parsing. Taking this approach, the PARSE function used by CONSTRUCT-HYPERGRAPH (Algorithm 16) might resemble the version given in Algorithm 19. Alternatively, there are parsing algorithms that can handle arbitrary CFGs, eliminating the need for grammar conversion. A well-known example is the Earley parsing algorithm [Earley, 1970], which performs grammar binarization internally. A more common choice for translation systems is the CYK+ [Chappelier and Rajman, 1998] algorithm, which is closely related to both the CYK and Earley algorithms.

All three parsing algorithms—CYK, Earley, and CYK+—have a $\mathcal{O}(|s|^3)$ upper bound and, at least in terms of worst-case complexity, there is no clear reason to choose one over the other. In practice, different parsing algorithms can have very different performance characteristics. A distinctive feature of translation grammars is that they tend to be extremely large: for the parallel training corpora typically used in research, the rule extraction methods of Chapter 2 can easily generate tens or hundreds of millions of distinct rules. Grammar size, and in particular the size of

---

Algorithm 19 A PARSE Function That Uses CYK

Input :	s	a source string
	G	a CFG
Output :	$\langle V_s, E_s \rangle$	the parse forest hypergraph for s parsed according to G

PARSE(s, G)

1   $G' = $ CONVERT-TO-CNF(G)
2   $\langle V'_s, E'_s \rangle = $ CYK(s, G')
3   $\langle V_s, E_s \rangle = $ FLATTEN$(\langle V'_s, E'_s \rangle)$
4   **return** $\langle V_s, E_s \rangle$

---

the non-terminal vocabulary, $|N|$, are well known to be significant factors in parser performance. For binarized or SAMT-style grammars, $|N|$ can easily be in the thousands. These characteristics can influence the performance of parsing algorithms. Consequently, the choice of algorithm, and its implementation, can matter quite a bit, and researchers have even developed specialized parsing algorithms for use in translation systems.

In this section, we will first describe the CYK+ algorithm. In order for CYK+ and related algorithms to be practical for translation-scale grammars, we need an efficient means of storing and accessing grammar rules. We will describe trie-based grammar storage. We will then discuss a variant of CYK+ that has been developed specifically with translation grammars in mind.

5.5.1   THE CYK+ ALGORITHM

CYK+[4] is a bottom-up parsing algorithm. Unlike CYK, which requires the input grammar to be in Chomsky Normal Form, CYK+ can handle arbitrary CFGs. In order to achieve $\mathcal{O}(|s|^3)$ complexity, CYK+ binarizes grammar rules internally.

CYK+ uses a chart to record both completed and partial results. Each cell of the chart contains two lists, referred to as the *type-1* list and the *type-2* list. For a CYK+ recognizer, the type-1 list is similar to the Boolean vector of the CYK recognizer: for the cell corresponding to sentence subspan $[i, j]$, the type-1 list contains items A such that $A \overset{*}{\Rightarrow} s_i \ldots s_j$. The type-2 list records the set of Earley-style *dotted rules* $\alpha\bullet$ such that $\alpha \overset{*}{\Rightarrow} s_i \ldots s_j$ and α is a prefix of some grammar rule (i.e., the grammar contains a rule $A \to \alpha\beta$, where α and β are symbol strings).

Pseudocode for a CYK+ recognizer is shown in Algorithm 20. The algorithm begins by trying to match rules of the form $A \to s_i \gamma$ (lines 1–2). If a match is found where γ is empty then A is added to the type-1 list of chart cell $[i, i]$ (line 3 of the MATCH procedure). If a match is

---

[4]In Chappelier and Rajman [1998] original description, the algorithm requires that grammar rules are either purely lexical or purely non-lexical, but the author's note that this restriction was made to simplify the algorithm and is easily eliminated. Since partially lexicalized rules are ubiquitous in translation grammars we describe a modified version here.

Algorithm 20 The CYK+ Recognition Algorithm

Input : String s; CFG, G, with no empty rules
Output : Boolean indicating whether s belongs to language defined by G

CYK-Plus-Recognize(G, s)

```
 1  for i = 1 to |s|
 2      Match(G, i, i, •, s_i)
 3  for width = 1 to |s|
 4      for i = 1 to |s| − width + 1                    // i = span start
 5          j = i + width − 1                           // j = span end
 6          for x = i + 1 to j                          // x = split-point
 7              for α• in type-2 list of chart[i, x − 1]
 8                  for A in type-1 list of chart[x, j]
 9                      Match(G, i, j, •, A)
10          if width > 1
11              for α• in type-2 list of chart[i, j − 1]
12                  Match(G, i, j, •, s_j)
13          for A in type-1 list of chart[i, j]
14              Match(G, i, j, •, A)
15  return TRUE iff S† is in type-1 list of chart[1, |s|]
```

Match($G, i, j, •, \cdot$)

```
 1  for each rule A → αβγ in G
 2      if γ is empty
 3          append A to type-1-list of chart[i, j]
 4      else
 5          append αβ• to type-2-list of chart[i, j]
```

---

found where γ is non-empty then the dotted rule $s_i•$ is added to the type-2 list (line 5 of the Match procedure).

Having completed this initialization stage, the algorithm proceeds to visit chart cells in order of increasing width. At each cell, the algorithm first attempts to extend existing dotted rules to cover the current span by adding a non-terminal symbol (lines 7–9) or a terminal (lines 11–12). It then checks for rules that begin with a non-terminal, which includes non-lexical unary rules of the form $A \to B$ (lines 13–14). Note that chains of unary rules are correctly handled since the Match procedure appends A to the type-1 list, which then becomes an argument to a

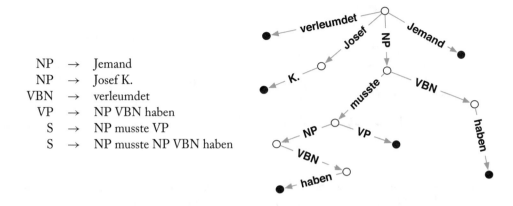

NP	→	Jemand
NP	→	Josef K.
VBN	→	verleumdet
VP	→	NP VBN haben
S	→	NP musste VP
S	→	NP musste NP VBN haben

Figure 5.2: The source-side projection of the grammar from Example 5.1 and the corresponding trie. The black circles indicate the nodes for which there are rules.

subsequent MATCH call later in the for loop. For a non-recognition version of the algorithm, cycles (like $A \Rightarrow B \Rightarrow C \Rightarrow A$) require special handling. Cycles are rarely useful in natural language parsing, and a standard technique is to break cycles by checking for repeated symbols, or even to remove unlexicalized unary rules from the grammar entirely.

Finally, the algorithm tests for the presence of the start symbol $S^\dagger$ in the type-1 list of the top-most cell.

Notice that the MATCH procedure contains a loop over all grammar rules with a given prefix. For a large grammar, a naive implementation that iterates over all rules would be prohibitively slow. The following section describes a better approach.

5.5.2 TRIE-BASED GRAMMAR STORAGE

Decoders typically store the translation grammar in a trie-based data structure (sometimes called a prefix tree). Each edge of the trie is labeled with a source-side terminal or non-terminal such that the sequence of labels along a path (from the root) to a node n represent the prefix α of some source-side rule $A \to \alpha\gamma$. A grammar rule $\langle A \to \alpha, B \to \beta \rangle$ is stored at the node with prefix path α, meaning that some nodes in the trie store no rules while others store one or multiple rules. At any given node, the rules are subgrouped by source and target left-hand side, $\langle A, B \rangle$.

Figure 5.2 gives an example of a grammar (only the source-side is shown) and its corresponding trie.

A trie can save space by compactly representing rules with common prefixes. However, the main advantage of using a trie is efficiency of access: the data structure is ideally suited for parsing algorithms like CYK+ where a rule match over a subspan $[i, k]$ is an extension (by one symbol) of a rule match over a shorter subspan $[i, j]$. The MATCH procedure from Algorithm 20 can be

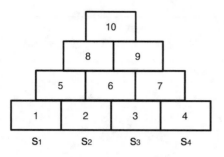 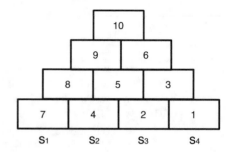

Figure 5.3: Order of span visits for Algorithms 20 (CYK+) and Algorithm 21 (recursive CYK+). For CYK+, the only inherent constraint on chart traversal is that it is bottom-up—the recursive CYK+ order would work equally well. The converse is not true: no other order is possible for recursive CYK+.

efficiently implemented if the grammar is stored in a trie: the trick is to store in the type-2 list, a pointer to a trie node along with each dotted rule (naturally, for a dotted rule $\alpha\bullet$, the pointer is to the trie node ending at path α). The loop in lines 1 to 5 then becomes two loops: the first (for the case that β is empty) is a loop over the rule left-hand sides stored at the trie node. The second is a loop over the outbound edges.

5.5.3 THE RECURSIVE CYK+ ALGORITHM

The CYK+ algorithm performs binarization dynamically, storing its internal representation of binarized rules—the dotted rules—in the chart's type-2 lists. For the large and highly lexicalized grammars used in translation, there can be a huge number of distinct binarized rules, making dotted rule storage expensive in terms of memory.

Sennrich [2014] proposes a variant of CYK+ that minimizes dotted rule storage by recursively expanding, and then discarding, every dotted rule as soon as it is constructed. To achieve this, the chart's cells must be visited in a specific order: both bottom-up and from right-to-left. Figure 5.3 illustrates this ordering. By examining the input sentence and the chart, the algorithm repeatedly proposes possible rule applications, which are tested by querying the grammar data structure. However, unlike standard CYK+, when visiting subspan $[i, j]$, the algorithm does not stop at proposing applications over $[i, j]$: immediately on finding a match, the algorithm tries to extend the rule application by matching a further symbol (and then another, and another—i.e., recursively). Thus, when visiting span $[i, j]$, the algorithm can find rule applications over any span $[i, k]$, where $k \geq j$. For example, when visiting cell 8 in Figure 5.3, the algorithm can potentially add items to the type-1 lists of cells 8, 9, and 10.

Pseudocode for a recursive CYK+ recognizer is given in Algorithm 21. The RECURSIVE-CYK-PLUS-RECOGNIZE function visits each subspan in the prescribed order (lines 1–7). For each subspan $[i, j]$, it does one of the following.

Algorithm 21 The Recursive CYK+ Recognition Algorithm

Input : String s; CFG, G, with no empty rules and no non-lexical unary rules
Output : Boolean indicating whether s belongs to language defined by G

RECURSIVE-CYK-PLUS-RECOGNIZE(G, s)

1 **for** $i = |s|$ **to** 1   // i = span start
2   **for** $j = i$ **to** $|s|$ // j = span end
3   **if** $i = j$
4   MATCH$(G, s, i, i, \bullet, s_i)$
5   **else**
6   **for** A in type-1 list of *chart[i,j-1]*
7   MATCH$(G, s, i, j\text{-}1, \bullet, A)$
8 **return** TRUE iff $S^{\dagger}$ is in type-1 list of *chart*$[1, |s|]$

MATCH$(G, s, i, j, {}_{,}\bullet, {}_{,})$

1 **for** each rule $A \to \alpha\beta$ in G
2   add A to type-1-list of *chart*$[i, j]$
3 **if** $j < |s|$
4   MATCH$(G, s, i, j + 1, {}_{,}{}_{,}\bullet, s_{j+1})$
5 **for** $k = j + 1$ **to** $|s|$
6   **for** A in type-1 list of *chart*$[j + 1, k]$
7   MATCH$(G, s, i, k, {}_{,}{}_{,}\bullet, A)$

- If $i = j$, it proposes a rule application over span $[i, i]$ with right-hand side s_i (line 4). The MATCH function tests this against the grammar, updating the type-1 list if a match is found, and then recursively attempts to expand the rule application.

- If $j > i$, RECURSIVE-CYK-PLUS-RECOGNIZE tries rule applications that begin with a non-terminal symbol over subspan $[i, j - 1]$ (lines 6–7). The MATCH function tests whether a proposed rule application is valid (by consulting the grammar data structure) and then recursively proposes extensions of the current rule application: either adding the next source word (line 4) or adding a non-terminal from an adjacent position in the chart (lines 5–7).

As presented, the algorithm does not handle non-lexical unary rules, but could be extended to do so. The recursive CYK+ algorithm yields the same result as the standard CYK+ algorithm, and has the same time complexity; it essentially performs the same steps, just in a different order. Its advantage lies in minimizing the dotted rule storage, thereby reducing memory consumption, and improving speed because storing and retrieving dotted rules typically involves RAM accesses with high latency.

5.6   STSG AND DISTINCT-CATEGORY SCFG

The string decoding algorithms presented so far have assumed that the grammar is an SCFG in shared-category form. They can easily be adapted to work with STSGs and distinct-category SCFGs.

5.6.1   STSG

Zhang et al. [2006] describe a simple, reversible procedure for converting a shared-category STSG, G, into an equivalent shared-category SCFG, G'. A one-to-one correspondence between derivations in G' and G means that an input sentence can be parsed with G' to produce a SCFG parse forest, which can then be converted into the equivalent STSG parse forest over G.

Zhang et al. [2006]'s method works as follows. For every STSG rule in the original grammar, two SCFG rules are produced. The first is effectively a flattened version of the original, with internal tree structure removed. To allow for the subsequent reversal of the conversion, the rule is given a left-hand side symbol that uniquely identifies the original rule. For instance, if the original STSG rule has identifier r_{4427} then a symbol V4427 is introduced into the SCFG non-terminal set (similarly to the introduction of virtual symbols in grammar binarization) and the SCFG rule is given the left-hand side V4427. The second SCFG rule is a unary non-lexical rule that rewrites the STSG's original root symbol as the newly introduced symbol.

Example 5.4   Suppose that rule r_{4427} is the following string-to-tree shared-category STSG rule:

The two resulting SCFG rules are:

$$
\begin{array}{lll}
q_1 & \text{VP} \rightarrow \text{V4427}_1 & \text{, V4427}_1 \\
q_2 & \text{V4427} \rightarrow \text{NP}_1 \text{ VBN}_2 \text{ haben} & \text{, have VBN}_2 \text{ NP}_1
\end{array}
$$

After parsing, the SCFG derivations are converted to STSG derivations by reducing pairs of hyperedges. For our example rules:

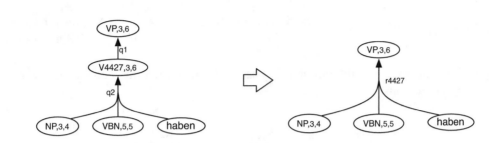

Once the STSG parse forest has been constructed, decoding can proceed as normal.

5.6.2 DISTINCT-CATEGORY SCFG

For a shared-category SCFG, the translation hypergraph was constructed by parsing the input sentence with the source-side CFG projection and then replacing the hyperedges of the resulting parse forest according to the inverse grammar projection. The correctness of that algorithm relies on two basic properties that hold for any shared-category SCFG G.

1. For any derivation d in G, the source tree of d is a CFG derivation in $\mathrm{proj}_s(G)$.

2. For any CFG derivation $d_s = r_1, r_2, \ldots, r_n$ in $\mathrm{proj}_s(G)$, there is a non-empty set of SCFG derivations in G that have d_s as their source tree. This set is $\{r'_1, r'_2, \ldots, r'_n : r'_i \in \mathrm{proj}'_s(r_i)\}$.

If G were a distinct-category SCFG, then only the first property would hold. The second fails since a derivation in $\mathrm{proj}_s(G)$ is not necessarily the source-side of any derivation in G.

Example 5.5   Let G be the distinct-category SCFG with the following rules:

r_1:	NP	$\to$	Josef K.	,	NP	$\to$	Josef K.
r_2:	VVPP	$\to$	verleumdet	,	VBN	$\to$	slandered
r_3:	VVPP	$\to$	verleumdet	,	VBN	$\to$	defamed
r_4:	VP	$\to$	$NP_1\ VVPP_2$	,	VP	$\to$	$VBD_2\ NP_1$
r_5:	VP	$\to$	VP_1 haben	,	VP	$\to$	have VP_1
r_6:	VP	$\to$	$NP_1\ VVPP_2$ haben	,	VP	$\to$	have $VBN_2\ NP_1$
r_7:	S	$\to$	Jemand musste VP_1	,	S	$\to$	Someone must VP_1
r_8:	S	$\to$	Jemand musste NP_1 $VVPP_2$ haben	,	S	$\to$	Someone must have $VBN_2\ NP_1$

r_9:   S →   Jemand musste NP_1 ,   S → NP_1 must have been
                   $VVPP_2$ haben VBN_2 by someone

The following derivation in $proj_s(G)$ can be formed using the source projections of rules r_1, r_2, r_4, r_5, and r_7:

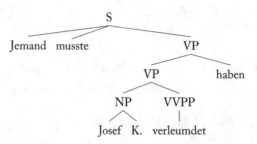

but no derivation in G has this source derivation. We can see this by looking at rule r_4, for which the source-side projection is the CFG rule VP → NP VVPP. If we check the grammar rules in $proj_s(G)$, we find that r_4 is the only rule with this source-side projection. But r_4 produces the target-side non-terminal VBD, which cannot be rewritten using any CFG rule in the target-side projection.

Examples like this occur in distinct-category SCFGs because the source and target CFGs mutually control the rewriting process: whether or not a synchronous rule can be applied depends on the non-terminals of both the source and target sides (of the rule and of the symbol string pair that is undergoing the rewrite). This property of mutually-controlled rewriting does not apply to shared-category SCFGs since the paired source and target non-terminals always match.

Fortunately, as we saw in Chapter 1, it is easy to convert any distinct-category grammar G to shared-category form G'. The conversion simply conjoins source and target non-terminals. For example, rule r_4 of Example 5.5 becomes:

$$(VP, VP) → (NP, NP)_1 (VVPP, VBD)_2 , (VVPP, VBD)_2 (NP, NP)_1.$$

Since there is a one-to-one mapping between the rules of G and G', it is trivial to convert derivations and hypergraphs from one form to the other. Thus, we can convert a distinct-category grammar to shared-category form, construct the translation hypergraph, and convert back to distinct-category form. Algorithm 22 gives the construction algorithm in pseudocode form. Once the hypergraph has been constructed, beam search can proceed as for a shared-category SCFG. The only difference is that vertex labels encode two non-terminal symbols (the conjoined source-target pair) instead of one.

Algorithm 22 Algorithm for constructing a distinct-category SCFG hypergraph

Input :	s	a source string
	G	a distinct-category SCFG
Output :	$\langle V_s, E \rangle$	translation hypergraph

CONSTRUCT-HYPERGRAPH(s, G)

1    $G' = $ CONJOIN-NON-TERMINALS(G)
2    $\langle V_s, E_s \rangle = $ PARSE$(s, \text{proj}_s(G'))$
3    $E = \varnothing$
4   **for** $e_s \in E_s$
5   **for** $r' \in \text{proj}'_s(\text{rule}(e_s))$
6            $r = $ SEPARATE-NON-TERMINALS(r')
7   add labeled hyperedge $\langle \text{head}(e_s), \text{tail}(e_s), r \rangle$ to E
8   **return** $\langle V_s, E \rangle$

5.7   HISTORICAL NOTES AND FURTHER READING

The presentation of string decoding given here, in line with most modern models and decoders, is firmly based on the approach presented in Chiang [2007]. For an account of earlier parsing-based approaches, see the brief history of syntax-based SMT in Section 1.5.

Translation, and particularly parsing-based approaches, are sometimes presented using the framework of *weighted deduction* (notably, Chiang [2007] presents the Hiero model as a weighted deductive proof system). This framework, which originated in the parsing literature, allows a particularly compact, modular, and uniform presentation and analysis of a wide range of translation models. For a good introduction to the use of weighted deduction in the context of statistical machine translation, see Lopez [2009].

The use of tries for storing grammar rules is not unique to machine translation: tries are also used in monolingual parsing (see, for instance, Klein and Manning [2001b]). Nor is the idea specific to syntax-based approaches (see, for instance, Germann et al. [2009]).

CHAPTER 6

Selected Topics

The central focus of this book has been on the use of syntax to model the ways that phrases are reordered between languages. This has taken six chapters, but even still, we are far from covering all of the ways that syntax is used in machine translation. In this chapter, we cover a number of considerations and extensions of the use of syntax that are important to know about, despite the fact that they did not fit within the core narrative presented in the previous chapters.

We begin with a central component of syntax-based translation that has so far been ignored: the monolingual parsers that produce all the syntax we care about! Section 6.1 looks at a number of ways that constituency structure and annotation are not optimal for machine translation, and how they can be altered in felicitous ways. It also describes how the upstream errors of parsers can be mitigated by extracting from and decoding from forests, instead of single-best output. This is followed in Section 6.2 by a discussion of the use of dependency parses for both tree-to-string and string-to-tree translation.

On its own, the presence of syntactic structure in translation rules is not enough to guarantee that translations are grammatically well formed, however it can provide a starting point for addressing issues of grammaticality that have proven challenging for statistical translation models. In Section 6.3, we look at some ways that target-side syntactic structure has been used as a foundation for developing linguistically-motivated extensions of the basic model. Finally, in Section 6.4 we look at the use of syntax in evaluation metrics.

6.1 TRANSFORMATIONS ON TREES

Monolingual constituency parsers like the Berkeley parser have thus far played a background role in this book. We have used their output directly to annotate one side of a parallel corpus in preparation for learning rules (Chapter 2) or to prepare input for tree-based decoding (Chapter 4). In so doing, we have ignored a number of issues. One problem is that parsers are not perfect; at least 7–10% of the constituents are likely to be wrong even under the best circumstances. Even if monolingual constituency parsing were perfect, it is not at all clear that the structure produced by monolingual parsers is optimal for machine translation. In this section, we will look at ways of altering the parser output in ways that better align with the needs of syntax-based translation. These methods include modifying the tree structure and the set and number of non-terminals used, letting the rules be combined more loosely with penalty-driven non-terminal mismatches, and, finally, mitigating the effects of errors in the one-best parse tree by working with forests.

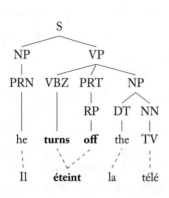 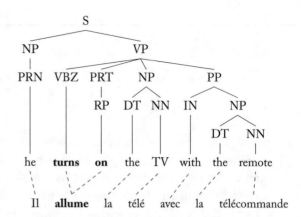

Figure 6.1: English–French sentence pairs with English derivations, showing alignment of phrasal verbs.

6.1.1   TREE RESTRUCTURING

One limitation of GHKM extraction is that only rules that span a syntactic constituent are extracted. For phrase-based SMT, it has long been known that translation pairs which are not syntactic constituents are also helpful [Koehn et al., 2003]. GHKM is able to learn non-constituent phrase pairs if they are embedded inside longer rules, but this often misses important generalizations.

As an example, consider the phrasal verbs *turn on* and *turn off* in Figure 6.1. Both phrasal verbs are translations of a single French word, *allumer* and *éteindre*, respectively. It is desirable to learn the translation units ⟨ allume , turns on ⟩ and ⟨ éteint , turns off ⟩. Such phrase pairs would allow the production of a sentence like *il éteint la télé avec la télécommande*, which combines rules from both sentences. This pair would be learned by a phrasal translation system. However, GHKM extraction on these alignments pairs produces the following rules:

$$
\begin{array}{llll}
r_1 & S \rightarrow & NP_1\ VP_2 & ,\ NP_1\ VP_2 \\
r_2 & VP \rightarrow & \text{éteint } NP_1 & ,\ \text{turns off } NP_1 \\
r_3 & NP \rightarrow & \text{allume } NP_1\ PP_2 & ,\ \text{turns on } NP_1\ PP_2 \\
r_4 & NP \rightarrow & \text{il} & ,\ \text{he} \\
r_5 & NP \rightarrow & \text{la télé} & ,\ \text{the TV} \\
r_6 & PP \rightarrow & \text{avec la télécommande} & ,\ \text{with the remote}
\end{array}
$$

The constituency constraint forces these phrase pairs to be part of much larger syntactic rules with different, conflicting predicate-argument structure. As such, GHKM is unable to produce the desired generalization of *il éteint la télé avec la télécommande*.

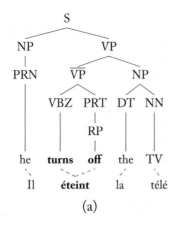

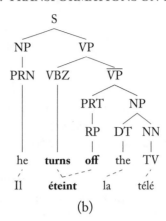

Figure 6.2: Left binarization (a) and right binarization (b) of the first derivation tree in Figure 6.1.

Various techniques have been proposed to restructure the training trees so that more useful rules can be learned. We now look at two of them: binarization and transformation-based learning.

Tree Binarization

Much of the problem is due to the flat structure of the VPs in the examples above, which is also somewhat arbitrary. One solution proposed by Wang et al. [2007] is called *tree binarization*. It works by binarizing trees before grammar learning, so as to break up wide constituents into many smaller ones with narrower spans, thereby increasing the number of extractable translation units. Note that this should not be confused with synchronous grammar binarization discussed in Section 5.3.1. Synchronous binarization is a post-processing operation that converts the n-ary SCFG rules of an already-learned grammar into weakly equivalent binary ones. In contrast, tree binarization yields an entirely different grammar with a different probability distribution. In both cases, however, binarization is reversible by deleting virtual nodes bottom-up, assigning each deleted virtual node's children to its parent.

There are many ways to binarize a parse tree. The two simplest are left-binarization and right-binarization. Left binarization of a node n with $r > 2$ children is performed by recursively replacing the leftmost two children of a node, N, with a new node, $\overline{N}$, until N has only two children. Right binarization is performed analogously by inserting new nodes to the right.

Binarization of the first derivation tree in Figure 6.1 results in the trees shown in Figure 6.2. By left-binarizing both sentences in Figure 6.1, GHKM extraction is able to extract the following additional synchronous rules (among others):

$$
\begin{array}{llll}
r_7 & \overline{\text{VP}} \rightarrow & \text{éteint} & , \text{ turns off} \\
r_8 & \overline{\text{VP}} \rightarrow & \text{allume} & , \text{ turns on} \\
r_9 & \text{VP} \rightarrow & \overline{\text{VP}}_1 \text{ NP}_2 & , \overline{\text{VP}}_1 \text{ NP}_2 \\
r_{10} & \text{VP} \rightarrow & \overline{\text{VP}}_1 \text{ PP}_2 & , \overline{\text{VP}}_1 \text{ PP}_2
\end{array}
$$

Here, the translations of *éteint* and *allume* can be stored as small translation units in the grammar, increasing the chance that they can be applied during translation. This allows us to produce a derivation of the input *il éteint la télé avec la télécommande*, yielding the translation *he turns off the TV with the remote*, by combining rules r_7 and r_{10} with rules r_1, r_4, r_5 and r_6 (which were binary in the original derivation tree).

In this example, left binarization had the desired effect, but there are other examples for which right binarization is more appropriate. One can also imagine different binarization schemes, such as identifying the head and binarizing outward, or trying to minimize the number of new rules. Wang et al. [2007] propose a "parallel binarization" scheme that constructs a binarization forest of possibilities for each tree in a treebank, and then uses Expectation-Maximization to learn the most probable global restructuring. This results in trees with mixed left-binarized and right-binarized nodes.

The increased generality of binarized treebanks comes at the cost of overgeneralizations during translation. Williams et al. [2015] describe that subcategorization constraints are violated more often by a synchronous grammar that is extracted from a binarized treebank than by one that is extracted from the original treebank. For instance, the constraint that finite verbs have exactly one subject in German (with the exception of coordinated structures and imperatives) is violated frequently by the grammar based on the binarized treebank. Williams et al. [2015] unbinarize dynamically during translation, employing a syntactic language model over the unbinarized trees to enforce subcategorization constraints. This helps to mitigate the overgeneralization problem caused by tree binarization.

Transformation-based Learning

Another tree restructuring technique has been proposed by Burkett and Klein [2012], who use six types of tree transformations to maximize the number of extractable nodes. An example is the `articulate` transformation type, shown in Figure 6.3. The transformation `articulate(VP,VBZ,PRT)` converts the derivation trees in Figure 6.1 into ones where the phrasal verb is extractable.

Burkett and Klein [2012] do not apply the transformations to all nodes, but use transformation-based learning [Brill, 1992] to greedily search for a sequence of transformations that maximally increases the number of extractable nodes on a small training set. An interesting aspect of this approach is that it tries to answer a fundamentally different question than previous work on tree binarization. Instead of searching for the "best" representation of a treebank according to some monolingual metric, the objective function takes into account the other side of the parallel corpus, and the alignments between the two texts. Thus, the algorithm will learn

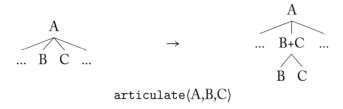

articulate(A,B,C)

Figure 6.3: Articulate transformation schematic from Burkett and Klein [2012].

different transformations for the same treebank if the alignment method or aligned language pair are changed.

6.1.2   TREE RE-LABELING

The same observations that apply to structure also apply to the grammar non-terminals: they are not necessarily optimal for learning translation rules. Consider the following simplified SCFG:

$$
\begin{aligned}
S &\rightarrow NP_1 VP_2 \quad, \quad NP_1 VP_2 \\
NP &\rightarrow you \qquad, \quad du \\
VP &\rightarrow sleep \qquad, \quad schlafen \\
VP &\rightarrow sleep \qquad, \quad schläfst
\end{aligned}
$$

The coarseness of the non-terminal label set here allows the overgeneration of ungrammatical sentences. When translating from English, both *du schlafen* and *du schläfst* can be produced. These are permitted by the grammar because the non-terminals encode only the most general information about the part-of-speech, and exclude morphological features of the noun phrase, such as grammatical person, gender, case, and number, which are relevant for morpho-syntactic phenomena such as agreement. Enriching non-terminals with morphological features could reduce the number of ill-formed sentences that the grammar generates:

$$
\begin{aligned}
S &\rightarrow NP\text{-}2\text{-}SG\text{-}NOM_1 VP\text{-}2\text{-}SG_2 \quad, \quad NP\text{-}2\text{-}SG\text{-}NOM_1 VP\text{-}2\text{-}SG_2 \\
NP\text{-}2\text{-}SG\text{-}NOM &\rightarrow you \qquad, \quad du \\
VP\text{-}3\text{-}PL &\rightarrow sleep \qquad, \quad schlafen \\
VP\text{-}2\text{-}SG &\rightarrow sleep \qquad, \quad schläfst
\end{aligned}
$$

Of course, this statement about the coarseness of non-terminals is true of parsing, as well. A long line of work there has established that automatically-refined non-terminal sets produce much higher accuracy parsers [Johnson, 1998, Matsuzaki et al., 2005, Petrov et al., 2006]. If this work is successful in parsing, where the task is to discriminate among structures over a grammatical input, it seems likely it should be helpful in language generation tasks like syntax-based MT, where the dangers of leaky grammars would seem to be more problematic. And indeed, state-splitting has been successfully applied to parse trees for GHKM extraction in string-to-tree systems [Chiang et al., 2009, Wang et al., 2010].

While finer-grained non-terminal sets can prevent some overgeneralizations, they are also problematic because they increase data sparsity and can prevent desirable derivations. For instance, singular and plural noun phrases are interchangeable in object position, and a full morphological annotation of all noun phrases symbols would needlessly constrain rule application. Having multiple variants of the same rule with different left-hand side symbols also increases the size of the grammar and the number of possible derivations that only differ in their non-terminal symbols. Hanneman and Lavie [2011] describe an algorithm for automatic label coarsening. Their objective is to maximize the probability of source symbols given the aligned target symbols, and vice-versa. This improves the quality of tree-to-tree translation in experiments on Chinese-English and French-English, with substantial reductions in the size of the joint non-terminal sets. A potential drawback of this objective is that symbol distinctions in one language can be important even if all symbols are mapped to a single symbol in the other language. For example, the function of noun phrases is marked with case in German, and encoding the function of noun phrases in the non-terminal symbol seems desirable to prevent overgeneralization, even if all noun phrase symbols are aligned to the same symbol NP in English.

While it may seem contradictory that both increasing and decreasing the size of the non-terminal set should improve translation performance, we expect various factors to play a role, including the language pair, the size of the original non-terminal set and whether syntax is used on the source, target, or both. Also, the drawbacks of non-terminal sets that are too coarse or too fine-grained can be compensated by other parts of the SMT system, for instance through separate models for agreement (see Section 6.3.1) that reduce overgeneralizations from overly coarse-grained symbols.

6.1.3 FUZZY SYNTAX

Another method of loosening the constraints imposed by syntax is to do away with the requirement that non-terminals match during rule application. This is often refered to as a "fuzzy" or "soft" syntax. Recall that by definition, CFG (and SCFG) derivations proceed by replacing a non-terminal in the derived string with any rule having that non-terminal on its left-hand side (Section 1.2.1). (For distinct-category SCFG, the non-terminal might be a pair.) We can soften this matching constraint by allowing a non-terminal A to be rewritten by any rule of the form $B \rightarrow \alpha$. Permitting mismatching in this way can be especially important when the grammars impose extensive constraints, such as using very, very large non-terminal sets (like SAMT), or in tree-to-tree decoding.

Chiang [2010] applied this fuzzy matching approach in a tree-to-tree setting. The process was controlled with a set of sparse features designed to allow the model to learn how often to match or mismatch rule applications. These features included counters *match* and $\neg match$ to count the number of rewrites where $A = B$ and $A \neq B$, respectively, and a feature $subst_{A \rightarrow B}$ that counts, for every pair of non-terminals, how often A is rewritten with a rule having B as its left-hand side. Separate features were used for source and target labels. The resulting models demonstrated improvement over a string-to-string baseline translating from both Arabic and Chinese into English. Fuzzy matching was an important piece of the performance gains, helping to loosen the tight constraints of tree-to-tree decoding.

In related work, Huck et al. [2014] collapsed rules that only differed in their source-side non-terminal symbols, but stored the set of non-terminal symbols with which the rule was seen in training. They described both dense and sparse features that penalized mismatches between the syntactic annotation of the input sentence and the rules that were applied during decoding.

6.1.4   FOREST-BASED APPROACHES

In previous chapters, we have seen two main uses of parse trees. The first is in grammar learning, where each sentence pair is annotated with a source-side or target-side parse tree (or sometimes both) prior to rule extraction. The second is in tree decoding, where each input sentence is parsed prior to decoding.

In a typical setting, both of these approaches are vulnerable to parsing errors since they use only the 1-best parse tree from a statistical parser. An obvious, and often effective, way to ameliorate this situation is to use the k-best parse trees. In the case of rule extraction, this involves running rule extraction k-times (first with the 1-best trees, then the 2-best trees, and so on) and then merging the resulting grammars. In the case of tree decoding, this involves translating the input k times and picking the output with the best model score. Clearly, this approach is impractical for large values of k. It is also wasteful, since many of the k-best trees will share subtrees and therefore much of the computational effort is spent recomputing previous results. Forest-based approaches provide more efficient means to represent and process a set of parse trees, or parse forest.

Forest Decoding

Forest decoding [Mi et al., 2008] is a natural extension of tree decoding. Instead of being given a single parse tree as input, the decoder is given a parse forest (in the form of a hypergraph). Typically, this parse forest is the pruned output of a statistical parser.

The main change to decoding is in hypergraph construction: the decoder must match grammar rules against a forest instead of a tree. Mi et al. [2008] generalize a simple tree-based rule matching algorithm for this purpose. Zhang et al. [2009] presents an alternative and more efficient algorithm (which we met previously in Section 4.4 when discussing efficient tree parsing). Once the hypergraph has been constructed, beam-search based decoding can proceed just as in tree decoding.

The input parse forest will contain a mix of plausible and less plausible hyperedges. If the parser produces a weighted forest then those forest weights can be used to inform translation. Typically, this means adding a feature function to the log-linear model to encode the input hyperedge probability.

Mi et al. [2008] demonstrate strong improvements for forest decoding over 1-best and 30-best baselines on a Chinese-to-English tree-to-string translation task. Compared with the baseline method of decoding k times with k-best parser outputs, forest decoding offers a much better speed-accuracy trade-off. Similar results have been reported for other language pairs: for instance, Neubig and Duh [2014] achieve large gains over tree decoding for both English-to-Japanese and Japanese-to-English translation. Zhang et al. [2011] report improvements on multiple language pairs using forests produced by combining alternative binarizations of the 1-best parse.

To be strictly consistent with our classification of syntax-based models (Section 1.4), forest decoding is a method for decoding with a tree-to-string or tree-to-tree model. In the literature, a model used with forest decoding is frequently referred to as a *forest-to-string* model.

Forest-based Rule Extraction

The other main use of parse trees is in grammar learning. Mi and Huang [2008] extend the GHKM algorithm (Section 2.4) to extract rules from a generalized form of alignment graph in which the parse tree is replaced with a parse forest. As in forest decoding, this forest is usually the pruned output of a statistical parser.

Mi and Huang's rule extraction algorithm involves three main changes compared to GHKM.

1. The notion of a frontier node is generalized to forest nodes. The identification of frontier nodes remains essentially unchanged.

2. The process of minimal rule formation is generalized to take account of the forest structure. The definition of a minimal rule remains essentially unchanged, but rule formation becomes more complicated since, in general, non-frontier nodes can be expanded in multiple ways. Mi and Huang describe a breadth-first algorithm that explores all possible expansions. They use a queue to keep track of the non-frontier nodes that require expansion.

3. To penalize the use of subtrees from non 1-best parse trees, Mi and Huang assign fractional counts to rules, so that rules extracted from the 1-best tree have a count of 1, but rules including non 1-best subtrees are penalized commensurately. Their method is based on the inside-outside algorithm from statistical parsing.

As for forest decoding, Mi et al. demonstrate strong improvements for forest-based rule extraction over 1-best and 30-best baselines on a Chinese-to-English tree-to-string translation task. Their results are further improved by combining forest-based rule extraction and forest decoding.

6.1.5   BEYOND CONTEXT-FREE MODELS

The context-free grammars that have been the focus of this book are a step up in the hierarchy of formal languages from word-based and phrase-based models, which can be formalized as regular

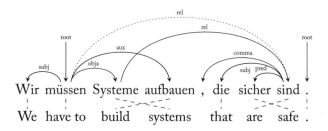

Figure 6.4: Non-projective German dependency tree.

grammars. Context-free grammars can model structures in natural language that regular grammars cannot, such as the hierarchical structure of subordinated clauses. However, there are structures in natural language that motivate the use of even more powerful, mildly context-sensitive models. Explorations with such models have been limited, but there are a few.

Non-projective Structures

In Figure 6.4, we see a German sentence with a discontinuous accusative object. Specifically, the relative clause that depends on the accusative object does not occur directly after the object, but after the end of the main clause. This discontinuity is visible in the tree via a crossing dependency edge, and trees with crossing edges are called non-projective [Ihm and Lecerf, 1963]. Non-projective structures cannot be derived by context-free grammars.

Just how prevalent such examples are depends highly on the languages under consideration. Buchholz and Marsi [2006] compiled statistics on various treebanks used for the CoNLL-X shared task on dependency parsing. In the treebanks used, between 0% (for Chinese) and 36% (for Dutch) of sentences contain at least one non-projective arc, with the median of the 13 treebanks being 12% (for Turkish).

Syntactic SMT models have similar options to parsers for dealing with non-projective structures. One option that goes back to Chomsky's early work [Chomsky, 1957] is to posit that discontinuities are surface phenomena, and that there is a context-free deep-syntactic structure which we can derive through a set of transformations such as *syntactic movement*. The Prague Dependency Treebank [Hajič et al., 2000] follows such a multi-layered approach, and its tectogrammatical (deep) layer has been used in SMT [Bojar et al., 2008]. The set of movements necessary can be complex [Hajičová et al., 2004].

A simpler, but linguistically less adequate option is to heuristically projectivize treebanks. Nivre and Nilsson [2005] propose a simple algorithm to projectivize dependency trees by "lifting" non-projective dependency edges. The non-projective tree in Figure 6.4 can be projectivized by lifting just one edge. The pseudo-projective dependency edge is shown as a dotted line. The downside of this projectivization is that it prevents the modeling of syntactic phenomena such as morphological agreement or subcategorization along the edges that have been lifted. This is problematic for our example because the relativizer *die* is an indirect dependent of its antecedent *Systeme*, and the morphological agreement between the two could be modeled only along the original dependency chain. This relation is lost in the pseudo-projective structure.

Mildly Context-sensitive Grammars for SMT

A more principled approach to dealing with non-projectivity is to increase the expressive power of the model, which also entails an increase in computational complexity. Mildly context-sensitive grammars place constraints on the non-projectivity allowed in the grammar to allow for polynomial parsing. A good introduction to theoretical and empirical aspects of constraints on non-projectivity can be found in Kuhlmann and Nivre [2006], and Kuhlmann [2013].

Translation models based on mildly context-sensitive grammars are an active research interest [e.g., Burbank et al., 2005, Carreras and Collins, 2009, Kaeshammer, 2015, Seemann et al., 2015, Zhang et al., 2008]. Unsurprisingly, the increase in computational cost compared to context-free models remains a major challenge. As such, such models often do not perform well, although they remain theoretically and scientifically interesting.

6.2   DEPENDENCY STRUCTURE

Our discussion so far has focused on context-free constituency representations. In this section, we broaden the scope to discuss models that have been developed for dependency grammars.

Projective dependency grammars describe context-free languages and are thus weakly equivalent to the context-free constituency grammars we discussed previously. For each projective dependency grammar, we can also induce a strongly equivalent context-free grammar [Gaifman, 1965]. This close relationship between dependency and constituency representations allows us to apply the same SCFG models and algorithms that we have discussed in the previous chapters on dependency structures.

All that is required is a simple mapping from dependency trees to constituency trees, and we illustrate one such mapping in Figure 6.5. The mapping uses a preterminal node for each word, labeled with its POS tag. Another constituent is added for each word, labeled with the incoming dependency edge label of the corresponding word. Each constituent has all direct dependents of the word, and the word's preterminal node, as its children. A special root node is added to ensure that there is a single root node per sentence. This mapping has been used for SMT by Hardmeier et al. [2011], and Sennrich et al. [2015].

While we can in principle use the previously discussed SCFG algorithms for projective dependency representations, some translation models have been specifically developed for dependency representations. We describe some prominent approaches and discuss the similarities and differences to the algorithms we presented in the previous chapters. The mapping from dependency trees into constituency format shown in Figure 6.5 will help us shed light on these.

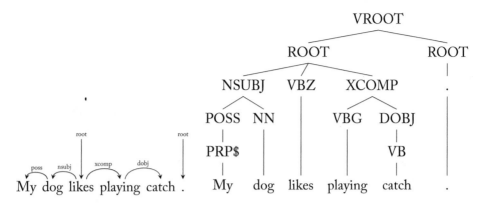

Figure 6.5: Dependency tree and its mapping into a constituency representation.

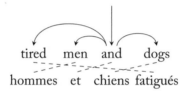

Figure 6.6: English–French sentence pair with alignment and English dependency tree.

6.2.1 DEPENDENCY TREELET TRANSLATION

Quirk et al. [2004] present a translation model based on a dependency representation. For training, they perform dependency parsing on the source sentence, and project these parses onto the target sentence via word alignments. They use *treelets* as their primary translation unit. They define a treelet to be a "connected subgraph of the dependency tree" Quirk et al. [2004]. This is more general than a *subtree*, which includes a node and all its descendants.

To illustrate what treelets are extracted from a small dependency tree, consider the dependency tree in Figure 6.6. From this dependency tree, the following subtree pairs are extracted:

1. tired   , fatigués
2. men   , hommes
3. and   , et
4. dogs   , chiens
5. tired men and dogs , hommes et chiens fatigués

Additionally, Quirk et al. [2004] extract the following treelets that are not subtrees:

6. men and dogs , hommes et chiens
7. men and   , hommes et
8. and dogs   , et chiens
9. men * dogs   , hommes * chiens

The last treelet is a treelet with a missing root, indicated by the wildcard character. This is a relaxation introduced by Quirk et al. [2004] to allow for more general rules, for instance for negation in French ("ne * pas").

To contrast these dependency extraction heuristics with those of the SCFG rule extraction algorithms that we saw in Chapter 2, we can assume a constituency representation of the dependency tree as in Section 6.2. Hierarchical rule extraction would still extract rules 1–5, but generalizes not by extracting treelets, but by replacing nodes in the subtree with non-terminal symbols:

10. NP → JJ_1 men and dogs   , hommes et chiens JJ_1
11. NP → JJ_1 men and NNS_2 , hommes et NNS_2 JJ_1
12. NP → JJ_1 NNS_2 and dogs , NNS_2 et chiens JJ_1
13. NP → JJ_1 men CC_2 dogs , hommes CC_2 chiens JJ_1

The SCFG rules 10–13 only represent a small selection of extractable rules. There are two major differences between the treelet pairs 6–9 and the SCFG rules 10–13 (the non-terminal symbols are shown for readability). First, the SCFG rules only allow for replacing one constituent with another, but not for their deletion or insertion. The treelet rules can be used to translate the sentence "men and dogs," whereas the SCFG rule set cannot. Tree binarization, introduced in the previous section, or SAMT-style extraction, discussed in Section 2.3, are two ways of increasing the generalization power of SCFG models. Second, the SCFG rules encode reordering information, whereas the treelets do not. Quirk et al. [2004] search over all possible orderings, and introduce a separate, discriminative reordering model. Since the number of possible reorderings is factorial, the search space is pruned heavily. Menezes and Quirk [2007] propose to extract *dependency order templates* at training time, which are unlexicalized treelet pairs, the source nodes being represented by their POS. As the treelets themselves, the order templates are scored via relative frequency estimates. During translation, treelets are combined with compatible order templates, as illustrated in Example 6.1, to create translation rules.

Example 6.1   Treelets and order templates required to translate "a very old man"

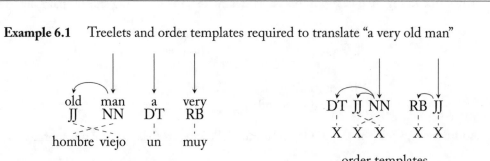

treelets   order templates

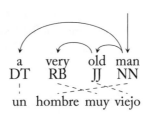

The space of possible reorderings is limited to those licensed by an order template, which reduces the search space over the original model. Note, however, that the model is still more general than a SCFG which only allows substitution of subtrees. Because the order templates enable search with less heavy pruning, the authors observe improvements in both translation quality and speed.

Menezes and Quirk [2008] further increase the generalization power of the model by modeling insertion and deletion via the order templates. Since the order templates are unlexicalized, this is more general than modeling them via unaligned words in treelet pairs. Menezes and Quirk [2008] motivate their insertion and deletion model with structurally divergent languages, such as when translating from English to Japanese, where determiners and pronouns are often deleted, but case markers inserted. Experimental results on translating from English to Japanese and Spanish indicate that their model is helpful for both translation directions, but that the type and frequency of deletions and insertions are very dependent on the language pair.

Modeling insertion and deletion via order templates is similar to SCFG rules that are unlexicalized except for unaligned words, which are being deleted (if they are on the source side) or inserted (if they are on the target side). As an example, consider the phrase "committee member," whose translation we could learn in a fully lexicalized rule (rule 14), or by combining an unlexicalized rule that models the insertion of "del" (rule 17) with the translation of the individual words.

14. NP $\rightarrow$ committee member , miembro del comité
15. NN $\rightarrow$ member , miembro
16. NN $\rightarrow$ committee , comité
17. NP $\rightarrow$ NN$_1$ NN$_2$, NN$_2$ del NN$_1$

Whether such (mostly) unlexicalized insertion and deletion rules are learned for SCFG grammars depends on the extraction heuristics. For instance, Chiang [2007] require at least one pair of aligned words in translation rules, which would make rule 17 invalid. GHKM extraction places no such restriction, but unlexicalized rules may be eliminated by other heuristics, such as scope pruning (discussed in Section 5.3.2).

A noteworthy component of the dependency treelet system is the *agreement model*, which is a simple bigram dependency language model. The motivation for this model is to model agreement phenomena, for instance learning a preference for the modifier-noun pair (`la`, `table`) over (`le`, `table`), even if the two words are separated by intervening modifiers. Although the target dependency trees are only obtained indirectly by projecting the source parse trees, Quirk et al. [2004] note that this agreement model is useful for their system, although they do not report empirical results on its impact.

6.2.2   STRING-TO-DEPENDENCY SMT

Dependency trees have also been shown to be useful as a target-side language model. The general ability to have gaps in rules (a capability of SCFGs) introduces the possibility of modeling long-distance dependencies between words, a capability that has thus far not been realized in this book. Shen et al. [2010] describe an approach that fills this gap. Its main components are a translation model that is similar to an unlabeled Hiero system, but restricted to be able to produce only *well-formed* dependency structures. These structures are composed from smaller structures, and their combination models the attachment of arguments to head-words in a trigram dependency model. This permits the modeling of relations between distant words, in constrast to *n*-gram models, which can only model local ones.

They divide well-formed dependency structures into two subcategories. *Fixed structures* consist of the root of a subtree, plus any number of children of the root. The extracted structure must be consecutive, and each child must be a complete subtree. This represents a head word that has taken zero or more arguments, and which may take more. Together, these constraints enforce the idea of constructing the target-language syntax bottom-up. Examples of well-formed and ill-formed structures are shown in Example 6.2.

Example 6.2   Consider the following English sentence along with its dependency structure:

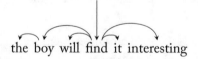

the boy will find it interesting

If we take this as the intended translated target-language sentence and structure, the following examples are well-formed substructures:

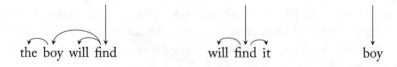

the boy will find   will find it   boy

Whereas the following two are ill-formed:

The first is ill-formed because *boy* has not yet had its arguments attached, and therefore is not yet completely built. The second is ill-formed because it is not a continuous segment of the original English sentence.

As a second type of well-formed structures, the authors defined *floating structures* in which the root of the subtree is unspecified. Relating back to the previous subsection's discussion of dependency treelets, this corresponds to the optional replacement of the treelet root with a wildcard. The definition of well-formed structures as unit of extraction is more general than only extracting full constituents, but less general than treelets.

Shen et al. define four operations to combine partial dependency structures: *left adjoining*, *right adjoining*, *left concatenation*, and *right concatenation*. The adjoining operations add a new child node to a fixed dependency structure, whereas the concatenation operations combine two siblings. The authors note that these operations are in principle sufficient to combine partial dependency structures into a full parse, but result in a large search space. Hence, they also use the substitution operation, using a single non-terminal label for floating structures, and the POS tag of the root for fixed structures. Mismatches between the label of the substitution site and the substituted structure are allowed, but incur a penalty. The adjoining and concatenation operations are implemented as special rules which are comparable to glue rules in hierarchical MT.

At decoding time, scores from a trigram dependency language model can be computed and scored as an additional weight in the log-linear model. This allows the decoder to model relations between words that are too distant to be modeled with *n*-gram models. In their evaluation, Shen et al. find that the restriction to well-formed dependency structures has a mixed effect when it is merely used to filter the rules of a hierarchical model. However, their main motivation for the use of dependency structure on the target side was to include the dependency language model. For that task, they obtain consistent improvements over a hierarchical baseline in their experiments on Chinese-to-English and Arabic-to-English.

6.3   IMPROVING GRAMMATICALITY

The previous chapters have mainly been devoted to describing algorithms for syntax-based SMT. In this section, we focus again on the question of *why* syntax-based algorithms are appropriate for SMT, and how a syntactic framework allows for solutions to problems that are hard to solve with phrase-based, or unlabeled hierarchical models.

As an introductory example in Chapter 1, we discussed reorderings between the source and the target language as a motivating example for syntax-based SMT. Failing to correctly reorder the words in the source text produces a "word salad" in the target language that may be hard to comprehend. Word order is one aspect of syntax, but for most languages, putting words in the right order is not sufficient to generate grammatically well-formed text. In this section, we will discuss other aspects of grammaticality, and how these aspects can be modeled in the framework of syntax-based SMT.

6.3.1   AGREEMENT

Inflectional languages typically mark features like gender and grammatical case on determiners, adjectives, nouns, and pronouns, and features like tense and number on verbs. In some syntactic relationships, feature agreement is required by the syntax of the language. In most Germanic and Romance languages, determiners and adjectives need to agree in case, number, and gender with their head noun, and finite verbs need to agree with their subject in number and person.

From a translation perspective, producing the right features in the translation is hard because feature types and values can differ substantially between languages. Consider the following example:

1. a bold decision

its translation into French,

2. une décision courageuse

and three alternative translations into German:

3. eine mutige Entscheidung

4. ein mutiger Entschluss

5. ein mutiges Urteil

Both German and French have grammatical gender, and mark the gender of the noun phrases through the inflection of determiners and attributes, whereas modern English has no grammatical gender. When translating into German or French, the translation of the determiners and attributes cannot be predicted from the source text, but is dependent on the head noun in the translation. This is highlighted by the fact that there are (at least) three possible translations of "decision" into German, the feminine noun "Entscheidung," the masculine "Entschluss," and the neuter "Urteil." Even when translating between two languages that both have the same feature types, feature values may differ, as between Example 2, the French noun "décision" being feminine, and Examples 4 or 5.

Agreement over short string distances can be modeled via n-gram language models, but agreement constraints can involve words that are distant in the surface string, which poses a problem for traditional n-gram models. This limitation of word-level n-gram language models has sparked considerable efforts on alternative models. Koehn and Hoang [2007] report improvements in grammatical coherence through language models on the level of morphological features, which are less sparse than surface word models. Ammar et al. [2013] use similar class-based language models, but trained on unsupervised clusters instead of linguistic features, and conclude that these models are effective at modeling morphological agreement. Neural Networks can better encode long n-grams than back-off models, and n-gram contexts of up to 32 have been used in the hope of better modeling long range dependencies [Ter-Sarkisov et al., 2014]. Recurrent Neural Networks are not limited to a fixed n-gram window, and can learn dependencies over longer distances [Elman, 1991]. Agreement has also been modeled outside of the main translation step, for instance through a rule-based error correction module [Rosa et al., 2012], or by first translating a morphologically underspecified representation of the text, and then generating the morphological features [Fraser et al., 2012, Toutanova et al., 2008].

Syntactic models facilitate the design of agreement models because words that need to agree are in clearly defined syntactic relationships. While the inflection prediction system by Toutanova et al. [2008] is implemented as n-best reranking, they use a treelet translation system as their base system, and the discriminative model for inflection prediction uses features based on source and target-side dependency structure, among others. Discriminative lexicon models that make use of syntactic context have also been integrated into the main translation pass of a tree-to-string translation system [Jeong et al., 2010].

Another class of models that can model agreement are dependency language models [Popel and Mareček, 2010, Quirk et al., 2004, Sennrich, 2015, Shen et al., 2010], which we will discuss in more detail in Section 6.3.4. Dependency language models are especially suitable to model agreement between words that are directly linked by a dependency arc, for which even a bigram model is sufficient. This applies to the aforementioned agreement requirements within (non-coordinated) noun phrases, and between subjects and verbs.

For other agreement phenomena, e.g., for the agreement between predicative adjectives and subjects in French, both the string distance and the syntactic distance can be high, which is problematic for both n-gram and syntactic language models with strong independence assumptions. Consider the subject and predicative adjective (highlighted) in the dependency tree in Figure 6.7. There is number agreement between the subject "elles" ('they') and the finite verb "peuvent" ("can"), but also between the subject and the predicative adjective "trouvées" ("found"). While the subject and the verb are directly linked in the dependency tree, the subject and the predicative adjective are only indirectly linked, and are predicted independently by dependency language models.

A more flexible method to enforce agreement constraints that is based on linguistic resources and manually designed constraints has been proposed by Williams and Koehn [2011], who model agreement in a unification grammar. They use a finite-state morphology to extract a lexicon of feature structures from the target side of the training corpus. The lexicon associates

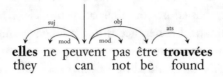

elles ne peuvent pas être **trouvées**
they   can   not be   found

Figure 6.7: French dependency tree, annotated according to the guidelines by Candito et al. [2010].

each target surface form with a set of feature structures. The rules in the synchronous grammar are augmented with constraints that identify which words or substitution sites need compatible feature structures, based on the syntactic relations. Example feature structures are shown in Example 6.3; an SCFG rule in Example 6.4.

Example 6.3 Two German feature structures[1] for the indefinite article "eine" and the noun "Welt" ("world"):

$$
\text{``eine''} \rightarrow
\begin{bmatrix}
\text{cat} & \text{ART} \\
\text{infl} &
\begin{bmatrix}
\text{case} & \text{nom} \\
\text{declension} & \text{mixed} \\
\text{agr} &
\begin{bmatrix}
\text{gender} & \text{f} \\
\text{num} & \text{sg}
\end{bmatrix}
\end{bmatrix}
\end{bmatrix}
\quad
\text{``Welt''} \rightarrow
\begin{bmatrix}
\text{cat} & \text{NN} \\
\text{infl} &
\begin{bmatrix}
\text{case} & \text{nom} \\
\text{agr} &
\begin{bmatrix}
\text{gender} & \text{f} \\
\text{num} & \text{sg}
\end{bmatrix}
\end{bmatrix}
\end{bmatrix}
$$

Example 6.4 SCFG rule augmented with unification constraints:

$$\text{SUBJ} \rightarrow \text{ART ADJA NN}$$

$\langle \text{SUBJ INFL} \rangle = \langle \text{ART INFL} \rangle$
$\langle \text{SUBJ INFL} \rangle = \langle \text{ADJA INFL} \rangle$
$\langle \text{SUBJ INFL} \rangle = \langle \text{NN INFL} \rangle$
$\langle \text{SUBJ INFL CASE} \rangle = \text{nom}$

The first three constraints ensure agreement between the article, adjective, and noun by unifying the respective feature structures. The resulting feature structure is made into the feature structure of the rule's left-hand side, which can be re-used in later rules, e.g., to enforce agreement with the verb. The final constraint is based on the rule's left-hand side label SUBJ, and encodes that German subjects require nominative case.

During translation, feature structures are unified where the constraints require compatibility, and translation hypotheses with incompatible feature structures are penalized or discarded. Discarding hypotheses with incompatible feature structures could theoretically guarantee perfect agreement. In practice, the approach relies on a high-quality lexicon, and missing or wrong entries can both result in agreement errors. Also, if data is sparse, the model may be unable to produce a correct translation, and may have to decide between allowing a wrongly inflected word form, or producing a grammatically correct, but semantically less plausible translation.

Despite the plethora of syntactic and non-syntactic models that aim to improve grammatical agreement, some problems are still unsolved. Agreement constraints become harder to model in coordinated structures, where the coordinated structure may have other feature values than its constituents. For example, the coordination of a masculine singular noun and a feminine singular noun in French is considered masculine plural for the purpose of agreement. In elliptical constructions, syntactic constituents that are relevant for agreement may be missing, and must be inferred from the context. Consider the three German translations of Example 6, where the noun in the second noun phrase is elided. The grammatical features of the elliptical noun phrase depend on the antecedent, which is underlined.

6. this is a bold <u>decision</u>, and hopefully **the right one**.

7. das ist eine mutige <u>Entscheidung</u>, und hoffentlich **die richtige**.

8. das ist ein mutiger <u>Entschluss</u>, und hoffentlich **der richtige**.

9. das ist ein mutiges <u>Urteil</u>, und hoffentlich **das richtige**.

Agreement phenomena may also cross sentence boundaries. Many languages, including most Romance and Germanic languages, require personal pronouns to agree in gender and number with their antecedent. For anaphora that cross sentence boundaries, the currently dominant approach of translating sentences independently of each other is unable to model these agreement constraints.Models specific to the problem of translating pronominal anaphora have been developed [Hardmeier and Federico, 2010], but pronoun translation remains an open challenge.

6.3.2 SUBCATEGORIZATION

Subcategorization [Chomsky, 1965], or the closely related concept of valency [Tesnière, 1959], is concerned with the number and types of syntactic arguments of words. Especially for verbs, there is a wide range of possible types of syntactic arguments, but specific verbs typically only allow for (or require) a small subset thereof. A well-known distinction is that between intransitive verbs that only take a subject as argument, such as "sleep"[2], and transitive ones that also take a direct object, such as "remember." There are various types of arguments, such as direct or indirect objects, prepositional objects (Example 2), or clausal objects (Example 3), and their interaction is complex. For instance, the verb "remind" may have both a direct and a clausal object (Example 4), where the direct objects denotes the receiver of the information, and the clausal object denotes the information. The verb "remember" takes either a direct or a clausal object (Examples 1 and 3, respectively), but not both, since both subcategory types are mapped to the same semantic role, the content of the memory.

1. he remembers his medical appointment.

2. I remind him of his medical appointment.

3. he remembers that he has a medical appointment.

4. I remind him that he has a medical appointment.

5. she was killed by the river.

Subcategorization is closely intertwined to the semantics of a word, for instance the number of participants in an action.[3] However, the mapping between syntax and semantics is complex. Multiple syntactic realizations can correspond to the same semantic frame, as do Examples 1 and 3, and a single syntactic structure can have multiple semantic interpretations. In Example 5, the prepositional phrase "by the river" could be interpreted as either the agent that killed her, or as an adjunct expressing the location of the murder.

For translation, subcategorization is challenging because subcategorization constraints need to be respected in the translation, which requires the modeling of additional inter-dependencies. Where the surface distance between a word and its arguments is long, n-gram models are insufficient to model these inter-dependencies. Also, the subcategorizations in the source sentence are imperfect evidence for those in the target sentence because subcategorization frames often differ between languages. For instance, the German verb "erinnern" takes a reflexive object in the meaning of "remember," and the content of the memory is realized as a prepositional object with the preposition "an." The German translation of Example 1 that respects these constraints is shown in Example 6. A literal translation in either direction, shown in Examples 7 and 8, is ungrammatical.

6. er erinnert sich an den Arzttermin.

7. *er erinnert den Arzttermin.

8. *he remembers himself to the medical appointment.

---

[2]While "sleep" is intransitive in its basic meaning, there are transitive meanings, as in "he sleeps a restless sleep."
[3]See Fisher et al. [1991] for an in-depth discussion.

Research that explicitly addresses the problem of subcategorization for SMT includes [Shilon et al., 2012, Weller et al., 2013].

Like for agreement, syntactic representations are an appropriate level of representation for subcategorization. While the surface distance between a word and its arguments varies, they are directly linked in the derivation tree, and various syntactic language models are in principle able to model subcategorization. Modeling subcategorization was a motivation for "head-driven," or lexicalized, probabilistic context-free grammars [Charniak, 2001, Collins, 2003]. By conditioning the probability of production rules on the head of the structure, lexicalized PCFGs can learn word-specific probability distributions, and thus model differences in subcategorization. Lexicalized PCFGs have been applied as language models in SMT [Charniak et al., 2003, Och et al., 2004, Post and Gildea, 2008], but early results were discouraging. Better success has been reported for dependency language models, which model subcategorization implicitly in the probability distribution of dependency bigrams [Quirk et al., 2004], or by explicitly predicting the subcategory type of each argument [Sennrich, 2015].

Subcategorization is not purely a fluency problem. Different meanings of a polysemous word often have different subcategorizations. For instance, "apply" has different meanings, and is translated differently, in the meaning of submitting oneself as a candidate for a job (German: "bewerben"), in the meaning of being relevant (German: "gelten"), and in the meaning of using something (German: "anwenden"). Examples 9–11 demonstrate the different meanings.

9. she applies for a job.

10. this rule applies to everyone.

11. he applies the wrong test.

In principle, composed GHKM rules can encode different translations for different subcategorizations of the same word, encoding both the correct translation and subcategorization in the target language:

$$S \rightarrow SUBJ_1 \text{ applies for } PN_2 \text{ . } , \quad SUBJ_1 \text{ bewirbt sich auf } PN_2 \text{ .}$$
$$S \rightarrow SUBJ_1 \text{ applies to } PN_2 \text{ . } , \quad SUBJ_1 \text{ gilt für } PN_2 \text{ .}$$
$$S \rightarrow SUBJ_1 \text{ applies } OBJA_2 \text{ . } , \quad SUBJ_1 \text{ wendet } OBJA_2 \text{ an .}$$

However, data will often be sparse, especially for languages that are highly inflected and/or have free word order. If more minimal rules are used, coverage improves, but the ability to disambiguate on the basis of subcategorization decreases.

A failure to account for cross-lingual differences in subcategorization not only hurts fluency, but can also cause semantic translation errors. Consider the English, German, and French analyses of "I like her" in Figure 6.8, where the English subject of "like" is expressed as object in German and French, and the English object is expressed as subject.

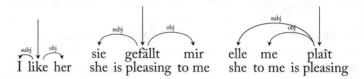

Figure 6.8: English, German and French dependency tree of *I like her* and corresponding translations.

Composed GHKM rules are in principle able to encode cases where grammatical roles are translated unusually, for instance in rule 7 in the following toy grammar, which can be combined with rules 2 and 3 to produce the correct translation.

1.	SUBJ	→	I	, ich
2.	SUBJ	→	I	, mir
3.	OBJ	→	her	, sie
4.	OBJ	→	her	, ihr
5.	V	→	like	, gefalle
6.	SENT	→	$SUBJ_1 \, V_2 \, OBJ_3$	, $SUBJ_1 \, V_2 \, OBJ_3$.
7.	SENT	→	$SUBJ_1$ like OBJ_2	, $SUBJ_2$ gefällt OBJ_1 .

However, rules 1, 4, 5, and 6, which are all minimal translation rules that express frequent translation pairs, are likely to score better, and result in the mistranslation "ich gefalle ihr," which expresses a different meaning, namely "she likes me."

Preventing semantic errors like this is still an open challenge in Machine Translation, and some models specifically model the semantic structure of sentences. One avenue of research is to incorporate semantic roles into syntax-based translation systems [Bazrafshan and Gildea, 2013, Liu and Gildea, 2008]. This line of work is based on the semantic role annotation from projects such as PropBank [Palmer et al., 2005] and FrameNet [Baker et al., 1998].

Another potential solution is to use an intermediate representation that abstracts away from shallow syntax and maps different realizations of the same meaning to the same expression. This reflects going one step higher in the famous Vauquois pyramid of translation. Research in this direction spans over more than half a century, and is beyond the scope of this book. However, we note that such semantic-based or interlingua-based approaches do not replace, but build on top of syntactic models, and syntactic knowledge is still required to analyze the source text, and generate syntactically well-formed output.

6.3.3   MORPHOLOGICAL STRUCTURE IN SYNCHRONOUS GRAMMARS

To some degree, Machine Translation is possible without an explicit model of morphology, and the models we discussed so far, as many phrase-based and hierarchical models, only require a segmentation of the text into words, or not even that for character-based translation [e.g., Vi-

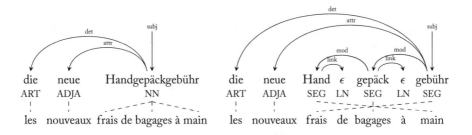

Figure 6.9: German noun phrase with dependency tree, and with/without hierarchical representation of compound.

lar et al., 2007]. However, for morphologically rich languages, treating words as atomic units is suboptimal. Morphological processes such as agglutination and compounding can produce complex morphological structures whose meaning is expressed as a syntactic structure in other languages. For instance, consider the German term "Handgepäckgebühr" ("carry-on bag fee"),[4] which is translated into French "frais de bagages à main." Without having seen the German term in the training data, its translation exceeds the capability of models that only operate on the level of words or larger units.

Compound splitting is an established technique for translation out of compounding languages [Koehn and Knight, 2003]. Applying compound splitting on the target side to produce new compounds is more complicated because compounds typically need to be merged, which requires their identification in the translation output [Stymne and Cancedda, 2011].

Context-free grammars cannot only represent syntactic structures, but also morphological structures [e.g., Heemskerk, 1993, Johnson et al., 2007]. Sennrich and Haddow [2015] represent the morphological structure of German compounds as part of the syntactic annotation. Figure 6.9 shows a representation of "Handgepäckgebühr" as a dependency tree, before and after splitting.

A dependency representation of morphological structure not only allows the extraction and use of morpheme-level translation rules, but also has the advantage over phrase-based and unlabeled hierarchical models that the output structure makes it easy to identify and merge split morphemes after decoding. Also, SCFG decoding constrains the reordering of morphemes, ensuring that compounds are not broken up by spurious reordering operations. The morpheme hierarchy within the compound also encodes morphosyntactic interactions, for instance the fact that in German, the last segment is the head of the compound and needs to agree with determiners and articles.

---

[4]While the English term is also a compound, it is written with spaces between the units. This minor spelling difference makes English compounds much easier to translate than German ones.

6.3.4   SYNTACTIC LANGUAGE MODELS

This chapter has highlighted various linguistic phenomena, syntactic, semantic, and morphological, which are relevant for producing accurate and grammatically well-formed translations. The accuracy of a translation, commonly referred to as *adequacy* [White et al., 1994], inherently depends on the source text, whereas the *fluency*, i.e., the degree to which the translation is grammatical and idiomatic, is independent from the source text. Traditionally, n-gram language models have been used to improve the fluency of translations, but they are limited to local fluency phenomena, and do not model the grammaticality of a sentence globally. Thus, errors such as agreement or subcategorization violations involving distant words, or even missing verbs, are common in SMT systems with n-gram language models [Williams and Koehn, 2014]. While this book is mainly devoted to learning and decoding with syntactic translation models, syntax can also be used in language modeling.

We briefly touched on the history of syntactic language models in Section 1.5. In this section, we will illustrate how syntactic language models can improve grammaticality with the example of dependency language models.

Like n-gram language models, dependency language models decompose the task of predicting the probability of a sentence $w_0, ..., w_n$ into predicting the probability of each word w_i, given some context. Whereas n-gram models use a history of previous words as context, dependency models define the context through the dependency structure. Quirk et al. [2004] define a simple bigram model that uses the direct ancestor in the dependency tree as context. The sequences resulting from following the dependency arcs have also been referred to as *syntactic n-grams* [Sidorov et al., 2013]. Example 6.5 shows a German dependency tree and the syntactic n-grams of size 2.

Example 6.5   Syntactic n-grams of size 2

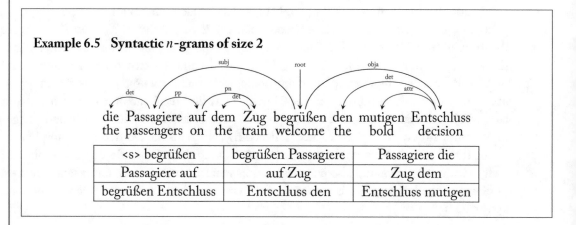

<s> begrüßen	begrüßen Passagiere	Passagiere die
Passagiere auf	auf Zug	Zug dem
begrüßen Entschluss	Entschluss den	Entschluss mutigen

A bigram dependency model is sufficient to enforce some grammaticality constraints. For instance, $p(\text{Passagiere}_{pl} \mid \text{begrüßen}_{pl})$ will be substantially higher than $p(\text{Passagier}_{sg} \mid \text{begrüßen}_{pl})$, since the latter violates gender agreement and is unlikely to occur in the training data. However, more sophisticated contexts may be required. In German prepositional phrases, gender and number is determined by the head noun, but case is governed by the preposition. To predict the correct determiner in the prepositional phrase, we need to condition the decision on the grandparent node, i.e., the preposition "auf," which governs the dative (or accusative) case: $p(\text{dem}_{\text{dat}} \mid \text{Zug}, \text{auf}) \gg p(\text{der}_{\text{nom}} \mid \text{Zug}, \text{auf})$.

Note that in German, like in English, there is number and person agreement between a verb and its subject, but not between a verb and its objects. In other words, we do not want to penalize the probability $p(\text{Entschluss}_{\text{sg}} \mid \text{begrüßen}_{\text{pl}})$, despite the mismatch in grammatical number. Including dependency labels in the context allows for a targeted modeling of subject—verb agreement, with $p(\text{Entschluss}_{\text{sg}} \mid \text{subj}, \text{begrüßen}_{\text{pl}}) \ll p(\text{Entschluss}_{\text{sg}} \mid \text{obja}, \text{begrüßen}_{\text{pl}})$. The labels also help to learn selectional preferences, for instance that the subject of "welcome" is likely to be an animate entity.

The context of dependency language models can also been filled with syntactic siblings [Shen et al., 2010], which is useful to model the order between siblings, or mutual exclusion of siblings. Sennrich [2015] defines a dependency language model that uses ancestor and sibling nodes as context, and both the word and the dependency label of each node:

$$p(\text{word} \mid \text{label, parent, label-of-parent, grandparent, label-of-grandparent,} \qquad (6.1)$$
$$\text{closest-sibling, label-of-closest-sibling}).$$

Depending on the number of ancestor and sibling nodes, the context can become quite large, and it is unclear how to formulate a back-off strategy. Thus, Sennrich [2015] implements the model as a feed-forward neural network, utilizing the network's power to generalize to unseen contexts.

Syntactic language models are especially attractive for syntax-based SMT because both can be trained on the same syntactic structures, and if the decoder produces syntactic derivations, it can provide the information required by a syntactic language model at little cost.

6.4   EVALUATION METRICS

The dominant method of automatically measuring the quality of a machine translation system is to compare an automatic translation to a human reference translation of the same text. The first such metric that was proposed, Bleu [Papineni et al., 2002], is still widely used today. A plethora of alternative metrics have been introduced since—just at the metrics shared task of the 2014 Workshop on Statistical Machine Translation, 29 metrics were compared, with the majority thereof new at the time [Machacek and Bojar, 2014].

The discussion of metrics is relevant for this book because popular translation quality metrics such as Bleu suffer from the same limitations as phrase-based translation models. n-gram quality metrics are most sensitive to local fluency, whereas inter-dependencies between distant words, such as agreement or subcategorization phenomena, are captured indirectly at best. There is thus a risk that these metrics vastly underestimate the quality of systems that are good at producing grammatically well-formed sentences, and not just a string of locally fluent fragments. Callison-Burch et al. [2006] discuss the fact that a rule-based system was ranked first in the human evaluation of the 2005 NIST MT evaluation, despite relatively poor BLEU scores, and conclude that it is inappropriate to use BLEU to "compar[e] systems which employ radically different strategies (especially comparing phrase-based statistical machine translation systems against systems that do not employ similar n-gram-based approaches)," or to try "to detect improvements for aspects of translation that are not modeled well by BLEU."

Translation quality metrics that operate on syntactic structures may be more suitable for the development and evaluation of syntax-based MT systems. During development, automatic metrics are regularly used to determine whether new model components are useful, and are typically employed as objective function for the optimization of the scaling parameters of the global log-linear model. A metric that is unable to detect that a new model improves an aspect of translation quality could lead to the new model being discarded as ineffective.

Liu and Gildea [2005] introduce two syntactic translation quality metrics. Both metrics assume the availability of parse trees of both the automatic translation and the human reference translation.

The subtree metric (STM) counts the number of subtrees of depth n in the translation output that also occur in the reference tree. Like BLEU, the metric is precision-based and clips the count of repeated subtrees to their count in the reference. Unlike BLEU, the units being counted are subtrees instead of n-grams, and subtree precision for different depths is averaged with the arithmetic mean, rather than the geometric mean. Also, the score does not include a brevity penalty, which is used in BLEU to penalize hypotheses that are too short.

$$STM = \frac{1}{D} \sum_{n=1}^{D} \frac{\sum_{t \in subtrees_n(hyp)} min(count_{hyp}(t), count_{ref}(t))}{\sum_{t \in subtrees_n(hyp)} count_{hyp}(t)}. \tag{6.2}$$

A second metric introduced by Liu and Gildea [2005] is the head-word-chain metric (HWCM). The metric is analogous to the subtree metric, but the unit is redefined to be chains of words linked by dependency relations:

$$HWCM = \frac{1}{D} \sum_{n=1}^{D} \frac{\sum_{g \in chain_n(hyp)} min(count_{hyp}(g), count_{ref}(g))}{\sum_{g \in chain_n(hyp)} count_{hyp}(g)}. \tag{6.3}$$

Example 6.6 shows a dependency tree and head-word chains that can extracted from it.

Example 6.6   Head-word chains of size 2

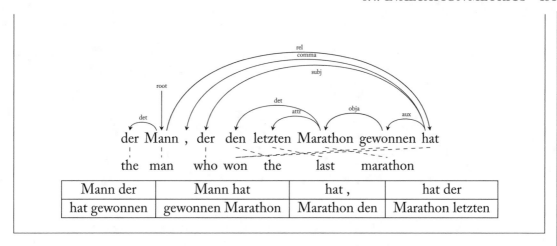

Note that the dependency chains correspond to the syntactic *n*-grams discussed in the context of dependency language models (Example 6.5). Appropriately, words that are in an agreement relationship, specifically determiners/attributes and their head noun, or subjects and their verb, are bigrams in this representation, which makes the metric sensitive to the quality of agreement. Word order in the surface string is ignored, which makes the metric insensitive to reordering errors, but could also be appropriate for languages with a free word order. Liu and Gildea [2005] find that both HWCM and STM correlate better with human judgments than BLEU. Owczarzak et al. [2007] define a metric which extract (labeled) dependency structures from LFG parse trees, and computes the f-score between the structures of the reference and the translation hypothesis.

A drawback of syntactic metrics is that they rely on a syntactic parse of the reference translation and the automatic system output. This requires language-specific resources for syntactic parsing, and it is hard to predict how well parsers will perform at annotating the texts produced by MT systems, which are typically far more noisy than the texts that parsers are trained on and developed for. A method of avoiding to parse the translation output was proposed by Yu et al. [2014], who only parse the reference translation, extract its head-word chains, and then use string matching to find correspondences of the head-word chains in the translation hypotheses. For models with target syntax, we can also directly use the internal tree structure of the automatic translation for the evaluation.

While human judgements are the final authority for evaluation, automatic evaluation metrics are used during system development, for instance for tuning the parameters of the log-linear model. BLEU is commonly used as objective function, but may not be the best choice. Sennrich [2015] optimized the log-linear parameters of a syntax-based SMT system on an interpolation of BLEU and (a variant of) HWCM. The inclusion of a syntactic metric as an objective function led to a higher weighting of a dependency language model, compared to optimizing on BLEU alone, and the resulting system produced better translations with fewer agreement errors than the system optimized on BLEU.

CHAPTER 7

Closing Remarks

7.1 WHICH APPROACH IS BEST?

Phrase-based and syntax-based translation are the two dominant paradigms in statistical machine translation. In many ways, syntax-based translation can be viewed as the natural successor to the phrase-based approach, just as phrase-based models succeeded word-based ones. While the purpose of this book was not to argue this case, consider many of the following supporting points that have been discussed herein. The rules that constitute syntax-based systems generalize phrases in a compelling way, by permitting gaps. Decoding with syntax is theoretically less computationally complex (polynomial in the input string, vs. NP-hard [Knight, 1999]). In practice, the reliance of syntax-based systems on parsers and their larger model sizes make them slower, but they expose easily-turned knobs that often permit near-parity in speed to phrase-based approaches. The structure provided by syntax-based translation allows reorderings over much longer distances to be explored in a systematic, empirically justified way.

At the same time, the paradigms are rightly aligned, not as old vs. new, but as competitive peers. Chronologically, their development has been largely parallel and intertwined. Syntax-based decoding, with its roots in 1960s-era compiler theory, precedes the stack-based decoding approach underlying phrase-based translation. But in terms of functioning systems, syntax-based approaches have lagged behind word- and phrase-based ones by a few years, from the original respective proposals in the late 1990s to the advent of each system's dominant instantiation in the mid 2000s. In applications where raw speed is of primary consideration, phrase-based decoding is the hands-down winner. Finally, many people also find phrase-based decoding to be conceptually simpler, whereas syntactic methods require a deeper understanding of natural language processing data structures and algorithms.

In light of these comparisons, it is natural to ask: which is the best approach?

It is impossible to answer such a question outside a particular use case and a set of objectives. For example, a key and growing use of machine translation is in *computer-aided translation* (CAT), whose goal is to assist translators and increase their efficiency. Distinct from post-editing, where translators correct the output of an MT system, CAT works with the translators during the translation process, making suggestions as they work through a sentence in a left-to-right manner. Although left-to-right syntax-based decoding algorithms have been developed, most syntax-based methods are non-directional and are hard to apply in this setting.

A more compatible use case for syntax-based output is in the consumption of automatically translated documents by human users, say, to enable one to understand a foreign news site. But even within that task, myriad questions must be answered. The issue is complicated by the fact that "syntax-based MT" encompasses a lot of different approaches (string-to-string, string-to-tree, and so on). The following guidelines provide a useful summary.

- *How different are the two languages?* Syntax-based approaches have worked best in settings with typologically distinct language pairs where reordering is more of an issue. This includes language pairs like Chinese—English, Arabic—English, and English—German.

- *What tools are available?* The use of syntax obviously requires the availability of linguistic parsing tools, whether dependency or constituency. With the exception of tree-to-tree models, a parser is required only on one side. This is fortunate because, in practice, English is often one of these language pairs, and means that many tools are likely available.

- *How important is quality?* Syntax-based approaches can achieve higher quality than phrase-based models for some language pairs, and are good candidates for settings where higher-quality translations produce a tangible benefit, such as reduced post-editing effort. If only the gist of a document is required, any hypothetical quality that could be gained from a syntax-based approach is unlikely to matter.

- *How much time is available to translate the page?* Computers are constantly getting faster, as are syntax-based decoding algorithms (Section 5.5.3). But given a fixed amount of computing infrastructure, it is likely that a phrase-based approach will yield a higher translation throughput. This is again related to the objectives being pursued: if speed and cost are of the utmost importance, phrase-based or string-to-string translation may be best. If the quality of the output is the highest concern, a deeper look into potential benefits of syntax, along with the potential tradeoffs, is warranted.

- *How well formed is the input?* Tree-to-string translation is dependent on a source-side parse. We have already noted that this parse is almost certainly an automatic one, and therefore will contain errors that have downstream effects on the MT system. These errors can grow quickly, however, when applied to ungrammatical text or text from a different domain used to train the parser. Thus, even for language pairs where such a tree-to-string system had been shown to be best, cascading errors could seriously affect performance.

- *How well formed does the output need to be?* As we saw in the previous chapter, an advantage of string-to-tree systems is the ability to model language-specific details related to text grammaticality. The ability to condition on rich target-side structure has only just begun to receive attention, and it is likely that future string-to-tree models will further capitalize on this advantage.

- *How much person-time is available for developing the system?* Syntactic approaches, particularly ones employing language-specific grammars and linguistic tools, require specialized attention. Lessons learned for a single language may not generalize. Independent work developing universal dependency grammar formalisms may help mitigate this.

Ultimately, the question is an empirical one. The wide range of available, well-documented and supported, open-source translation systems—many of which include both phrase-based and syntax-based decoders—means that the choice of which paradigm to use is one that can be answered by the tried-and-true method of experimentation.

7.2   WHAT'S NEXT?

As the saying goes, it's dangerous to make predictions, especially about the future. In many ways, the question of what lies ahead for statistical machine translation is a question of what lies ahead for machine translation in general. There are, however, a few areas of early and trending work that we think have particular bearing on the syntax question.

The balance between universality and specificity   Most recent work on syntax-based approaches has been focused on constituency-grammar. This presents a problem: relatively few languages have well-developed constituency grammars, and even fewer have treebanks that can be used to train such grammars. As noted above, pairing with English allows the use of syntax in learning SCFG rules, which can then be applied in either direction. But in order to really utilize the parse tree, we are effectively limited to tree-to-string systems *out of* English and string-to-tree ones *into* it. This raises an important question in MT research: whether to focus our efforts on what's common to most translation pairs, or to focus on language-specific issues. The former approach is reflected in efforts such as the *Universal Dependencies Project* [McDonald et al., 2013], and there is certainly much to be learned from it. On the other hand, it is clear that there is also much to gain from language-specific efforts, as well. This can also be viewed as a classic trade-off between engineering and science. Exactly where the inflection point shifts in favor of specificity for a particular language pair, and when and whether it's worthwhile to chase this long tail, remains an important issue.

Morphology   Syntax-based MT constructs richer representations of the source and target sentences than does phrase-based MT, but at the very bottom, they are the same: word tokens are represented as unrelated integers. There is no modeling of the complex relationships between words reflected in inflectional and derivational morphology. It is quite clear that this misses important generalizations, and that this can impact the entire translation pipeline, beginning with word segmentation and alignment. But morphology is another area where the desire for language universals is pitted against the need for specific human-informed models of particular languages. Most languages do not have morphological analyzers, and many of the tools that do exist are hand-built symbolic (not statistical) ones. Although there is hope that morphology can eventually be approached in a language-neutral way, we expect that in the interim there will be lots of language-specific work required.

Semantics   The fundamental goal of translation is to preserve the meaning of the source text. Syntactic models do not explicitly model semantic equivalence, and there are many situations where semantic representations generalize over syntactic variations, such as the active-passive shift. A compelling extension to syntactic models is therefore semantic models that more explicitly capture the meaning of translation units, and ensure that meaning is preserved during translations. There have been promising pilot studies in the semantic annotation of parallel corpora [e.g., Bos, 2014, Sulem et al., 2015, Xue et al., 2014], but research is still at an early stage. (Similar, in many ways, to the status of work on syntax in the early 2000s). Given the dependence of semantics on syntax, we expect that syntax will remain an important component of these efforts.

Neural networks   Finally, over the past few years, neural networks have proven to be a disruptive technology in statistical machine translation. An important open question is whether these approaches will establish themselves as a third translation paradigm, on par with phrase-based and syntax-based ones. That is a distinct possibility. However, it is also likely that neural networks will continue to complement syntax-based machine translation. The relatively recent advance in neural approaches described in Devlin et al. [2014], for example, was in fact integrated into a syntax-based (Hiero) translation system. In both cases, it is safe to say that neural networks will significantly shape the future of machine translation.

APPENDIX A

Open-Source Tools

There are many open-source packages for hierarchical and syntax-based model extraction and translation. We here provide a list of some popular tools.

Name	Description	License	Last Updated
cdec	Hiero extractor and SCFG decoder written in C++. cdec-decoder.org	Apache 2.0	2016
GHKM	The original GHKM extractor, written by Michel Galley. Java-based. github.com/joshua-decoder/galley-ghkm	GPL 2.0	2012
Jane	Hiero extraction, hierarchical and phrase-based translation. C++. www-i6.informatik.rwth-aachen.de/jane	Non-commercial	2014
Joshua	Hierarchical and phrase-based decoder. Java. joshua-decoder.org	Apache 2.0	2016
Moses	Phrase-based and syntax-based decoder. Includes tools for extracting Hiero, SAMT, and GHKM grammars. C++. statmt.org/moses	LGPL	2016
NiuTrans	Phrase-based, hierarchical, and syntax-based decoder. C++. www.nlplab.com/NiuPlan/NiuTrans.html	GPL 2.0	2014
SAMT	The original SAMT extractor. Hadoop-based. www.cs.cmu.edu/~zollmann/samt	GPL	2010
Thrax	Hadoop-based Java-tool for Hiero and SAMT grammar extraction. Included with Joshua, available separately at github.com/joshua-decoder/thrax	BSD 2-clause	2015
Travatar	Tree-to-string decoder written in C++. www.phontron.com/travatar	LGPL	2016
UCAM-SMT	Hierarchical phrase-based statistical machine translation system based on OpenFST. ucam-smt.github.io	Apache 2.0	2015

Bibliography

Waleed Ammar, Victor Chahuneau, Michael Denkowski, Greg Hanneman, Wang Ling, Austin Matthews, Kenton Murray, Nicola Segall, Alon Lavie, and Chris Dyer. The CMU machine translation systems at WMT 2013: syntax, synthetic translation options, and pseudo-references. In *Proc. of the 8th Workshop on Statistical Machine Translation*, pages 70–77, Sofia, Bulgaria, August 2013. Association for Computational Linguistics. 141

Abhishek Arun, Chris Dyer, Barry Haddow, Phil Blunsom, Adam Lopez, and Philipp Koehn. Monte Carlo inference and maximization for phrase-based translation. In *Proc. of the 13th Conference on Computational Natural Language Learning (CoNLL-2009)*, pages 102–110, Boulder, CO, June 2009. Association for Computational Linguistics. DOI: 10.3115/1596374.1596394. 22

Collin F. Baker, Charles J. Fillmore, and John B. Lowe. The Berkeley FrameNet project. In *Proc. of the 36th Annual Meeting of the Association for Computational Linguistics and 17th International Conference on Computational Linguistics*, vol. 1, pages 86–90, Montreal, Quebec, Canada, 1998. Association for Computational Linguistics. DOI: 10.3115/980845.980860. 146

Kathy Baker, Steven Bethard, Michael Bloodgood, Ralf Brown, Chris Callison-Burch, Glen Coppersmith, Bonnie Dorr, Wes Filardo, Kendall Giles, Ann Irvine, Mike Kayser, Lori Levin, Jusin Martineau, Jim Mayfield, Scott Miller, Aaron Philips, Andrew Philpot, Christine Piatko, Lane Schwartz, and David Zajic. Semantically informed machine translation (SIMT). Technical report, Johns Hopkins University Human Language Technology Center of Excellence, 2009. 39

Yehoshua Bar-Hillel, Micha A. Perles, and Eli Shamir. On formal properties of simple phrase structure grammars. *Zeitschrift für Phonetik, Sprachwissenschaft und Kommunikationsforschung*, (14), pages 143–172, 1961. DOI: 10.1524/stuf.1961.14.14.143. 78

Marzieh Bazrafshan and Daniel Gildea. Semantic roles for string to tree machine translation. In *Proc. of the 51st Annual Meeting of the Association for Computational Linguistics*, vol. 2, Short Papers, pages 419–423, Sofia, Bulgaria, 2013. 146

Phil Blunsom and Miles Osborne. Probabilistic inference for machine translation. In *Proc. of the 2008 Conference on Empirical Methods in Natural Language Processing*, pages 215–223, Honolulu, HI, October 2008. Association for Computational Linguistics. DOI: 10.3115/1613715.1613746. 22

Ondřej Bojar, Silvie Cinková, and Jan Ptácek. Towards English-to-Czech MT via tectogrammatical layer. *Prague Bull. Math. Linguistics*, 90, pages 57–68, 2008. DOI: 10.2478/v10108-009-0007-5. 133

Ondřej Bojar, Christian Buck, Christian Federmann, Barry Haddow, Philipp Koehn, Johannes Leveling, Christof Monz, Pavel Pecina, Matt Post, Hervé Saint-Amand, Radu Soricut, Lucia Specia, and Aleš Tamchyna. Findings of the 2014 Workshop on Statistical Machine Translation. In *Proc. of the 9th Workshop on Statistical Machine Translation*, pages 12–58, Baltimore, MD, June 2014. Association for Computational Linguistics. DOI: 10.3115/v1/w14-3302. xiv

Ondřej Bojar, Rajen Chatterjee, Christian Federmann, Barry Haddow, Matthias Huck, Chris Hokamp, Philipp Koehn, Varvara Logacheva, Christof Monz, Matteo Negri, Matt Post, Carolina Scarton, Lucia Specia, and Marco Turchi. Findings of the 2015 Workshop on Statistical Machine Translation. In *Proc. of the 10th Workshop on Statistical Machine Translation*, pages 1–46, Lisbon, Portugal, September 2015. Association for Computational Linguistics. DOI: 10.18653/v1/w15-3001. xiv

Johan Bos. Semantic annotation issues in parallel meaning banking. In *Proc. of the Tenth Joint ACL-ISO Workshop of Interoperable Semantic Annotations (ISA-10)*, pages 17–20, Reykjavik, Iceland, 2014. 156

Eric Brill. A simple rule-based part of speech tagger. In *Proc. of the 3rd Conference on Applied Natural Language Processing*, ANLC '92, pages 152–155, Trento, Italy, 1992. Association for Computational Linguistics. DOI: 10.3115/974499.974526. 128

Peter F. Brown, Vincent J. Della Pietra, Stephen A. Della Pietra, and Robert L. Mercer. The mathematics of statistical machine translation: Parameter estimation. *Computational Linguistics*, 19 (2), pages 263–311, June 1993. 19, 20

Sabine Buchholz and Erwin Marsi. CoNLL-X shared task on multilingual dependency parsing. In *Proc. of the 10th Conference on Computational Natural Language Learning (CoNLL-X)*, pages 149–164, New York City, 2006. Association for Computational Linguistics. DOI: 10.3115/1596276.1596305. 133

Andrea Burbank, Marine Carpuat, Stephen Clark, Marcus Dreyer, Pamela Fox, Declan Groves, Keith Hall, Mary Hearne, I. Dan Melamed, Yihai Shen, Andy Way, Benjamin Wellington, and Dekai Wu. Final report of the 2005 language engineering workshop on statistical machine translation by parsing. Technical Report, Johns Hopkins University Center for Speech and Language Processing. 134

David Burkett and Dan Klein. Transforming trees to improve syntactic convergence. In *Proc. of the 2012 Joint Conference on Empirical Methods in Natural Language Processing and Computational Natural Language Learning*, pages 863–872, Jeju Island, Korea, July 2012. Association for Computational Linguistics. 128, 129

Chris Callison-Burch, Miles Osborne, and Philipp Koehn. Re-evaluating the role of BLEU in machine translation research. In *Proc. the 11th Conference of the European Chapter of the Association for Computational Linguistics*, pages 249–256, Trento, Italy, 2006. 150

Marie Candito, Benoît Crabbé, and Pascal Denis. Statistical French dependency parsing: treebank conversion and first results. In *Proc. of the 7th International Conference on Language Resources and Evaluation (LREC'10)*, Valletta, Malta, May 2010. European Language Resources Association (ELRA). 142

Xavier Carreras and Michael Collins. Non-projective parsing for statistical machine translation. In *Proc. of the 2009 Conference on Empirical Methods in Natural Language Processing*, pages 200–209. Association for Computational Linguistics, 2009. DOI: 10.3115/1699510.1699537. 134

Jean-Cédric Chappelier and Martin Rajman. A generalized CYK algorithm for parsing stochastic CFG. In *Proc. of the 1st Workshop on Tabulation in Parsing and Deduction*, pages 133–137, 1998. 114, 115

Eugene Charniak. Immediate-head parsing for language models. In *Proc. of the 39th Annual Meeting on Association for Computational Linguistics*, ACL '01, pages 124–131, 2001. DOI: 10.3115/1073012.1073029. 28, 145

Eugene Charniak, Kevin Knight, and Kenji Yamada. Syntax-based language models for statistical machine translation. In *MT Summit IX*, New Orleans, 2003. 28, 29, 145

Ciprian Chelba and Frederick Jelinek. Exploiting syntactic structure for language modeling. In *Proc. of the 36th Annual Meeting on Association for Computational Linguistics*, 1998. DOI: 10.3115/980451.980882. 29

Colin Cherry and Dekang Lin. A comparison of syntactically motivated word alignment spaces. In *Proc. the 11th Conference of the European Chapter of the Association for Computational Linguistics*, Trento, Italy, 2006. 28

Colin Cherry and Chris Quirk. Discriminative, syntactic language modeling through latent SVMs. In *Proc. of the 8th Conference of the Association for Machine Translation in the Americas*, 2008., Waikiki, HI, October 2008. 30

David Chiang. A hierarchical phrase-based model for statistical machine translation. In *Proc. of the 43rd Annual Meeting on Association for Computational Linguistics*, pages 263–270, Ann Arbor, MI, 2005. DOI: 10.3115/1219840.1219873. 29

David Chiang. Hierarchical phrase-based translation. *Computational Linguistics*, 33(2), pages 201–228, 2007. ISSN 0891-2017. DOI: 10.1162/coli.2007.33.2.201. 29, 34, 61, 100, 123, 137

David Chiang. Learning to translate with source and target syntax. In *Proc. of the 48th Annual Meeting of the Association for Computational Linguistics*, pages 1443–1452, Uppsala, Sweden, 2010. 28, 130

David Chiang, Kevin Knight, and Wei Wang. 11,001 new features for statistical machine translation. In *Proc. of Human Language Technologies: The 2009 Annual Conference of the North American Chapter of the Association for Computational Linguistics*, pages 218–226, Boulder, CO, 2009. DOI: 10.3115/1620754.1620786. 25, 129

Noam Chomsky. *Syntactic Structures*. Mouton, The Hague, Netherlands, 1957. DOI: 10.1515/9783110218329. 133

Noam Chomsky. *Aspects of the Theory of Syntax*. MIT Press, Cambridge, MA, 1965. 143

Tagyoung Chung, Licheng Fang, and Daniel Gildea. Issues concerning decoding with synchronous context-free grammar. In *Proc. of the 49th Annual Meeting of the Association for Computational Linguistics: Human Language Technologies*, pages 413–417, Portland, OR, June 2011. 42, 74

Jonathan Clark, Chris Dyer, and Alon Lavie. Locally non-linear learning for statistical machine translation via discretization and structured regularization. *Transactions of the Association for Computational Linguistics*, 2, pages 393–404, 2014. 23

John Cocke and Jacob T. Schwartz. Programming languages and their compilers: Preliminary notes. Technical report, Courant Institute of Mathematical Sciences, New York University, NY, 1970. 67

Michael Collins. Head-driven statistical models for natural language parsing. *Computational Linguistics*, 29, pages 589–637, 2003. DOI: 10.1162/089120103322753356. 145

John DeNero, Mohit Bansal, Adam Pauls, and Dan Klein. Efficient parsing for transducer grammars. In *Proc. of Human Language Technologies: The 2009 Annual Conference of the North American Chapter of the Association for Computational Linguistics*, pages 227–235, Boulder, CO, 2009a. DOI: 10.3115/1620754.1620788. 111, 112

John DeNero, Adam Pauls, and Dan Klein. Asynchronous binarization for synchronous grammars. In *Proc. of the ACL-IJCNLP 2009 Conference Short Papers*, pages 141–144, Singapore, 2009b. Association for Computational Linguistics. DOI: 10.3115/1667583.1667627. 111

Jacob Devlin, Rabih Zbib, Zhongqiang Huang, Thomas Lamar, Richard Schwartz, and John Makhoul. Fast and robust neural network joint models for statistical machine translation. In *Proc. of the 52nd Annual Meeting of the Association for Computational Linguistics*, vol. 1, Long Papers, pages 1370–1380, Baltimore, MD, 2014. DOI: 10.3115/v1/p14-1129. 156

Yuan Ding and Martha Palmer. Machine translation using probabilistic synchronous dependency insertion grammars. In *Proc. of the 43rd Annual Meeting of the Association for Computational Linguistics (ACL'05)*, pages 541–548, Ann Arbor, MI, June 2005. DOI: 10.3115/1219840.1219907. 100

Bonnie Dorr. Machine translation divergences: A formal description and proposed solution. *Computational Linguistics*, 20 (4), pages 597–633, 1994.

Jay Earley. An efficient context-free parsing algorithm. *Communications of the ACM*, 13(2), pages 94–102, February 1970. DOI: 10.1145/357980.358005. 114

Jason Eisner. Learning non-isomorphic tree mappings for machine translation. In *Proc. of the 41st Annual Meeting on Association for Computational Linguistics*, 2003. DOI: 10.3115/1075178.1075217. 28, 99

Jeffrey L. Elman. Distributed representations, simple recurrent networks, and grammatical structure. In *Machine Learning*, pages 195–225, 1991. DOI: 10.1007/bf00114844. 141

Licheng Fang, Tagyoung Chung, and Daniel Gildea. Terminal-Aware Synchronous Binarization. In *Proc. of the 49th Annual Meeting of the Association for Computational Linguistics: Human Language Technologies*, pages 401–406, Portland, OR, June 2011. 111

Cynthia Fisher, Henry Gleitman, and Lila R. Gleitman. On the semantic content of subcategorization frames. *Cognitive Psychology*, 23(3), pages 331–392, July 1991. DOI: 10.1016/0010-0285(91)90013-e. 144

Heidi J. Fox. Phrasal cohesion and statistical machine translation. In *Proc. of the ACL-02 Conference on Empirical Methods in Natural Language Processing*, Philadelphia, PA, July 2002. DOI: 10.3115/1118693.1118732. 29

Alexander Fraser, Marion Weller, Aoife Cahill, and Fabienne Cap. Modeling inflection and word-formation in SMT. In *Proc. of the 13th Conference of the European Chapter of the Association for Computational Linguistics*, pages 664–674, Avignon, France, 2012. 141

Alexander Fraser, Helmut Schmid, Richárd Farkas, Renjing Wang, and Hinrich Schütze. Knowledge sources for constituent parsing of German, a morphologically rich and less-configurational language. *Computational Linguistics*, 2013. DOI: 10.1162/coli_a_00135. 45

Haim Gaifman. Dependency systems and phrase-structure systems. *Information and Control*, 8(3), pages 304–337, 1965. DOI: 10.1016/s0019-9958(65)90232-9. 134

Michel Galley, Mark Hopkins, Kevin Knight, and Daniel Marcu. What's in a translation rule? In *Proc. of the Main Conference on Human Language Technology Conference of the North American Chapter of the Association of Computational Linguistics*, Boston, MA, May 2004. 29, 40, 41

Michel Galley, Jonathan Graehl, Kevin Knight, Daniel Marcu, Steve DeNeefe, Wei Wang, and Ignacio Thayer. Scalable inference and training of context-rich syntactic translation models. In *Proc. of the 21st International Conference on Computational Linguistics and the 44th Annual Meeting of the Association for Computational Linguistics*, Sydney, Australia, July 2006. DOI: 10.3115/1220175.1220296. 18, 19, 20, 23, 26, 29, 40, 42, 43

Giorgio Gallo, Giustino Longo, Stefano Pallottino, and Sang Nguyen. Directed hypergraphs and applications. *Discrete Applied Mathematics*, 42(2–3), pages 177–201, 1993. DOI: 10.1016/0166-218x(93)90045-p. 67

Ulrich Germann, Eric Joanis, and Samuel Larkin. Tightly packed tries: How to fit large models into memory, and make them load fast, too. In *Proc. of the Workshop on Software Engineering, Testing, and Quality Assurance for Natural Language Processing (SETQA-NLP 2009)*, pages 31–39, Boulder, CO, June 2009. Association for Computational Linguistics. DOI: 10.3115/1621947.1621952. 123

Spence Green, Daniel Cer, and Christopher D. Manning. An empirical comparison of features and tuning for phrase-based machine translation. In *Proc. of the 9th Workshop on Statistical Machine Translation*, pages 466–476, Baltimore, MD, June 2014. Association for Computational Linguistics. DOI: 10.3115/v1/w14-3360. 25

Jan Hajič, Alena Böhmová, Eva Hajičová, and Barbora Vidová-Hladká. The Prague Dependency Treebank: A Three-Level Annotation Scenario. In A. Abeillé, Ed., *Treebanks: Building and Using Parsed Corpora*, pages 103–127. Amsterdam, Kluwer, 2000. DOI: 10.1007/978-94-010-0201-1. 133

Eva Hajičová, Jiří Havelka, Petr Sgall, Kateřina Veselá, and Daniel Zeman. Issues of projectivity in the Prague Dependency Treebank. *Prague Bulletin of Mathematical Linguistics*, (81), pages 5–22, 2004. 133

Greg Hanneman and Alon Lavie. Automatic category label coarsening for syntax-based machine translation. In *Proc. of the 5th Workshop on Syntax, Semantics and Structure in Statistical Translation*, SSST-5, pages 98–106, Portland, OR, 2011. Association for Computational Linguistics. ISBN 978-1-932432-99-2. 130

Christian Hardmeier and Marcello Federico. Modelling Pronominal Anaphora in Statistical Machine Translation. In Marcello Federico, Ian Lane, Michael Paul, and François Yvon, Eds., *Proc. of the 7th International Workshop on Spoken Language Translation (IWSLT)*, pages 283–289, 2010. 143

Christian Hardmeier, Jörg Tiedemann, Markus Saers, Marcello Federico, and Prashant Mathur. The Uppsala-FBK systems at WMT 2011. In *Proc. of the 6th Workshop on Statistical Machine Translation*, pages 372–378, 2011. 134

Kenneth Heafield. KenLM: faster and smaller language model queries. In *Proc. of the 6th Workshop on Statistical Machine Translation*, pages 187–197, Edinburgh, Scotland, July 2011. Association for Computational Linguistics. 78

Kenneth Heafield, Philipp Koehn, and Alon Lavie. Language model rest costs and space-efficient storage. In *Proc. of the 2012 Joint Conference on Empirical Methods in Natural Language Processing and Computational Natural Language Learning*, pages 1169–1178, Jeju Island, Korea, July 2012. Association for Computational Linguistics. 83

Kenneth Heafield, Philipp Koehn, and Alon Lavie. Grouping language model boundary words to speed K-best extraction from hypergraphs. In *Proc. of the 2013 Conference of the North American Chapter of the Association for Computational Linguistics: Human Language Technologies*, Atlanta, GA, June 2013. 92, 93, 94, 95, 96, 97

Josée S. Heemskerk. A probabilistic context-free grammar for disambiguation in morphological parsing. In *Proc. of the 6th Conference on European Chapter of the Association for Computational Linguistics*, EACL '93, pages 183–192, Utrecht, The Netherlands, 1993. DOI: 10.3115/976744.976767. 147

Mark Hopkins and Greg Langmead. Cube pruning as heuristic search. In *Proc. of the 2009 Conference on Empirical Methods in Natural Language Processing*, pages 62–71, Singapore, 2009. Association for Computational Linguistics. DOI: 10.3115/1699510.1699519. 100

Mark Hopkins and Greg Langmead. SCFG decoding without binarization. In *Proc. of the 2010 Conference on Empirical Methods in Natural Language Processing*, pages 646–655, Cambridge, MA, October 2010. Association for Computational Linguistics. 111, 112, 113

Liang Huang. Forest reranking: discriminative parsing with non-local features. In *Proc. of the 45th Annual Meeting of the Association for Computational Linguistics*, pages 586–594, Columbus, OH, June 2008. Association for Computational Linguistics. 100

Liang Huang and David Chiang. Better k-best parsing. In *Parsing '05: Proc. of the 9th International Workshop on Parsing Technology*, pages 53–64, Vancouver, Canada, 2005. Association for Computational Linguistics. DOI: 10.3115/1654494.1654500. 61, 63, 67

Liang Huang and David Chiang. Forest rescoring: faster decoding with integrated language models. In *Proc. of the 45th Annual Meeting of the Association of Computational Linguistics*, pages 144–151, Prague, Czech Republic, June 2007. 29, 61, 89, 90, 92, 100

Liang Huang, Kevin Knight, and Aravind Joshi. Statistical syntax-directed translation with extended domain of locality. In *Proc. of the 7th Conference of the Association for Machine Translation in the Americas*, pages 66–73, 2006. 29, 100

Liang Huang, Hao Zhang, Daniel Gildea, and Kevin Knight. Binarization of synchronous context-free grammars. *Computational Linguistics*, 35(4), pages 559–595, 2009. DOI: 10.1162/coli.2009.35.4.35406. 110

Matthias Huck, Hieu Hoang, and Philipp Koehn. Preference grammars and soft syntactic constraints for GHKM syntax-based statistical machine translation. In *Proc. of SSST-8, 8th Workshop on Syntax, Semantics and Structure in Statistical Translation*, pages 148–156, Doha, Qatar, 2014. Association for Computational Linguistics. DOI: 10.3115/v1/w14-4018. 131

Peter Ihm and Yves Lecerf. Éléments pour une grammaire générale des langues projectives. Centre commun de recherche nucléaire, Etablissement d'Ispra, Centre de traitement de l'information scientifique. CETIS, 1963. 133

Minwoo Jeong, Kristina Toutanova, Hisami Suzuki, and Chris Quirk. A discriminative lexicon model for complex morphology. In *The 9th Conference of the Association for Machine Translation in the Americas*. Association for Computational Linguistics, 2010. 141

Mark Johnson. PCFG models of linguistic tree representations. *Computational Linguistics*, 24(4), pages 613–632, 1998. 129

Mark Johnson, Thomas L. Griffiths, and Sharon Goldwater. Bayesian inference for PCFGs via Markov chain Monte Carlo. In *Proc. of Human Language Technologies 2007: The Conference of the North American Chapter of the Association for Computational Linguistics*, 2007. 147

Miriam Kaeshammer. Hierarchical machine translation with discontinuous phrases. In *Proc. of the 10th Workshop on Statistical Machine Translation*, pages 228–238, Lisbon, Portugal, September 2015. Association for Computational Linguistics. DOI: 10.18653/v1/w15-3028. 134

Ronald M Kaplan, Klaus Netter, Jürgen Wedekind, and Annie Zaenen. Translation by Structural Correspondences. In Sergei Nirenburg, Harold L. Somers, and Yorick A. Wilks, Eds., *Readings in Machine Translation*. MIT Press, 2003. 27

Tadao Kasami. An efficient recognition and syntax-analysis algorithm for context-free languages. Technical report, Air Force Cambridge Research Lab, Bedford, MA, 1965. 67

Martin Kay. Functional unification grammar: A formalism for machine translation. In *Proc. of the 10th International Conference on Computational Linguistics and 22nd Annual Meeting on Association for Computational Linguistics*, pages 75–78, Stroudsburg, PA, 1984. DOI: 10.3115/980491.980509. 27

Dan Klein and Christopher D. Manning. Parsing and hypergraphs. In *7th International Workshop on Parsing Technologies*, pages 123–134, Bejing, China, 2001a. DOI: 10.1007/1-4020-2295-6_18. 67

Dan Klein and Christopher D. Manning. Parsing with treebank grammars: Empirical bounds, theoretical models, and the structure of the penn treebank. In *Proc. of 39th Annual Meeting of the Association for Computational Linguistics*, pages 338–345, Toulouse, France, July 2001b. DOI: 10.3115/1073012.1073056. 123

Kevin Knight. Decoding complexity in word-replacement translation models. *Computational Linguistics*, 25(4), pages 607–615, 1999. 153

Kevin Knight and Jonathan Graehl. An Overview of Probabilistic Tree Transducers for Natural Language Processing. In Alexander F. Gelbukh and Alexander F. Gelbukh, Eds., *CICLing*, vol. 3406 of *Lecture Notes in Computer Science*, pages 1–24. Springer, 2005. 6, 98

Philipp Koehn. *Statistical Machine Translation*. Cambridge University Press, New York, NY, 2010. DOI: 10.1017/cbo9780511815829. xv

Philipp Koehn and Hieu Hoang. Factored Translation Models. In *Proc. of the 2007 Joint Conference on Empirical Methods in Natural Language Processing and Computational Natural Language Learning (EMNLP-CoNLL)*, pages 868–876, Prague, Czech Republic, 2007. Association for Computational Linguistics. 141

Philipp Koehn and Kevin Knight. Empirical Methods for Compound Splitting. In *Proc. of the 10th Conference on European Chapter of the Association for Computational Linguistics*, pages 187–193, Budapest, Hungary, 2003. DOI: 10.3115/1067807.1067833. 147

Philipp Koehn, Franz Josef Och, and Daniel Marcu. Statistical phrase-based translation. In *Proc. of the 2003 Conference of the North American Chapter of the Association for Computational Linguistics on Human Language Technology*, pages 48–54, Edmonton, Canada, 2003. Association for Computational Linguistics. DOI: 10.3115/1073445.1073462. 19, 20, 29, 36, 40, 126

Philipp Koehn, Abhishek Arun, and Hieu Hoang. Towards better machine translation quality for the German-English language pairs. In *Proc. of the 3rd Workshop on Statistical Machine Translation*, pages 139–142, Columbus, OH, June 2008. Association for Computational Linguistics. DOI: 10.3115/1626394.1626412. 2

Marco Kuhlmann. Mildly Non-Projective Dependency Grammar. *Computational Linguistics*, 39(2), pages 355–387, 2013. DOI: 10.1162/coli_a_00125. 134

Marco Kuhlmann and Joakim Nivre. Mildly non-projective dependency structures. In *21st International Conference on Computational Linguistics and 44th Annual Meeting of the Association for Computational Linguistics*, Sydney, Australia, 2006. DOI: 10.3115/1273073.1273139. 134

Jan Landsbergen. Montague Grammar and Machine Translation. In Sergei Nirenburg, Harold L. Somers, and Yorick A. Wilks, Eds., *Readings in Machine Translation*. MIT Press, 2003. 27

Junhui Li, Philip Resnik, and Hal Daumé III. Modeling syntactic and semantic structures in hierarchical phrase-based translation. In *Proc. of the 2013 Conference of the North American Chapter of the Association for Computational Linguistics: Human Language Technologies*, pages 540–549, Atlanta, GA, June 2013. 74

Zhifei Li and Sanjeev Khudanpur. A scalable decoder for parsing-based machine translation with equivalent language model state maintenance. In *Proc. of the NAACL-HLT/AMTA Workshop on Syntax and Structure in Statistical Translation*, page 10, 2008. DOI: 10.3115/1626269.1626271. 83

Percy Liang, Ben Taskar, and Dan Klein. Alignment by agreement. In *Proc. of the Main Conference on Human Language Technology Conference of the North American Chapter of the Association of Computational Linguistics*, pages 104–111, 2006. DOI: 10.3115/1220835.1220849. 31

Dekang Lin. A path-based transfer model for machine translation. In *Proc. of the 18th International Conference on Computational Linguistics (Coling 2004)*, pages 625–630, Geneva, Switzerland, Aug. 23–27 2004. DOI: 10.3115/1220355.1220445. 100

Ding Liu and Daniel Gildea. Syntactic features for evaluation of machine translation. In *Proc. of the ACL Workshop on Intrinsic and Extrinsic Evaluation Measures for Machine Translation and/or Summarization*, pages 25–32, Ann Arbor, MI, 2005. 150, 151

Ding Liu and Daniel Gildea. Improved tree-to-string transducer for machine translation. In *Proc. of the 3rd Workshop on Statistical Machine Translation*, pages 62–69, Columbus, OH, 2008. Association for Computational Linguistics. DOI: 10.3115/1626394.1626402. 146

Yang Liu, Qun Liu, and Shouxun Lin. Tree-to-string alignment template for statistical machine translation. In *Proc. of the 21st International Conference on Computational Linguistics and the 44th Annual Meeting of the Association for Computational Linguistics*, pages 609–616, 2006. DOI: 10.3115/1220175.1220252. 29, 100

Adam Lopez. Statistical machine translation. *ACM Comput. Surv.*, 40(3), pages 1–49, 2008. DOI: 10.1145/1380584.1380586. xv

Adam Lopez. Translation as weighted deduction. In *Proc. of the 12th Conference of the European Chapter of the Association of Computational Linguistics (EACL 2009)*, pages 532–540, Athens, Greece, March 2009. Association for Computational Linguistics. DOI: 10.3115/1609067.1609126. 123

Matous Machacek and Ondřej Bojar. Results of the WMT14 metrics shared task. In *Proc. of the 9th Workshop on Statistical Machine Translation*, pages 293–301, Baltimore, MD, June 2014. Association for Computational Linguistics. DOI: 10.3115/v1/w14-3336. 149

Daniel Marcu and William Wong. A phrase-based, joint probability model for statistical machine translation. In *Proc. of the ACL-02 Conference on Empirical Methods in Natural Language Processing*, vol. 10, pages 133–139, Stroudsburg, PA, 2002. Association for Computational Linguistics. DOI: 10.3115/1118693.1118711. 19

Mitchell P. Marcus, Mary Ann Marcinkiewicz, and Beatrice Santorini. Building a large annotated corpus of English: The Penn Treebank. *Computational Linguistics*, 19(2), page 330, 1993. 43

Takuya Matsuzaki, Yusuke Miyao, and Jun'ichi Tsujii. Probabilistic CFG with latent annotations. In *Proc. of the Annual Meeting of the Association for Computational Linguistics (ACL)*, Ann Arbor, MI, June 2005. DOI: 10.3115/1219840.1219850. 129

Austin Matthews, Paul Baltescu, Phil Blunsom, Alon Lavie, and Chris Dyer. Tree transduction tools for cdec. *The Prague Bulletin of Mathematical Linguistics*, (102), pages 27–36, 2014. DOI: 10.2478/pralin-2014-0011. 98

Ryan McDonald, Joakim Nivre, Yvonne Quirmbach-Brundage, Yoav Goldberg, Dipanjan Das, Kuzman Ganchev, Keith Hall, Slav Petrov, Hao Zhang, Oscar Täckström, Claudia Bedini, Núria Bertomeu Castelló, and Jungmee Lee. Universal dependency annotation for multilingual parsing. In *Proc. of the 51st Annual Meeting of the Association for Computational Linguistics*, vol. 2, Short Papers, pages 92–97, Sofia, Bulgaria, August 2013. 155

I. Dan Melamed. Multitext grammars and synchronous parsers. In *Proc. of the 2003 Conference of the North American Chapter of the Association for Computational Linguistics on Human Language Technology*, pages 79–86, Edmonton, Canada, 2003. Association for Computational Linguistics. DOI: 10.3115/1073445.1073466. 110

Arul Menezes and Chris Quirk. Using dependency order templates to improve generality in translation. In *Proc. of the Second Workshop on Statistical Machine Translation at ACL 2007*. Association for Computational Linguistics, July 2007. DOI: 10.3115/1626355.1626356. 136

Arul Menezes and Chris Quirk. Syntactic models for structural word insertion and deletion during translation. In *Proc. of the 2008 Conference on Empirical Methods in Natural Language Processing*, pages 735–744, Honolulu, HI, October 2008. Association for Computational Linguistics. DOI: 10.3115/1613715.1613808. 137

Haitao Mi and Liang Huang. Forest-based translation rule extraction. In *Proc. of the 2008 Conference on Empirical Methods in Natural Language Processing*, pages 206–214, Honolulu, HI, October 2008. Association for Computational Linguistics. DOI: 10.3115/1613715.1613745. 132

Haitao Mi, Liang Huang, and Qun Liu. Forest-based translation. In *Proc. of the 45th Annual Meeting of the Association for Computational Linguistics*, pages 192–199, Columbus, OH, June 2008. Association for Computational Linguistics. 100, 131, 132

Moses Contributors. Moses Syntax Tutorial. http://www.statmt.org/moses/?n=Moses.Sy ntaxTutorial. Accessed November 28, 2015. 25

Graham Neubig and Kevin Duh. On the elements of an accurate tree-to-string machine translation system. In *Proc. of the 52nd Annual Meeting of the Association for Computational Linguistics*, vol. 2, Short Papers, pages 143–149, Baltimore, MD, June 2014. DOI: 10.3115/v1/p14-2024. 132

Joakim Nivre and Jens Nilsson. Pseudo-projective dependency parsing. In *Proc. of the 43rd Annual Meeting of the Association for Computational Linguistics*, pages 99–106, Ann Arbor, MI, 2005. DOI: 10.3115/1219840.1219853. 133

Franz Josef Och and Hermann Ney. Discriminative training and maximum entropy models for statistical machine translation. In *Proc. of the 40th Annual Meeting on Association for Computational Linguistics*, pages 295–302, Pennsylvania, PA, 2002. DOI: 10.3115/1073083.1073133. 18, 21, 36

Franz Josef Och and Hermann Ney. A systematic comparison of various statistical alignment models. *Computational Linguistics*, 29(1), pages 19–51, 2003. DOI: 10.1162/089120103321337421. 31

Franz Josef Och, Daniel Gildea, Sanjeev Khudanpur, Anoop Sarkar, Kenji Yamada, Alexander Fraser, Shankar Kumar, Libin Shen, David Smith, Katherine Eng, Viren Jain, Zhen Jin, and Dragomir Radev. A smorgasbord of features for statistical machine translation. In *Proc. of the Main Conference on Human Language Technology Conference of the North American Chapter of the Association of Computational Linguistics*, pages 161–168, Boston, MA, 2004. 30, 145

Karolina Owczarzak, Josef van Genabith, and Andy Way. Labelled dependencies in machine translation evaluation. In *Proc. of the 2nd Workshop on Statistical Machine Translation*, pages 104–111, Prague, Czech Republic, 2007. Association for Computational Linguistics. DOI: 10.3115/1626355.1626369. 151

Martha Palmer, Daniel Gildea, and Paul Kingsbury. The Proposition Bank: a corpus annotated with semantic roles. *Computational Linguistics Journal*, 31(1), 2005. 146

Kishore Papineni, Salim Roukos, Todd Ward, and Wei-Jing Zhu. BLEU: A method for automatic evaluation of machine translation. In *Proc. of the 40th Annual Meeting on Association for Computational Linguistics*, pages 311–318, Philadelphia, PA, 2002. DOI: 10.3115/1073083.1073135. 149

Slav Petrov, Leon Barrett, Romain Thibaux, and Dan Klein. Learning accurate, compact, and interpretable tree annotation. In *Proc. of the 21st International Conference on Computational Linguistics and the 44th Annual Meeting of the Association for Computational Linguistics*, pages 433–440, Sydney, Australia, 2006. DOI: 10.3115/1220175.1220230. 17, 45, 129

Martin Popel and David Mareček. Perplexity of n-Gram and Dependency Language Models. In Petr Sojka, Ales Horák, Ivan Kopecek, and Karel Pala, Eds., *Text, Speech and Dialogue*, vol. 6231 of *Lecture Notes in Computer Science*, pages 173–180. Springer, 2010. ISBN 978-3-642-15759-2. 141

Matt Post and Daniel Gildea. Parsers as language models for statistical machine translation. In *Proc. of the 8th Conference of the Association for Machine Translation in the Americas*, 2008. 30, 145

Arjen Poutsma. Data-oriented translation. In *Proc. of the 14th International Conference on Computational Linguistics (Coling 2000)*, Saarbrücken, Germany, 2000. DOI: 10.3115/992730.992738. 28

Chris Quirk, Arul Menezes, and Colin Cherry. Dependency Tree Translation: Syntactically Informed Phrasal SMT. Technical Report MSR-TR-2004-113, Microsoft Research, 2004. 100, 135, 136, 138, 141, 145, 148

Chris Quirk, Arul Menezes, and Colin Cherry. Dependency treelet translation: Syntactically informed phrasal SMT. In *Proc. of the 43rd Annual Meeting of the Association for Computational Linguistics*, Ann Arbor, MI, June 2005. DOI: 10.3115/1219840.1219874. 29, 100

Rudolf Rosa, David Mareček, and Ondřej Dušek. DEPFIX: A system for automatic correction of Czech MT outputs. In *Proc. of the 7th Workshop on Statistical Machine Translation*, pages 362–368, Montreal, Canada, 2012. Association for Computational Linguistics. 141

Lane Schwartz, Chris Callison-Burch, William Schuler, and Stephen Wu. Incremental syntactic language models for phrase-based translation. In *Proc. of the 49th Annual Meeting of the Association for Computational Linguistics: Human Language Technologies*, pages 620–631, Portland, OR, June 2011a. 30

Lane Schwartz, Chris Callison-Burch, William Schuler, and Stephen Wu. Erratum to incremental syntactic language models for phrase-based translation. In *Proc. of the 49th Annual Meeting of the Association for Computational Linguistics: Human Language Technologies*, pages 620–631, Portland, OR, June 2011b. Association for Computational Linguistics. http://dowobeha.github.io/papers/acl11.erratum.pdf 30

Nina Seemann, Fabienne Braune, and Andreas Maletti. String-to-tree multi bottom-up tree transducers. In *Proc. of the 53rd Annual Meeting of the Association for Computational Linguistics and the 7th International Joint Conference on Natural Language Processing*, vol. 1, Long Papers, pages 815–824, Beijing, China, July 2015. DOI: 10.3115/v1/p15-1079. 134

Rico Sennrich. A CYK+ variant for SCFG decoding without a dot chart. In *Proc. of SSST-8, 8th Workshop on Syntax, Semantics and Structure in Statistical Translation*, pages 94–102, Doha,

Qatar, October 2014. Association for Computational Linguistics. DOI: 10.3115/v1/w14-4011. 118

Rico Sennrich. Modelling and optimizing on syntactic n-grams for statistical machine translation. *Transactions of the Association for Computational Linguistics*, 3, pages 169–182, 2015. 141, 145, 149, 151

Rico Sennrich and Barry Haddow. A joint dependency model of morphological and syntactic structure for statistical machine translation. In *Proc. of the 2015 Conference on Empirical Methods in Natural Language Processing*, pages 2081–2087, Lisbon, Portugal, 2015. Association for Computational Linguistics. DOI: 10.18653/v1/d15-1248. 147

Rico Sennrich, Philip Williams, and Matthias Huck. A tree does not make a well-formed sentence: Improving syntactic string-to-tree statistical machine translation with more linguistic knowledge. *Computer Speech and Language*, 32(1), pages 27–45, 2015. DOI: 10.1016/j.csl.2014.09.002. 134

Libin Shen, Jinxi Xu, and Ralph Weischedel. String-to-dependency statistical machine translation. *Computational Linguistics*, 36(4), pages 649–671, 2010. DOI: 10.1162/coli_a_00015. 30, 138, 139, 141, 149

Reshef Shilon, Hanna Fadida, and Shuly Wintner. Incorporating linguistic knowledge in statistical machine translation: translating prepositions. In *Proc. of the Workshop on Innovative Hybrid Approaches to the Processing of Textual Data*, pages 106–114, Avignon, France, April 2012. Association for Computational Linguistics. 145

Grigori Sidorov, Francisco Velasquez, Efstathios Stamatatos, Alexander Gelbukh, and Liliana Chanona-Hernández. Syntactic dependency-based n-grams as classification features. In *Proc. of the 11th Mexican International Conference on Advances in Computational Intelligence*, vol. Part II, pages 1–11, San Luis Potosí, Mexico, 2013. Springer-Verlag. DOI: 10.1007/978-3-642-37798-3_1. 148

Sara Stymne and Nicola Cancedda. Productive generation of compound words in statistical machine translation. In *Proc. of the 6th Workshop on Statistical Machine Translation*, pages 250–260, Edinburgh, Scotland, 2011. Association for Computational Linguistics. 147

Elior Sulem, Omri Abend, and Ari Rappoport. Conceptual annotations preserve structure across translations: a French-English case study. In *Proc. of the 1st Workshop on Semantics-Driven Statistical Machine Translation (S2MT 2015)*, pages 11–22, Beijing, China, 2015. Association for Computational Linguistics. DOI: 10.18653/v1/w15-3502. 156

Aram Ter-Sarkisov, Holger Schwenk, Fethi Bougares, and Loïc Barrault. Incremental Adaptation Strategies for Neural Network Language Models. In *Proc. of the 3rd Workshop on Continuous Vector Space Models and their Compositionality*, Bejing, China, 2015. 141

Lucien Tesnière. *Elements de Syntaxe Structurale*. Editions Klincksieck, Paris, 1959. 143

Kristina Toutanova, Hisami Suzuki, and Achim Ruopp. Applying morphology generation models to machine translation. In *Proc. of the 45th Annual Meeting of the Association for Computational Linguistics*, 2008. 141

David Vilar and Hermann Ney. On LM heuristics for the cube growing algorithm. In *Annual Conference of the European Association for Machine Translation*, pages 242–249, Barcelona, Spain, May 2009. 90

David Vilar, Jan-Thorsten Peter, and Hermann Ney. Can we translate letters? In *Proc. of the Second Workshop on Statistical Machine Translation*, pages 33–39, Prague, Czech Republic, June 2007. Association for Computational Linguistics. DOI: 10.3115/1626355.1626360. 146

Andrew Viterbi. Error bounds for convolutional codes and an asymptotically optimum decoding algorithm. *IEEE Transactions on Information Theory*, 13(2), pages 260–269, September 1967. DOI: 10.1109/tit.1967.1054010. 67

Wei Wang, Kevin Knight, and Daniel Marcu. Binarizing syntax trees to improve syntax-based machine translation accuracy. In *Proc. of the 2007 Joint Conference on Empirical Methods in Natural Language Processing and Computational Natural Language Learning (EMNLP-CoNLL)*, 2007. 127, 128

Wei Wang, Jonathan May, Kevin Knight, and Daniel Marcu. Re-structuring, re-labeling, and re-aligning for syntax-based machine translation. *Computational Linguistics*, 36(2), pages 247–277, June 2010. DOI: 10.1162/coli.2010.36.2.09054. 129

Warren Weaver. Translation. In William N. Locke and A. Donald Booth, Eds., *Machine Translation of Languages: Fourteen Essays*, pages 15–23. John Wiley & Sons, 1955. 27

Jonathan Weese, Juri Ganitkevitch, Chris Callison-Burch, Matt Post, and Adam Lopez. Joshua 3.0: syntax-based machine translation with the Thrax grammar extractor. In *Proc. of the 6th Workshop on Statistical Machine Translation*, 2011. 39

Marion Weller, Alexander Fraser, and Sabine Schulte im Walde. Using subcategorization knowledge to improve case prediction for translation to German. In *Proc. of the 51st Annual Meeting of the Association for Computational Linguistics*, vol. 1, Long Papers, pages 593–603, Sofia, Bulgaria, August 2013. 145

Benjamin Wellington, Sonjia Waxmonsky, and I. Dan Melamed. Empirical lower bounds on the complexity of translational equivalence. In *Proc. of the 21st International Conference on Computational Linguistics and the 44th Annual Meeting of the Association for Computational Linguistics*, Sydney, Australia, July 2006. DOI: 10.3115/1220175.1220298. 28

John S. White, Theresa O'Connell, and Francis O'Mara. The ARPA MT evaluation methodologies: evolution, lessons, and future approaches. In *Proc. of the 1st Conference of the Association for Machine Translation in the Americas*, pages 193–205, Columbia, MD, 1994. 148

Philip Williams and Philipp Koehn. Agreement constraints for statistical machine translation into German. In *Proc. of the 6th Workshop on Statistical Machine Translation*, pages 217–226, Edinburgh, UK, 2011. Association for Computational Linguistics. 141

Philip Williams and Philipp Koehn. GHKM rule extraction and scope-3 parsing in Moses. In *Proc. of the 7th Workshop on Statistical Machine Translation*, pages 388–394, Montréal, Canada, June 2012. Association for Computational Linguistics. 44

Philip Williams and Philipp Koehn. Using feature structures to improve verb translation in English-to-German statistical MT. In *Proc. of the 3rd Workshop on Hybrid Approaches to Machine Translation (HyTra)*, pages 21–29, Gothenburg, Sweden, April 2014. Association for Computational Linguistics. DOI: 10.3115/v1/w14-1005. 30, 148

Philip Williams, Rico Sennrich, Maria Nadejde, Matthias Huck, and Philipp Koehn. Edinburgh's syntax-based systems at WMT 2015. In *Proc. of the 10th Workshop on Statistical Machine Translation*, pages 199–209, Lisbon, Portugal, 2015. Association for Computational Linguistics. DOI: 10.18653/v1/w15-3024. 128

Dekai Wu. Trainable coarse bilingual grammars for parallel text bracketing. In *Proc. of the 3rd Workshop on Very Large Corpora (VLC)*, 1995. DOI: 10.1007/978-94-017-2390-9_15. 28

Dekai Wu. A polynomial-time algorithm for statistical machine translation. In *Proc. of the 34th Annual Meeting on Association for Computational Linguistics*, Santa Cruz, CA, June 1996. DOI: 10.3115/981863.981884. 28, 100

Dekai Wu. Stochastic inversion transduction grammars and bilingual parsing of parallel corpora. *Computational Linguistics*, 23(3), pages 377–403, 1997. 28, 33, 110

Wenduan Xu and Philipp Koehn. Extending hiero decoding in Moses with cube growing. *The Prague Bulletin of Mathematical Linguistics*, (98), pages 133–142, 2012. DOI: 10.2478/v10108-012-0015-8. 90

Nianwen Xue, Ondřej Bojar, Jan Hajič, Martha Palmer, Zdenka Urešová, and Xiuhong Zhang. Not an interlingua, but close: comparison of English AMRs to Chinese and Czech. In *Proc. of the 9th International Conference on Language Resources and Evaluation (LREC'14)*, Reykjavik, Iceland, 2014. European Language Resources Association (ELRA). 156

Kenji Yamada and Kevin Knight. A Syntax-based statistical translation model. In *Proc. of the 39th Annual Meeting on Association for Computational Linguistics*, Toulouse, France, July 2001. DOI: 10.3115/1073012.1073079. 28, 41

Kenji Yamada and Kevin Knight. A decoder for syntax-based statistical MT. In *Proc. of the 40th Annual Meeting on Association for Computational Linguistics*, Philadelphia, PA, July 2002. DOI: 10.3115/1073083.1073134. 28

Victor H. Yngve. A Framework for Syntactic Translation. In Sergei Nirenburg, Harold L. Somers, and Yorick A. Wilks, Eds., *Readings in Machine Translation*. MIT Press, 2003. 27

Daniel H. Younger. Recognition and parsing of context-free languages in time n3. *Information and Control*, 10(2), pages 189–208, 1967. DOI: 10.1016/s0019-9958(67)80007-x. 67

Hui Yu, Xiaofeng Wu, Jun Xie, Wenbin Jiang, Qun Liu, and Shouxun Lin. RED: A reference dependency based MT evaluation metric. In *COLING 2014, 25th International Conference on Computational Linguistics, Proc. of the Conference: Technical Papers*, August 23–29, 2014, Dublin, Ireland, pages 2042–2051, 2014. 151

Hao Zhang, Liang Huang, Daniel Gildea, and Kevin Knight. Synchronous binarization for machine translation. In *Proc. of the Main Conference on Human Language Technology Conference of the North American Chapter of the Association of Computational Linguistics*, pages 256–263, New York City, 2006. Association for Computational Linguistics. DOI: 10.3115/1220835.1220868. 110, 120

Hao Zhang, Licheng Fang, Peng Xu, and Xiaoyun Wu. Binarized forest to string translation. In *Proc. of the 49th Annual Meeting of the Association for Computational Linguistics: Human Language Technologies*, pages 835–845, Portland, OR, June 2011. Association for Computational Linguistics. 132

Hui Zhang, Min Zhang, Haizhou Li, and Chew Lim Tan. Fast translation rule matching for syntax-based statistical machine translation. In *Proc. of the 2009 Conference on Empirical Methods in Natural Language Processing*, pages 1037–1045, Singapore, August 2009. Association for Computational Linguistics. DOI: 10.3115/1699571.1699647. 98, 131

Min Zhang, Hongfei Jiang, Haizhou Li, Aiti Aw, and Sheng Li. Grammar comparison study for translational equivalence modeling and statistical machine translation. In *Proc. of the 22nd International Conference on Computational Linguistics (Coling 2008)*, pages 1097–1104, Manchester, UK, August 2008. DOI: 10.3115/1599081.1599219. 134

Andreas Zollmann and Ashish Venugopal. Syntax augmented machine translation via chart parsing. In *Proc. of the Workshop on Statistical Machine Translation*, pages 138–141, New York City, 2006. Association for Computational Linguistics. DOI: 10.3115/1654650.1654671. 29, 36

Authors' Biographies

PHILIP WILLIAMS

Philip Williams is a Research Associate at the University of Edinburgh, where he completed his Ph.D. in 2014. His main research interest is the integration of linguistic information into statistical machine translation. In his thesis, he applied unification-based constraints to syntax-based statistical machine translation. He is the main contributor to the syntax-based models in the Moses toolkit.

RICO SENNRICH

Rico Sennrich is a Research Associate at the University of Edinburgh. He received his Ph.D. in Computational Linguistics from the University of Zurich in 2013. His research focuses on data-driven natural language processing, in particular machine translation, syntax, and morphology. His contributions to syntax-based machine translation include a more efficient algorithm for SCFG decoding, and novel models for syntactic language modelling and productive generation of compounds. He developed syntax-based SMT systems for English-German that were tied for first place in the shared translation tasks of WMT 2014 and 2015.

MATT POST

Matt Post is a Senior Research Scientist at the Human Language Technology Center of Excellence at Johns Hopkins University, where he has been since completing his Ph.D. at the University of Rochester in 2011. Since 2012, he has co-organized the WMT Conference on Statistical Machine Translation. He is the maintainer of the Apache Joshua statistical machine translation toolkit.

PHILIPP KOEHN

Philipp Koehn is a Professor of Computer Science at Johns Hopkins University, where he is affiliated with the Center for Language and Speech Processing. He also is the Chair of Machine Translation at the University of Edinburgh. He received his Ph.D. in 2003 from the University of Southern California. He is the creator and maintainer of Moses, the de facto statistical machine translation system, used throughout the world in both research and industry. He is a co-founder of the WMT Conference on Statistical Machine Translation, and author of the 2009 textbook *Statistical Machine Translation*.

Author Index

Index

Printed in the United States
by Baker & Taylor Publisher Services